Speech and Political Practice

SUNY Series in the Philosophy of the Social Sciences

Lenore Langsdorf, Editor

SPEECH AND POLITICAL PRACTICE

RECOVERING THE PLACE OF HUMAN RESPONSIBILITY

✾

MURRAY JARDINE

STATE UNIVERSITY OF NEW YORK PRESS

Published by
State University of New York Press, Albany

For information, address State University of New York Press,
State University Plaza, Albany, N.Y. 12246

Production by M. R. Mulholland
Marketing by Anne M. Valentine

Library of Congress Cataloging-in-Publication Data

Jardine, Murray, 1954–
    Speech and political practice : recovering the place of human
responsibility / Murray Jardine.
        p.   cm. — (SUNY series in the philosophy of the social
sciences)
    Includes bibliographical references and index.
    ISBN 0-7914-3685-3. — ISBN 0-7914-3686-1 (pbk.)
    1. Language and languages—Philosophy.   2. Objectivism
(Philosophy)   3. Narration (Rhetoric)   4. Speech acts (Linguistics)
5. Political science.   6. Ethics.   I. Title.   II. Series.
P106.J34   1998
401-dc21   97-19490
                                                                  CIP

10 9 8 7 6 5 4 3 2 1

To my mother and the memory of my father

CONTENTS

ACKNOWLEDGMENTS

This book is the result of a long and very fruitful apprenticeship to three outstanding teachers. The issues it examines first arose for me while taking undergraduate courses from Clarke Cochran and became fully articulated thanks to Tom Spragens, who directed the dissertation upon which the book is based, while the major thesis was inspired by several graduate seminars with Bill Poteat. Without any one of these three, the book could never have been written.

I would like to thank my other graduate teachers, Michael Gillespie, Ruth Grant, and Romand Coles. In addition to reading and critiquing the original dissertation, they have given me many important ideas and have forced me to formulate carefully my own thoughts. I am also grateful to Jerry Perkins and Bill Oden, who introduced me to political science and political theory, respectively.

Many colleagues and students have read parts of the manuscript, assisted in research, or have contributed to this project in a more general way through discussion and friendship. I would especially like to thank David Buist, Elizabeth Newman, John Berkman, Keith Boeckelman, Jim Stoner, Garry Jennings, Cecil Eubanks, Ellis Sandoz, Ray Blackwood, Steve Wild, Donald Byrne, Ronn Daniel, Keith Smith, Reed Brodsky, Spencer Banzhaf, Sindey Fazio, Judy Fazio, Shane Landry, Catherine Fairchild Calhoun, Amanda Jones, Danny Tesvich, Richard Moore, Ashley Perkins, Sandra Jeansonne, Jason Rush, Patrick Conlan, Amy Weinstein, James Powell, Ashley Tate, Elizabeth Freeman, Ross Romero, Todd Meyers, Pete Petrakis, Bill Simmons, and Matt Chociej.

I would also like to express my appreciation for the invaluable guidance provided by Clay Morgan at SUNY Press and by Lenore Langsdorf, editor of SUNY's Philosophy of the Social Sciences series.

Although all of the above people have in some way contributed to this book, I am ultimately responsible for it and therefore for any errors or shortcomings it may contain.

Finally, I would like to thank the following publishers for kindly granting permission to reprint from their publications:

From "On the Obsolescence of the Concept of Honour," by Peter Berger. *European Journal of Sociology* xi (1970): 339–347. Copyright © 1970 by *The European Journal of Sociology*. Used by permission.

INTRODUCTION:
POLITICAL THEORY
AND HUMAN FINITUDE

In the twilight of the nineteenth century, Friedrich Nietzsche proclaimed that the twentieth century would witness "the advent of nihilism." Nihilism, for Nietzsche, meant the complete breakdown of moral limits on human actions; in a nihilistic world "everything is permitted." Put differently, nihilism is the utter loss of any sense of human finitude. Nihilism, according to Nietzsche, was the end result of the Enlightenment, with its dream of progress toward human autonomy through scientific rationality. By attempting to turn themselves into gods, controlling their own destiny, humans would instead turn themselves into beasts, or rather something worse than beasts, with unlimited power to control and to destroy but with no moral constraints on the use of that power.

What seemed a century ago to be the raving of a madman has now become the most conventional of academic wisdom. Perhaps the most pervasive theme in contemporary political theory is that the Enlightenment is over. The modern world of Western bourgeois culture seems to be exhausted, its ideal of progress having degenerated into the technological nihilism of total war and insatiable consumerism. As we approach the twenty-first century it is widely anticipated that we are entering a new historical era, a "postmodern" age, which will require a new understanding of political order to replace the disintegrating modern worldview. If the central feature of late modernity is the breakdown of any sense of human limits, then essential to any new model of political life will be some way of reestablishing such a sense of limits, or human finitude.

My purpose in writing this book is to address this central question of finitude. I will do so by considering how a political community may critically judge its own practice, and thus how it may set limits both to the actions of its members and to what it may demand of its members. This approach to reestablishing a sense of human finitude will emerge from a consideration of the uniquely human capacity for speech, and will ultimately rearticulate the human sense of place.

To understand why certain characteristics of the human speech act can and should provide limits for political practice, it will be helpful to consider briefly the modern Enlightenment understanding of political order, as well as the major alternatives that have emerged following its demise.

Any vision of political order inevitably embodies certain assumptions about the structure of reality and how human beings attain knowledge of that reality; indeed, because they shape the vocabulary of social practice, these assumptions largely determine the possibilities inherent in a human society. The breakdown of a political community is really the collapse of a cosmology. Hence, any attempt to construct an alternative to a dying political order must ultimately examine the epistemological and ontological assumptions underlying that order. Only in this way can the new political vision understand the root causes of the old order's breakdown.

Modern political theory and practice are inextricably tied to the Enlightenment conception of acceptable knowledge. For modernity, valid knowledge must take the form of exact, exhaustively specifiable, impersonal "facts." Such "objective" knowledge can be obtained only if the knowing subject—the human being who ascertains facts—ruthlessly eliminates all unexamined assumptions and prejudices from the mind and proceeds by well-defined logical procedures to derive truth, i.e., facts, from an unbiased examination of the relevant experiential evidence. Ontologically, reality is structured in such a way that it can be exhaustively described by such facts, and experiences purporting to describe dimensions of reality that cannot be so treated are regarded as derivative or even unreal.

As has been extensively documented in the twentieth century, the Enlightenment project of obtaining exact, impersonal, objective knowledge has failed, mainly because it is impossible for the subject to obtain the independence from context required by this epistemological model. Human beings inescapably approach any cognitive task from within the confines of a "paradigm," or particular set of presuppositions, and cannot subject their assumptions or methodology to full critical assessment. The application of the Enlightenment model of acceptable knowledge has thus had the effect of progressively shrinking the domain of intelligible human experience. In the seventeenth and eighteenth centuries, what is now called "religious belief" conflicted with the model of exact, impersonal knowledge and was relegated to the realm of mere opinion; by the late nineteenth century, morality, which the Enlightenment philosophers had thought could be placed on a firm, secular footing by skeptical rationalism, was in serious danger of becoming a matter of subjective value; and by the mid-twentieth century it had become an open question whether even the hardest sciences could meaningfully be described as objective. This potential disintegration of even scientific knowledge into a thoroughgoing subjectivism is, at one level, what has caused the breakdown of any limits to human action in late modernity, as it has become difficult, if not impossible, to determine the relative validity of competing truth claims and thus rule out any belief system and its practical implications as unacceptable.

Politically, the Enlightenment's normative model has conceived of human societies as collections of autonomous individuals pursuing their own personal goals subject only to a neutral framework of laws that prevents these individuals from interfering with each other's actions. The task of political theory in this model is to maximize individual freedom by articulating a set of neutral, impersonal rules that does not favor any individual or group of individuals, or any particular way of life, over others. This is the basic project of modern liberalism, although liberals notoriously disagree over precisely what institutionally-embodied set of rules—whether the free market of nineteenth-century liberalism or the activist state favored by twentieth-century liberals—actually maximizes individual autonomy. Marxism differs from liberalism only in that it assumes that destroying the oppressive and discriminatory institutions of capitalism will eventually eliminate the need for any rules and thus for the state that enforces them, replacing regulation with voluntary cooperation. Human progress for both liberalism and Marxism consists in applying scientific knowledge to develop the material resources and institutional framework necessary to allow full individual autonomy. In either case, the essential political ideal—the society of independent individuals pursuing their goals without subordination to hierarchical command—corresponds to the modern conception of acceptable knowledge, in several ways.

The autonomous individual pursuing his (or more recently, her) own independently chosen goals corresponds to the autonomous subject achieving neutral, unbiased knowledge, as does the liberal political theorist, establishing universal, neutral rules to order the society of autonomous individuals, or the critical Marxist, using a scientific understanding of the historical process to unmask ideological delusions embedded in the liberal's supposedly neutral rules. Additionally, the idea that individuals should be autonomous to pursue their own goals is itself partly a result of the relegation of questions about ultimate human ends to the realm of the subjective; since such questions lie outside the public sphere of objectively ascertainable facts, their resolution must be left up to the private judgment of each individual person. The collapse of the idea of neutral, purely objective knowledge has meant the collapse of the modern liberal political project as well, as it brings about the recognition that any set of rules inevitably privileges certain individuals, groups, or ways of life, which in turn has led to the despairing conclusion that since reality is ultimately only a chaos of subjective interpretations, no true knowledge is possible and human societies are finally ordered only by sheer power.

Practically, although modernity at its best has achieved some impressive successes in limiting arbitrary personal power and improving the material conditions of life, the modern attempt to create a society of autonomous individuals has ultimately had the paradoxical result of vastly increasing the potential for tyranny. Even at the earliest stages of the Enlightenment, Thomas Hobbes had observed that the logical outcome of conceiving society as a collection of purely isolated individuals was perpetual conflict, or a "war of all against all," which would require an authoritarian government to maintain order. A more subtle analysis was made by Alexis de Tocqueville in the nineteenth century, when he suggested that the attempt to replace older ascriptive hierarchies with neutral, impersonal rules would eventually have the effect of subjecting every conceivable detail of everyday life to bureaucratic regulation—a system of "administrative despotism" rather than violent authoritarianism. In the twentieth century, various social commentators, most notably Max Weber and more recently Michel Foucault, have refined Hobbes's analysis even further by cataloging the ways in which the attempt to liberate the individual from premodern hierarchies and social roles through enlightened education has actually turned each individual into an object of administration by an army of experts. Finally, as numerous sociological studies have demonstrated, the conditions of isolation and anomie produced by modern individualism are fertile ground for demagoguery and ideological fanaticism. The combination of these practical results of the goal of individual autonomy and the breakdown of any ethical or even epistemological limits has turned this century into an orgy of destruction, both in the worldwide ideological wars of the first half of the century and more recently in the wanton waste of the consumer economy as it attempts to anesthetize the malaise experienced throughout contemporary Western societies.[1]

In terms of a theoretical response to the situation of late modernity, it seems to me that it is possible to discern the emergence of at least three different approaches to reconstructing political order.

Nietzsche was the first fully to comprehend the disintegration of modernity into nihilism. He did not view this situation with despair but rather saw it as an epochal opportunity. Accepting that reality is indeed nothing more than a chaos of interpretations, and that all political order is a form of domination, Nietzsche saw that power rests with the strongest, which for him meant the most persuasive—those who could create the most aesthetically appealing interpretation of the human condition. The collapse of modern scientific rationalism and its illusion of utilitarian truth would allow the recreation of an aristocratic order based upon the persuasive capacities of an artistic elite.

In the twentieth century, there have been two major appropriations of Nietzsche's philosophy. One has been the vulgarization found in the Nazi and fascist pseudo-aristocracies. The other, originating with Martin Heidegger's response to Nietzsche, associated with such theorists as Foucault and Jacques Derrida, and sometimes referred to as "postmodernism," has, contrary to both Nietzsche and Heidegger, an egalitarian political vision. For these thinkers, the recognition that reality is a chaos of interpretations implies that one who wants to live most fully should be open to "otherness"—that is, to other interpretations of the world and their practical manifestations that bourgeois rationalism has suppressed and silenced. Additionally, the postmodernists see Nietzsche's insight into the inevitability of power and domination as a tool with which any hierarchy can be discredited. Political orders such as modern technocracies, which legitimate themselves through supposedly objective truth claims, can be shown to be nothing more than interpretations of the world that benefit those in power. Hence, egalitarian freedom would be found not in the easily-corrupted utopias of Marxism and anarchism, but rather would take the form of a continual effort to deconstruct the disciplinary matrix of any social system that might develop; liberation comes not from tearing down the existing society and replacing it with a new one but from creating tolerance and autonomy by constantly discrediting would-be structures of domination. The postmodernists see the Nietzschean insight as liberating, but in a different way than Nietzsche did. If attempts to construct neutral systems of rules based on supposedly objective truth have paradoxically intensified the potential for domination, perhaps recognizing the relativity of truth and thus the inevitably of domination may actually permit its amelioration through an aesthetic appreciation of the other.[2]

The postmodernist project is open to at least four crucial objections. First, and most fundamentally, it could be argued that postmodernism is not really *post*-modern at all but rather only a kind of disappointed modernism, since, like Nietzsche, it does not really question the

Enlightenment conception of valid knowledge but simply draws the conclusion that since no knowledge claims can meet the modern standard of objective truth, there is ultimately no truth. Second, from a practical standpoint, it is not clear why recognizing reality as a chaos of competing interpretations implies openness and tolerance. This was not Nietzsche's conclusion. If domination is inevitable, why attempt to limit it? Why not simply engage in ruthless domination? The assumption that we would want to avoid or limit domination seems to be a product of the Western humanist tradition, with its idea of a rationally structured reality, which the postmodernists claim to repudiate. Third, to the extent that contemporary Western, and especially American, societies already have developed a substantially aesthetic orientation, as manifested in the consumer capitalist economy, a postmodernist politics may simply be coopted by the forces it proposes to critique. What could be more postmodern than MTV? Finally, and more ominously, a postmodernist politics, by attempting to discredit existing structures of domination, could destroy political orders, such as liberal capitalism, where domination is at least somewhat restrained, and allow them to be replaced with overtly tyrannical political movements, whether of the left or of the right, whose leaders have simply answered the second question raised above with an unbridled assertion of the will to power. This is to say that postmodernism does not really seem to have resolved the issue of limits that any viable political theory must. Or, to paraphrase Allan Bloom, those who have given Nietzsche a tolerant, egalitarian interpretation do not seem to realize that they may be playing with fire.[3]

A different response to the breakdown of the Enlightenment project has been to revive the classical conception of political order as articulated paradigmatically by Aristotle. This approach is most closely associated with political theorists such as Leo Strauss and his followers. In the classical cosmology, reality is a fixed, hierarchical natural order where every being has a place and a function. Human knowledge comes from practice, from participating in the natural order by fulfilling the purpose appropriate to one's place. The political community is concerned not with achieving maximal autonomy for individuals but rather with teaching individuals the virtues appropriate to their places in the society and thus in the cosmos. Individuals achieve happiness not by pursuing self-chosen goals but by virtuously fulfilling their naturally ordained roles.[4]

The classical model of political order is compelling in many ways, but from the standpoint of late modernity, it has at least two fatal flaws. First, however much we may have become disillusioned with the modern goal of individual autonomy, the hierarchical social organization implied in premodern political theory is not palatable to us because we fear its potential for arbitrary personal power. Indeed, this is so partly because of the breakdown of the modern idea of neutral knowledge: we suspect hierarchies precisely because of the capacity for domination inherent in claims to epistemological privilege. Any postmodern political order, it seems, must be democratic in some sense, although perhaps not in the manner envisaged by liberalism and socialism.

Second, and even more importantly, the unchanging natural order which is the fundamental assumption of classical political theory has been one of the prime casualties of modern science. This is true in two senses—first in that we now know that we can indeed control and change nature through science, and more fundamentally in that we now realize that "nature" is not something that exists independently of us, but rather is (at least partly) our own interpretive construct.[5] Indeed, this is where lies one of the crucial contradictions in the Enlightenment paradigm. Early modernity assumed a fixed natural order (albeit one that was mechanistic rather than functional), but also assumed that humans could understand this order well enough to control it—without realizing that such control would itself imply a changeable nature. It is precisely the late modern recognition of the extent of human agency, wrought partly by the development of science, that has made establishing limits such a difficult task. If the Enlightenment ideal of progress represents a denial of human finitude, it nevertheless must be admitted that the premodern anthropology underestimates human capacities. We cannot reestablish moral limits on human action by crawling back into the cosmic womb.

A corollary to this second objection is that the classical cosmology is problematic because it may well be the precursor of the Enlightenment model of acceptable knowledge. The classical conception of an unchanging natural order, independent of human agency and with a definitive, context-neutral meaning for each component of that order, is very similar to the modern notion of an impersonal, acontextual fact. In both cases knowledge that does not transcend human interpretation to reach the level of pure, detached theory is regarded as mere opinion. The modern rejection of the transcendent as undemonstrable may not be so much a rebellion against Plato as his logical successor.[6]

The third discernible response to the breakdown of the modern project is represented by recent developments in the philosophies of language and science, both of which have been heavily influenced by the later work of Ludwig Wittgenstein, by political theorists such as Eric Voegelin and Hannah Arendt, whose work in certain ways parallels and even anticipates these developments, and by more recent political theorists such as Jürgen Habermas, Charles Taylor, and Alasdair MacIntyre, who have explicitly or implicitly built on Wittgensteinian foundations. Recent work in philosophy of language and science has recognized that adequate descriptions of these phenomena will not be found through reconstructions of them in terms of strictly specifiable logical relations, but rather in explications of the overall context of these activities, including the structures of the communities that sustain them. Obtaining reliable knowledge is not a matter of somehow abstracting oneself from any context to achieve objectivity, but of learning the communal practices appropriate within various contexts. Or, to put it in Habermas's terminology, the model of human rationality that is emerging from these endeavors is communicative rather than subject-centered.[7]

Richard Bernstein has argued that these developments can be described as an attempt to go "beyond objectivism and relativism." By objectivism, Bernstein means the Enlightenment conception of acceptable knowledge already described, i.e., that which takes the form of exactly specified, impersonal facts. As we have seen, relativism is simply the flip side, or logical outcome, of objectivism, since once we have taken the objectivist model of acceptable knowledge as our standard, the discovery that no knowledge claims can meet this standard forces us to conclude that there can be no valid knowledge. Recent philosophy of science and philosophy of language, however, have shown that we can have reliable knowledge that does not conform to the objectivist Enlightenment model, and that regarding the world as a chaos of interpretations is not the only alternative to objectivism.[8]

Politically, the theorists whom I have grouped together differ significantly, but it can be said that the emerging model of rationality just described implies that human existence should be understood in the context of a community, rather than in terms of isolated individuals, and that political communities can order themselves not through neutral ahistorical rules, or through a natural hierarchy, but through communicative activities, or in other words, through speech. For Habermas, this means paradigmatically debate about the common good, and much of his theoretical attention has been directed at an explication of how to structure such debate. Others, most notably MacIntyre and theologian Stanley Hauerwas, have been concerned with reviving virtue as a central ethical category, and have argued that the stories that make up a community's history can provide the examples of virtuous action that can guide the individual members of the community.[9] This model of political order is similar to Aristotle's, except that the historical narratives of a community take the place of his functional natural order. In this understanding, political order is not something given in the eternal structure of the cosmos, but rather something humans speak into existence, just as human activities generally are not governed by any natural telos, but instead are structured by communicative contexts.

The understanding of human community implied in the work of MacIntyre and Hauerwas seems to have the appealing features of pre-modern political theory without its weaknesses. It can provide examples of virtue and a context for discussion of the common good, but it does not depend on a static cosmology, and it does not necessarily imply rigid hierarchies: anyone can tell a story. When the narrative model is examined more closely, however, a difficult question immediately arises. Put most simply, how can we tell a good story from a bad story? After all, the Nazis had stories too. The story of a human community may well rationalize oppression, exploitation, and conquest. If we are to ground political order in communal narratives that teach virtue and thus set limits on what individuals can do, then we must have some standards that will set limitations on what the community can do to individuals, not to mention other communities.

My own project can be stated most simply as providing one possible answer to this question. I will argue that a good narrative, as opposed to a bad one, provides the members of the community based upon it with a *place*. By a "place" I mean a location that allows a person to orient himself or herself in the world. A place, by showing individual persons where they are, allows them to develop an understanding of their own identity and its relation to others, which in turn will ultimately set limits on both individual and collective actions.

There are many important kinds of places available to human beings. Geographical location is an obvious example of place, but even such matters as dress can be important places, as they can give one a sense of orientation in a social context; the increasing informality of dress in late modern societies is one of many indications that we are losing our sense of place. The idea of place is central to classical political thought and practice, as for example in the place that the polis provides for Aristotle's citizens, and an important theme in twentieth-century political theory has been the modern loss of any sense of place.

My own understanding of place, however, is different from the premodern understanding of place in one crucial respect. The premodern understanding of place is taken from the model of Aristotle's finite cosmos. Place is taken to mean something static because it is part of the ultimately unchanging natural order, and so it has historically taken such forms as an attachment to a geographical location or some kind of relatively fixed station in a social hierarchy. This understanding of place is vulnerable to the criticisms made earlier of the attempt to revive classical political theory, i.e., that we are wary of social hierarchies because of their potential for domination, and, more fundamentally, that we no longer find the idea of an unchanging natural order believable. My argument will transcend the limitations of the premodern conception of place by deriving place not from nature but from human speech. That is, I will examine the places that inhere in the structure of the speech act, or actually in the structures of various types of speech act. Rather than being geographical locations or places in a social hierarchy, the places I will discuss will be places of faithfulness—that is, places of orientation that imply certain responsibilities—inherent in specific speech situations. This approach is congruent with what I earlier referred to as the emerging communicative understanding of rationality, and in fact one way to describe my project would be to say that it is an attempt to contribute to the debate concerning communicative rationality, broadly understood, by developing some rudiments of a speech-oriented political vocabulary. Doing so may provide some ideas about how we can regain a sense of place without abandoning legitimate modern achievements such as democracy and scientific knowledge.

In order adequately to articulate such a speech-based conception of place, my argument will have to proceed in a somewhat indirect manner. It will first be necessary to explain how a consideration of the speech act could reestablish a sense of finitude, or limits. In order to do this, I will begin by developing the problem of limits in more detail, using a more technical terminology. In chapter 1, I will examine the development of modern political theory to argue that what we have lost in late modernity is any conception of necessity, such as was supplied by the premodern natural order; we live in a radically contingent world. I will simultaneously argue that the source of this radical contingency is ultimately the Enlightenment's objectivist conception of knowledge. I will then examine several contemporary political theories to show that they fail to regain a sense of necessity because they do not fully escape the objectivist model of valid knowledge. My task will then be conceptualized as developing a non-objectivist conception of necessity appropriate for political practice.

I will make two further arguments to show how this can be accomplished through a consideration of the speech act. In chapter 2, I will examine the critique of objectivism that has emerged from recent philosophy of science; describing the characteristics of objectivism will make clear what pitfalls to avoid when constructing a non-objectivist conception of necessity. Then, in chapter 3, I will draw on the literature that examines the differences between oral and literate cultures to argue that the superordination of visual experience that occurs with literacy is an important experiential source of objectivist modes of thought. That is, I will argue that objectivist categories of thinking can tend to arise when the written or printed word, which has the same characteristics as the objectivist model of knowledge, is tacitly used as an epistemological paradigm, something that is likely to happen in a culture where print literacy is widespread. From this I will conclude that a non-objectivist conception of necessity must draw upon motifs peculiar to, or at least more predominant in, oral/aural experience. Although this part of the argument is not explicitly political, it is vital. This is certainly not because there is any need for yet another critique of objectivism; explicitly objectivist doctrines no longer have any appeal for most political theorists. Rather, it is because the real problem for political theorists and others attempting to escape the objectivist/relativist dualism is that such categories of thought arise from and are reinforced by very concrete everyday experiences (such as the visual orientation produced by literacy), so that reforming our epistemological and thus our political orientation will require attention to its experiential context.

After having established why a consideration of the speech act would be an appropriate method for constructing a non-objectivist conception of necessity, I will proceed to examine oral/aural experience to develop this concept. Chapter 4 will show that if necessity is conceived in terms of speech and hearing, rather than in terms of visual experience, it is not mutually exclusive with contingency, but rather can coexist with even absolute contingency. It is possible to speak of a contextual necessity that sets limits even in a situation of infinite possibilities. In an ethical or political context the standard of necessity is that the speaker must remain faithful to his or her words, although considerable explanation will be required to clarify just what this means.

In chapter 5, I will apply this understanding of necessity to MacIntyre's discussion of narrative to produce the concept of place introduced above. A speech-based place will turn out to be a human activity that limits the elements of a narrative tradition by establishing standards for recognizing faithful or unfaithful speech in specific contexts. This explication of place will provide some definite criteria for what constitutes a good or bad narrative: only narratives that can allow such places to develop can be considered acceptable. I will then make this concept of place more concrete by developing examples of specific places, such as apprenticeship, ritual, and prophecy, appropriate to political practice, thus showing more specifically how the place implied in human speech can provide limits on individual and collective action.

Finally, in the Conclusion, I will relate my discussion of speech-based place to some of the current debates concerning morality and community, specifically arguing that speech-based places can bring about a new public realm relevant to postindustrial societies. The purpose of this discussion will not be to establish a comprehensive vision of political order, nor to resolve once and for all the question of the good life and moral rightness, but rather to contribute to a new vocabulary for political order with which such issues can be debated; one central implication of the movement beyond objectivism and relativism and its attention to linguistic context is that the crucially important aspects of most political theories are not explicit doctrines concerning the good society but rather the vocabularies developed in constructing those doctrines.

One of the central implications of the discussion will be that if we want to regain a sense of place, and therefore of finitude, we must redress somewhat the imbalance between sight, on the one hand, and speech and hearing, on the other, in our sensory and therefore conceptual orientation; I will show throughout the discussion how my concept of place can help bring this about. Additionally, my discussion of our sensory orientation and its relation to our political vocabulary will illuminate a more general issue. Many twentieth-century political theorists, as diverse in orientation as Foucault and Voegelin, have argued that modernity has been characterized by a severe restriction of the range of human experience; partly as a result of, and partly as a contributing factor to the objectivist paradigm, large areas of potential human experience, such as the religious dimension, have been disregarded as irrelevant to any public, or even private, aspect of human existence. These theorists have urged a reconsideration of human experiences forgotten or repressed by modernity. My discussion of oral cultures and related issues will both explicate some of the reasons for the modern restriction of experience and indicate some approaches to expanding our experiential horizons.

I mentioned above that my project could be described as a contribution to the debate concerning communicative rationality by articulating some rudimentary elements of a speech-based political vocabulary. Another way to describe it might be as a contribution to a Wittgensteinian political theory. As I have mentioned, Wittgenstein's later writings have been the starting point for much of the theoretical work that attempts to move beyond objectivism and relativism. Although I have not discussed Wittgenstein systematically, I have used his insights throughout the discussion, and, more importantly, the entire argument proceeds from an orientation developed through close study of his later work.

Another possible description of my project could be as an attempt to establish an epistemological grounding for what is sometimes referred to as "communitarian" political theory. This term has been applied to theorists such as MacIntyre, Taylor, Robert Bellah, William Sullivan, Michael Sandel, Michael Walzer, and others, although not all of these writers have themselves accepted the label. What communitarian theorists have in common are, first, a critical stance toward liberal individualism, and second, the conviction that ethical standards must emerge from the practice of concrete historical communities, rather than from universal, abstract principles. The communitarians have so far been quite successful in critiquing liberal political theory and its claim to neutrality, but they have been considerably less successful in replying to charges of relativism, historicism, and even romanticism that have been levelled against their conceptions of community and narrative, a matter I will discuss in some detail in chapter 1. By grounding MacIntyre's analysis of narrative in certain features of the speech act, my discussion could be said to provide one possible epistemological foundation—or, to use a safer term, framework—for the communitarian project, broadly defined. Additionally, by providing a Wittgensteinian epistemological framework for communitarian theory, my project can contribute to replacing the now somewhat stale liberal-communitarian debate with what I think would be a more fruitful communitarian exchange with post-Nietzscheans, neo-Aristotelians, and especially critical theorists such as Habermas.

Before beginning my argument, I should address three important issues. First, the concept of place that I have just briefly described may sound somewhat similar to Habermas's universal pragmatics. There is indeed some resemblance, but there are also important differences. Most importantly, my concept of place is inseparable from the idea of narrative, and in fact I will present it as necessary to fill in some of the conceptual gaps in MacIntyre's formulations. Also, while one of Habermas's most important claims has been that all communication is oriented toward the goal of achieving understanding, my argument will require only that all communication is at some level intelligible and that all speech contexts are intelligibly connected. Actually, although it would be misleading to describe my project as a synthesis of MacIntyre and Habermas, partly because my focus is mainly on MacIntyre, my concept of place could be understood as occupying a middle ground between these two theorists and their respective formulations of human rationality.

The second matter that should be briefly clarified concerns my use of anthropological studies of oral-literate differences. Specifically, the argument described above, i.e., that a consideration of the spoken word can provide the conceptual resources to escape objectivism, may strike the reader as counterintuitive, since Derrida and others have argued that writing *breaks up*, rather than causes, an objectivist orientation. I shall discuss this matter in more detail later, but here I will simply point out that scholars who study oral-literate differences agree that on this point at least, Derrida is indeed mistaken. Objectivism seems to be an epistemological paradigm peculiar to literate cultures.

On the other hand, by focusing on the phenomenological effects of literacy as an experiential source of objectivism, I do not mean to imply that such a visual orientation is the *only* source of objectivist/relativist thinking. Clearly there are many sources. I want to concentrate on literacy as an important experiential source of objectivism, however, because examining its subtle perceptual and conceptual effects can help unravel some fundamental confusions in current attempts to escape objectivism, and because, more generally, a consideration of human speech from this perspective can yield some extremely important insights into political practice.

Additionally, it might be wondered why I am discussing differences between oral and literate cultures when there is now substantial evidence that we are experiencing the beginnings of something different from either, a new postliterate electronic-image culture based on television and computers. From this standpoint, my discussion of oral-literate distinctions could seem outdated and therefore irrelevant. I will in fact briefly discuss the literature on the electronic media, but I want to focus mainly on oral-literate dichotomies for two reasons. First, for my purposes, the critical issue is the change from an oral/aural to a visual orientation, which was first effected by print literacy and which has not been reversed (indeed, has almost certainly been intensified) by the new electronic media. Second, although the literature on orality and literacy has developed to the point where certain conclusions appear to be generally accepted and therefore can be applied in a philosophical discussion, no such consensus has yet arisen about the effects of the electronic media, partly because the subject matter itself is changing so rapidly. Therefore, any discussion of electronic-image culture would be somewhat speculative. As I have mentioned, I will briefly address some of the issues currently raised in debates about the future of post-industrial or information-based societies.

Finally, I should point out that the understanding of place that I will develop is not really new; indeed it is quite "premodern." The ancient Hebrews, who did not even have a word for "nature" but who rather understood the world as something brought into existence and ordered by an ever-faithful speaker, seem to have regarded the fundamental human place as that of a responsible speaker before God. The biblical stories can be regarded as attempts to articulate this understanding of human place. My discussion could ultimately be understood as an attempt to examine some of the implications of this model of reality for postmodern[10] political theory and practice.

1

The Concept of a Narrative Practice as an Alternative to Objectivism

If nihilism means that everything is permitted, then a nihilistic world would be characterized by what we might call radical contingency. In a radically contingent world, all moral and epistemological categories are open to question; nothing is necessary in the sense that it simply *is*, independent of human agency. Whereas the ethical and political practice of the premodern world was structured by the overriding necessity of an immutable natural order where every being had a place and a function, and even early modernity could confidently rely on the necessity of a mechanically predictable if ultimately purposeless nature to determine appropriate social behavior, the late modern situation is one of unrelenting skepticism about every truth claim because we see all such claims as contingent human interpretations, with no grounding other than changing perceptions. For late modernity, nothing *is*; everything changes, or rather, everything can be changed by human interpretation. Nihilism has resulted from our recent recognition of the extent to which the world we experience is our own creation. If we want to escape from the nihilism of late modernity by regaining a sense of necessary limitations, then it would appear that we must articulate a conception of necessity that is compatible with the interpretive dimension of human existence.

As I have indicated, my project is an attempt to articulate a vocabulary for judging the validity of the communal narratives discussed by Alasdair MacIntyre and others, with the specific goal of demonstrating how limits may be established on individual actions within a community and on the actions a community may take toward both its own individual members and other communities. I will do this by developing the concept of a speech-based place to modify and extend MacIntyre's explication of the role of narrative—or as I will conceptualize it, narrative practice—in political communities. I will approach this task in turn by developing the idea of an oral/aural place as a non-objectivist concept of necessity. Doing so would, I believe, accomplish the task adumbrated above—of articulating a conception of necessity that is compatible with the interpretive dimension of human existence. I have already discussed why any attempt to establish moral limits on political practice must go beyond the dichotomy of objectivism and relativism; in this chapter, I will explain why a concept of necessity grounded in the human capacity for speech could be a fruitful approach to this issue. This will allow me to establish a context for the chapters that discuss matters that might initially seem rather distantly related to ethics and politics.

We can begin to establish such a context by examining more closely the late modern situation of nihilism or radical contingency. To state the formulation just given in more detail, we could say that nihilism results from the ambiguous nature of modernity. On the one hand, modern humanity has discovered a hitherto underestimated capacity to understand, control, and even change the world, resulting in both previously unimaginable material wealth and relatively egalitarian social and political structures. On the other hand, these developments which have led to the modern idea of progress have been accompanied— and ultimately, it seems, overwhelmed—by an ever-growing epistemological and moral skepticism as our ability to control the world changes precisely those natural and human aspects of reality that we had earlier taken as the unchanging foundations of knowledge.

I will introduce my own project by arguing very briefly that this ambiguous situation of modernity results from what might be called our partial rejection of the classical natural order as articulated by Aristotle. That is, the modern objectivist paradigm has abandoned Aristotle's teleology but not his requirement that order and truth must be ultimately independent of human agency. The tensions produced by this situation have produced modern nihilism. This argument is certainly not original; it has been explicitly made by Jürgen Habermas and it is implied by MacIntyre and indeed most of the work that attempts to go beyond the objectivist/relativist dichotomy.[1] My own innovation is that I will develop this idea using the concepts of necessity and contingency; instead of saying that late modernity has destroyed all limits or that it has become nihilistic, I will argue that modernity has destroyed the cosmological conception of necessity available to the premodern world without providing a substitute, so that human knowledge and action have become radically contingent, and that the source of this radical contingency is ultimately the Enlightenment's objectivist conception of knowledge, which implies a very narrow understanding of necessity.

The implication of this discussion will be the need for a non-objectivist concept of necessity such as I will attempt to construct.

I should point out that I will hardly attempt to demonstrate this claim exhaustively, something that would obviously require a much longer argument; I simply want to establish the plausibility of the basic conceptual framework which will allow me to develop the idea of place. I should also reiterate that my discussion does not imply that my evaluation of modernity is entirely negative; I have already mentioned some of modernity's successes and indicated that I do not consider a return to anything like premodern political order a serious or desirable possibility. My discussion will, however, pay close attention to the destructive tendencies in modernity in order to illuminate more clearly the late modern situation.

Necessity and Contingency in Modern Political Theory

We have already mentioned that for Aristotle, human fulfillment comes from practicing the virtues appropriate to one's place in the political community and thus in the natural order. The individual can be taught to develop good habits that will enable him[2] to contribute to the healthy maintenance of the society, since by nature it is only here that he can actually be a fulfilled, completed human being. The natural order of things, which consists of the various potentialities of natural beings, sets limits to the possible actions of the individual and in turn sets limits to what the society may demand of the individual. Nature, society, and individual fit together into a harmonious whole. Man has a fixed place in the cosmic scheme of things which allows him to understand himself and his purpose.

One way to conceptualize Aristotle's cosmos is to say that it is characterized by an unchanging necessity, or that the natural essences of beings set necessary limits on occurrences, including ultimately the kinds of social structures that will allow humans to function properly. We could say that in the classical cosmos, events are only *relatively* contingent, since they are all ultimately derivable from the essences of natural beings. That is, no truly new or novel or *absolutely* contingent event can occur; although change takes place, all possible occurrences are determined by the relatively narrow limits established by the unchanging structures of the various natural beings so that nothing is ever created and reality contains a finite set of possibilities.

This necessity, or rather perceived necessity, although it sets definite limits on human actions, is problematic for modernity because it implies that humans have no free will—that is, no truly creative capacity—and indeed no way fundamentally to reorder relations of social hierarchy, since they are grounded in the immutable order of nature. From the modern standpoint, the classical political order has very limited possibilities because it is a component of a closed cosmos.

This closed cosmos was shattered by the biblical understanding of the world as absolutely contingent upon the paradigmatic personal speaker, God, who speaks it into existence and whose words remain ultimately always faithful. The world is absolutely or radically contingent in this view because God's speech acts actually create it from nothing and the world so created has infinite possibilities. Events are not derivable from unchanging natural essences because none exist; the possibility exists for truly novel occurrences. Similarly, humans, since they are created in God's image, also have a creative power in their capacity for speech and can actually change the world.[3] The conceptual revolution produced by this model lies at the basis of modern inductive, experimental science and the modern political ideals of freedom, equality, and democracy, but it has destroyed the basis for political theory available to the classical world by breaking down the necessary relations among natural beings and their ends. To gain a better understanding of modernity, we must examine these implications more closely.

For both Plato and Aristotle, the reality we experience with our senses is ultimately only a series of shifting images under which lies the true reality, the world of the Forms or the essences of natural beings. Aristotle had more confidence than Plato in the immanent world, but even for him induction is an inferior form of knowledge, and true science consists in deductive knowledge. Hence, ancient science rarely rose above the level of sophisticated classificatory systems. The implications of the biblical picture, however, are that we can be confident that the appearances we experience are ordered such that they will remain consistent in time; an experiment performed at T_1 will yield results comparable with one performed at T_2. We can determine general laws from particular experience, since God's faithfulness means that the particular experiences will be consistent and comparable; in Aristotle's understanding of knowledge, such an approach will never yield the true essences of beings, which are the real basis of knowledge.[4]

Similarly, if the order of the contingent world depends upon the faithful words of God, it cannot be a self-contained hierarchical whole of eternal essences or potentialities, and there will tend to be a flattening out of the hierarchies that define it, including those among people. Man and woman, slave and free, and all nationalities will be equal under their creator. Additionally, since every person, even the most humble, has the creative power of speech, every human life is of infinite value. Thus, political and social hierarchies and forms of bondage will eventually become suspect.

We can see here how the biblical picture apparently contains the seeds of what is generally recognized as the promise of modernity—freedom, democratic equality, and scientific knowledge. But it seems that we can also see the origins of modern nihilism. For in this picture, humanity is radically displaced. Our place is no longer fixed in the cosmos and the polis; rather, it is wherever we meet God. We become restless wanderers, changing even our names. Even the tomb could not be a permanent place for God incarnate. Humanity's understanding of itself cannot be found in nature but rather in the story of its faithfulness to God's call. Therefore, if this faithfulness becomes problematic, the world may become an absolutely contingent, placeless chaos.[5]

This fundamental shift in orientation to and understanding of reality was not achieved immediately, of course. Only after many centuries of gradual changes in vocabulary and conceptual frameworks did the implications of a world radically contingent upon a transcendent creator-God begin to become clear. Not until the nominalist movement of the later Middle Ages was it decisively grasped that the biblical picture could allow no fixed essences or potentialities such as are central to Aristotle's entire comprehension of reality. Here we have the conceptual breakthrough that revolutionizes the Western conception of motion and thus allows modern mathematical physics to develop. This breakthrough, however, appears to have been made only at a huge cost; given the extent to which the medieval conception of God itself depended upon Aristotle's teleology, trust in God could become highly problematic when that teleology was destroyed, and the universe created by God could become a chaotic void. With nominalism we see the beginnings of what may be the fundamental modern dilemma: how to order a world that is potentially radically contingent.[6]

It is indeed the case that as the hierarchical cosmos of the medieval order crumbled, many of modernity's most prized achievements—scientific knowledge, greater social and political equality, and a greater sense of individual responsibility—began to develop, beginning with the Reformation and the scientific revolution and continuing through various modern reform movements. But also from a very early point, the potentially chaotic implications of a radically contingent world began to manifest themselves. Although there are many aspects to modernity, one fruitful way of understanding modern political theory is to see it as a series of attempts to come to grips with this question, each one only radicalizing the problem beyond the previous one.

Modern objectivism, with its model of exact, impersonal, context-neutral "facts," can be understood as an attempt to establish necessity in the radically contingent world of nominalism, where there are no natural, unchanging essences or teloi. Indeed, René Descartes' protypical formulation of the objectivist paradigm—that the only true knowledge is that which takes the form of "clear and distinct" ideas, themselves found by systematic skepticism—is explicity conceived as a response to the possibility that the world in which we live was created by a malevolent trickster. But as much as modern thought is based on the rejection of Aristotelian essences, objectivism still contains a residual element of the Aristotelian cosmos in that it still assumes that the world's order—the "facts" obtained by skeptical reason—must be unchanging and must exist independently of human agency. The tension created by early modernity's apparent rejection of the classical cosmos and its retention of remnants thereof eventually generates late modernity's nihilism.

This tension can be seen quite clearly in the natural right theory of Hobbes and John Locke. Hobbes retained the concept of nature—of an ultimately unchanging order independent of human agency—but in a radically changed form. For Hobbes, nature is an inertial universe of matter in motion. There are no essences or natural ends to which beings are drawn; there are merely the redirections of inertial motion following collisions between particles of matter, describable by mathematical laws. Humans do not discern natural essences, including their own moral potentiality; in Hobbes's empiricist epistemology, the human subject simply receives its knowledge and passions from outside sensations. Politically, then, there is no highest good for man or natural order for communal life; the world consists simply of isolated individuals pursuing their own individual desires formed by natural passions. These radically dissociated individuals will frequently come into conflict over the scarce resources necessary to satisfy their desires, so that the natural state of man is a perpetual war of all against all. However, since men are mechanisms whose movements are predictable, it can be known with certainty that all of them have one common fear, i.e., violent death. Therefore, sufficient peace and order to allow individuals to pursue their own goals without conflict can be attained through an overpowering sovereign force, based on the fear of violent death, which establishes through authoritative acts of speech the fundamental rules of society, such as the definition of property. The rules established by the sovereign are to remain unquestioned, although within this framework substantial freedom of action is allowed. The basis for the modern liberal state, which has as its purpose not the promotion of the good life but merely the provision of sufficient order to allow individuals to pursue their own desires without imposing on each other, is established.

Locke arrives at similar but importantly different political conclusions. The state is again simply a device to maintain order for individuals to pursue their private goals, but since, for Locke, the state of nature is relatively peaceful, minimal government is necessary. Indeed, individuals retain most of their natural rights when entering civil society and are allowed, in fact obliged, to overthrow the government if it attempts to take away those rights. Maintaining order requires not authoritarian government but limited, constitutional government.

Hobbes and Locke substantially articulate the political experience of the modern English-speaking world, at least until quite recently. Hobbes's Leviathan is the model of the modern Anglo-American liberal semi-secularized Protestant church-state. It exists, as noted, to maintain sufficient order for individuals peacefully to go about their business, it establishes basic laws which order transactions between individuals, it promotes scientific rationality as a means to improve the conditions of material life (that is, to provide for self-preservation), and it is ultimately grounded in an effectively unquestioned constitutional order which contains as a crucial component a civil theology centered around Protestant moral virtues (understood by Hobbes as the rules necessary to keep people out of each other's way), the clearest exemplar of which is the unofficial national religion of the United States, or what has been called the "American Civil Religion."[7]

Hobbes's world is contingent ontologically in that there are no natural essences, only bodies in inertial motion, ethically in that there is similarly no universal end or goal for men, and politically in that society is not something given in the natural order but rather a creation of humans for convenience. On the other hand, there is still a substantial ontological necessity derived from the mathematical laws governing motion, which in turn creates the ethical necessity embodied in the universal fear of violent death and the political necessity of the liberal state's neutral rules. Indeed, the necessity of Hobbes's mechanically determined universe is in certain ways much more rigid than that of Aristotle's functional cosmos, although it ultimately does allow a greater range of possibilities.

Hobbes's assumption that all humans desire self-preservation can be understood as a remnant, however degenerate, of premodern natural law theories, but Locke's theory shows even more clearly early liberalism's dependence on necessary limits remaining from premodern ethical and political thinking. The most important feature of Locke's theory is tacitly articulated in his conception of the law of nature. Locke's law is different from Hobbes's in that it is a preexisting moral obligation which all (or almost all) can be expected to know, rather than being merely an individual prudential calculation ratified by the state. This difference is why Locke's state of nature is more peaceful than Hobbes's: much of what Hobbes's sovereign does to maintain order, including deciding what counts as property, is built into the structure of Locke's state of nature. Thus, by bringing an essentially Aristotelian element—a moral obligation independent of existentially organized political society—into the picture, without which his theory would be incoherent, or would simply be the same as Hobbes's, Locke indicates the fundamental importance for English-speaking political order and bourgeois culture of a slowly eroding set of premodern (civic republican and biblical) beliefs, which help to legitimate the state (that is, which provide the substance of Hobbes's civil religion) and to temper the disintegrative effects of a purely self-interested individualism, which would otherwise lead to the necessity of the authoritarian state envisioned by Hobbes.[8] Additionally, the partial transformation of these older beliefs into such modern manifestations as the Protestant work ethic and early liberal conceptions of rational self-improvement could in certain respects make the social order of liberalism quite harsh, with forcible education or exclusion of those failing to conform to the bourgeois model of the independent self.[9]

In sum, then, natural right theory presents us with a much more contingent, changeable world than is the case with Aristotle, but there are still very substantial elements of necessity derived from residual elements of pre-Enlightenment thinking. As these limiting elements become purged in later modern thought, setting down definitive moral and political principles becomes a much more difficult matter.

There are two routes from the natural right liberalism of Hobbes and Locke to the deontological liberalism of Immanuel Kant, one represented by David Hume and the other by Jean-Jacques Rousseau. Both can be understood as recognitions of residual Aristotelian elements in natural right theory and as consequent further radicalizations of the world's contingency. Hume points out that if we push the empiricist model of knowledge to its logical conclusion, we must admit that causation is really only something we habitually impute to perceived regularity; it is not, as far as we can know, something actually "out there." Hence, immutable laws of nature governing the motions of bodies, from which are derived the principles of natural right, turn out to be, in effect, remnants of Aristotelian ontology still lodged in our imaginations. Extending Hume's argument, we could say that ethically, even Hobbes's grim formulation of natural right as nothing more than self-preservation turns out to be a kind of back-door Aristotelian telos; if human likes and dislikes vary radically, there is no reason for thinking that the even the desire for self-preservation is universal. Thus, natural right theory founders because it fails fully to recognize the implications of its own assumptions.

Politically, the effects of this theoretical impasse were minimal for the English-speaking world itself, which continued to build relatively stable and effective democratic polities on the basis of a logically incoherent but existentially powerful combination of biblical, republican, and natural right elements. Only relatively recently has this amalgam showed striking signs of being unable to provide an adequate conceptual framework for dealing with the political problems of a technological age. The situation in continental Europe, however, was much less stable. The political theories of Rousseau and the German thinkers more clearly articulate the tensions of societies where traditional communities, social hierarchies, and forms of political legitimation have started to come unravelled under the forces of modernization but where no clearly satisfactory institutional successors are emerging, that is, where traditional elements of necessity are eroding and nothing is taking their place.

Rousseau's criticism of Hobbes and Locke, that they read social attributes into their "natural" men, can be understood in two ways. First, we can interpret it as an articulation of the fact that, however individualistic natural right theory may appear on the surface, a tacit Aristotelian conception of man as a social being remains, however tenuously, in the structure of the theory, corresponding to the residual Aristotelian elements in early empiricist epistemology. Second, we can say that Rousseau, living in eighteenth-century France, is experiencing a much more thoroughgoing disintegration of premodern social structures and belief systems than Hobbes or Locke experienced in seventeenth-century England, or indeed until English-speaking peoples generally experienced until well into the nineteenth or even the twentieth century. The key to the political successes of the Anglo-American democracies, in one sense, is that since they entered the modern world first, they entered it only partially. They have been, until recently, essentially early modern societies. The continental societies were forced to deal with a later and more thoroughgoing confrontation with a world becoming radically contingent.

Rousseau's political theory articulates this radical contingency in the form of human freedom from nature, or, as he understands it, human potential toward perfectibility. Man in his natural state is asocial and indeed is not really man, being propelled only by inchoate desires, the most important of which is self-preservation, and by sympathy for other proto-humans. Social cooperation develops only slowly as an ad hoc response to natural desires. As it does develop, however, man begins to understand himself as man, as a moral being rather than a natural being, potentially free and perfectible. Unfortunately, social cooperation as it has developed to the present has resulted in the ultimate enslavement of all, including the rulers. But a transformation is possible, and the good society of *The Social Contract* can be created through an act of will. Man can gain true moral freedom through participation in a democratic society where no one dominates or is dominated.

Rousseau puts forward a vision similar to Aristotle's except that all men can be citizens and that freedom from nature, or natural desire, not the fulfillment of a natural end, is what is achieved. But this vision of a free humanity contains an ominous paradox. Since participation in the democratic politics of the good society is precisely what does, or can, lift man from his natural, pre-moral, pre-human state, his freedom and humanity are entirely dependent upon this participation in society. Participation, however, means submitting to the general will, since this is what directs the society and thus creates the individual as a free moral being in the society. Those who disagree with the general will have then, through their mistaken decision, lost their freedom, and they must be forced to be free. Since, in turn, any aspect of life can be relevant to the good of the community, it follows that there can be no limits to the action of the state in forcing one to be free. With Rousseau we see the first articulation of the possibility of modern totalitarianism. Rousseau's conception of freedom becomes paradoxically potentially totalitarian not because it is a positive conception, but because there are no limits to it. The individual becomes radically free from nature in willing the society that creates him as a moral being. But precisely because this means that he is in effect creating himself, his freedom is indeterminate and could result in anything. Rousseau's attempt to create a republic of virtue using a liberal conception of human nature creates an intensified version of Hobbes's Leviathan. And, of course, the French Revolution was, in part, the social embodiment of this paradox. The revolutionaries were not limited by pre-Enlightenment practice to the extent that the earlier English revolutionaries were, so the revolution, in attempting to bring about freedom, instead eventually supplanted the decaying *ancien regime* with an even worse form of tyranny. With Rousseau the world is even closer than with Hobbes to being radically contingent upon human will; not only does man will society, he now wills himself.

Kant's philosophy is an attempt to deal with the implications of Hume's critique of natural right and Rousseau's conception of human freedom. It recognizes the greater extent of human agency implied by Hume and Rousseau but seeks to avoid the indeterminate, or radically contingent, world to which it seems to lead. Kant attempts to do this by arguing that the human subject does not just passively receive sensations but does in a sense actively project a conceptual framework onto the world it perceives. What keeps this framework from being simply an arbitrary creation is that it is limited by certain universal categories, such as causation and non-contradiction, which we cannot possibly conceive as being otherwise. Human intersubjectivity, or understanding of the phenomenal world, and human moral action are thus limited by these categories of the understanding, which in a sense take the place of Aristotle's cosmos. In the case of morality, the fundamental limit is set by the impossibility of the rational will contradicting itself. Hence, the basic moral law derived from pure practical reason is that the agent should always act in such a way that the maxim he acts upon could become a universal law. Kant thought that this meant that the agent should always treat any rational being (including himself) as an end rather than as a means. This amounts to a more abstract restatement of Hobbes's and Locke's law of nature, or to put it differently, the law of nature purged of heteronomy. In this regard, its major effect on liberalism would be to move it away from a primary concern with economics and material well-being to a more thoroughgoing attempt to construct a neutral state, governed by rules of equal justice and an expanded conception of tolerance, such as is found in the theories of reform liberals such as John Rawls.[10]

Later continental philosophers, however, argued that Kant's solution does not succeed, since the limits he perceives to human understanding (and thus the structure of subjectivity and intersubjectivity) turn out simply to be hypostasized elements of Newtonian physics and Euclidean geometry, and the limit he places on human moral freedom, the universalizability of the categorical imperative, turns out to be an empty formalism from which any moral position could be derived; the fundamental liberal moral rule of non-imposition of values does not follow. In other words, Kant suffers the same fate as the earlier natural right theorists: what he had taken to be the necessary structure of the knowing subject and derivative necessary moral laws turned out to be merely contingent features of his own existential situation. Different subjects may project different conceptual frameworks onto the world.

From here it is a fairly short step to the proto-emotivism of Weber, who realized how indeterminate Kant's conception of the moral will was, and who can be said to have painted a picture of the later bourgeois world to which Kantian philosophies such as Rawls's would most fully apply. In the bureaucratic pluralism described by Weber, there is a schizophrenic split between the phenomenal world, the public realm of necessity, technocracy, and utilitarian individualism, and the noumenal world, the private realm of contingency, value-noncognitivism, and expressive individualism. These realms reinforce each other in a kind of Tocquevillian scenario, with the relentless pressure of bureaucratic control and maneuver in the public realm forcing the individual further and further into his own isolated subjectivity in the private realm, thus making him more susceptible to regularization and normalization in public, and so on. The rational freedom of Kant's noumenal self has become simply the radical contingency of demonic value choices, and the ends of public policy are the outcome of an indeterminate struggle that is rational only in the methods used to conduct it.

Although Rawls has modified his theory considerably since its first presentation in *A Theory of Justice*, his initial formulation of what he called the original position can be understood as a very apt metaphor for the radical contingency of life in the technocratic Weberian order. Beginning with individuals preparing to establish principles of justice by social contract under a veil of ignorance, unaware of their own abilities, preferences, and position in the society they will join, Rawls argues that these people will choose to be governed by a system of rights and liberties that allows equal freedom for all and by a principle of distribution such that all inequalities work to the advantage of the least advantaged, since these principles are what one would rationally choose to maximize one's advantage, that is, to maximize the benefits of the worst possible outcome under the given conditions of high uncertainty. The deontological selves inhabiting the original position, stripped of all attributes except the capacity for rational choice, are, as Rawls himself points out, an articulation of the need to divest all selves of their social history in order to provide for true equality of opportunity;[11] and the great uncertainty provided by the veil of ignorance could be recognized as an articulation of the uncertainty of successfully carrying out one's life plans in an individualistic, competitive society. In both cases, Rawls's formulation captures the tenuousness of individual identity in a world where the natural moral order of Aristotle or even natural right theory has been lost and nothing has taken its place—that is, where the ethical and political necessity previously provided by a nature of which humans are a part has disappeared.

While the Weberian world just described is, from a moral standpoint, radically contingent, it is still subject to necessity in that Weber (and later bourgeois culture) thought that in the realm of science, at least, objective facts were still ascertainable. Karl Marx and Nietzsche, however, while chronologically earlier than Weber, can be said to have pushed his logic to its ultimate conclusion to show that even "facts" are really human creations. In so doing, they complete the process of destroying any conception of necessity to limit human actions.

With Marx the problem we saw in Rousseau and Kant, that man is partly natural and thus determined but also capable of transcending natural necessity and becoming free, returns but in radically historicized form. Marx accepts the Hegelian understanding of history as a progressively synthetic process but grounds it not in a spiritual process of consciousness but rather in economics. Man must eat to live, and it is in producing the necessities of life that he produces himself as a self-conscious social being. Thus, although human social structures are determined, or at least limited in manifestation, by the technological forces of production, the dialectic of needs—the creation of new needs from the creation of tools necessary to satisfy existing needs—can eventually progress to the point where humans can transcend the limitations of their economic nature to create an abundance great enough to fulfill everyone's needs, thus allowing all to be truly free.

Marx's theory creates a world more radically contingent than that of Weber in two ways. First, since all ideas are ultimately the creation of the forces of production, all notions of morality, justice, and even, to a certain extent, empirical social fact, are timebound, historically relative, and simply express the sociological position of those who hold them. Second, since the historical process of production, with its contingent moralities, leads inevitably to the final realm of communism, anything that advances this end result would logically become permissible. The only element of necessity left in this picture is the vision of the communist society, since even the necessity provided by the technological forces of production is ultimately overcome. But unlike even Rousseau's goal of the egalitarian republic, which has some basis in concrete historical examples and clearly embodies moral principles already available, Marx's communist society is so different from anything hitherto existing that it becomes quite difficult to tell, as a practical matter, just what could bring it about. The goal of communism removes all limitations on the actions of those who would move history toward its culmination—not, as is so often stated, because of the certainty it provides to Marxist ideologues, but precisely because of the almost total uncertainty embodied in the vision of a perfectly free humanity.

Nietzsche, finally, can be understood as radicalizing the conception of human agency found in Marx and thus completing the process begun by Rousseau's recognition of the contradictions in natural right theory. Man is an animal whose fundamental characteristic is not economic activity but rather an unlimited capacity for creation through interpretation. The world in which he lives is therefore nothing more nor less than a chaotic clash of such interpretations. There is no being, only perpetual becoming, so man's notions of right, wrong, good, evil, and even rationality are simply values that he has posited, bridges that he has thrown across the abyss. "Truth" is not that which corresponds to the functional or mechanical natural order or even that which allows man to transcend his current situation through greater economic productivity but simply the most persuasive interpretation generated by the will to power. Recognizing this means that man—or at least the most persuasive men, the artists who create beauty—can cast off the egalitarian mediocrity of liberalism or socialism and the disenchanting analysis of science to create a new aristocratic order. But since this situation has no determinate end, even the tenuous necessity supplied by the good societies of Rousseau and Marx have disappeared. Nothing is left but endless new horizons. Just as Hobbes's instrumental rationalism is prophetic of the nineteenth century, Nietzsche's aesthetic irrationalism is prophetic of the twentieth century.

This prophetic role can perhaps be seen most clearly, not in the fascist appropriation of the will to power or even the deconstructive criticism of postmodernism, but in the overtly irrationalist ideological transformation that has followed the demise of reform liberalism and democratic socialism in the English-speaking world. The recently triumphant neoclassical liberalism of Friedrich Hayek, Milton Friedman, and Robert Nozick asserts that the utterly arbitrary distribution of rewards deriving from unregulated capitalism is the very guarantor of individual freedom, since any "patterned" distribution of rewards imposes someone's values on others. Legitimation comes not from a just distribution of rewards, since none can exist, but from the freedom that capitalism allows to will one's own values and act on them, i.e., from the system's capacity to provide an ever greater variety of demonic value choices. The moral orientation of contemporary capitalism is no longer rational self-improvement but rather aesthetic self-expression.

The story that I have sketched here attempts to articulate the late modern situation as a loss of any conception of necessity that can allow us to set limits on human actions. We have increasingly destroyed the necessity of Aristotle's ordered cosmos and left ourselves in a radically contingent universe. The form of this contingency can be seen changing, as it becomes more extreme in extent, from the inertial motion of Hobbes to the freedom of the will in Rousseau and Kant, from there to the historical materialism of Marx, and finally to the chaos of interpretations described by Nietzsche. It is this radical contingency, which tears down all limits, that makes the twentieth century unique in its coexistence of spectacular human capacities and grotesque human degradation.

Practically, it seems to me that this radical contingency has manifested itself in two ways in the twentieth century—first in the overt nihilism of the totalitarian movements during the first half of the century, and more recently in the subtler nihilism of the emerging global postindustrial capitalist economy.

The first half of this century engendered mass political movements that transformed vulgarized versions of the nineteenth-century German philosophies into vehicles for secular salvation, resulting not only in unprecedented violence and destruction, as Nietzsche himself had anticipated, but more fundamentally in the thoroughgoing denial of human finitude characteristic of the totalitarian attempt to take the Enlightenment idea of progress to its logical conclusion and actually create a new kind of human being. The world wars and revolutions of this century have been the most obvious manifestations of this breakdown of any limits on human action.

The half-century since the end of World War II has been characterized by relative peace and unprecedented prosperity, but at the same time by a profound sense of cultural exhaustion. The immediate postwar period seemed briefly to recapture a sense of stability as the corporate managerial order, or "new class," which replaced the shattered institutions of classical liberalism in the industrial societies, did achieve some legitimacy, even to the extent of partially reviving nineteenth-century notions of progress. Within a generation, however, Keynesian economic policies seemed to have exhausted their possibilities and popular culture gave clear signs that the widespread alienation that developed under earlier industrialism had actually intensified; the postwar order did not resolve the fundamental dilemmas of bourgeois civilization which had become manifest in the early twentieth century.

More recently, the revival of laissez-faire ideology and the collapse of communism has given some the impression that the late twentieth century has seen the triumph of a "free-market democracy" which has actually restored a sense of human limits.[12] Nothing could be further from the truth. While the left sees recent developments as the reestablishment of hierarchical domination, and the right interprets the end of the Cold War as the triumph of capitalist realism over Marxist fantasy, the transformation of capitalism to a postindustrial economy and its expansion to global proportions is better understood as the most complete practical manifestation of the radical contingency of late modern existence articulated by Nietzsche. Not only has the new global information economy resulted in a significant increase in inequality of income and wealth, it has uprooted both elites and masses in a more thoroughgoing way than could even have been imagined earlier in the century.

At the elite level, the transformation of capitalism has resulted in the rise of an even newer version of the "new class," deriving its power not from technical expertise but from the production and manipulation of cultural symbols. This transnational dominant class of "symbolic analysts," unlike the earlier entreprenurial or managerial classes, has little sense of institutional loyalty, as it works on a largely freelance basis. Also, rather than insulating itself from market forces, or attempting to carve out a private life of suburban domesticity separate from its public life of work, as older dominant classes within capitalism attempted to do, the new elite would better be described as living lives of frenzied market activity where public and private are collapsed into a blur of perpetual image-creation.

At the mass level, meanwhile, the postwar middle class of white collar and unionized blue collar workers sees its work being done by computers or low-wage Third World labor, and finds itself sliding into a vast class of service workers who receive not only low pay but more importantly few fringe benefits and virtually no job security. Indeed, the new computer technologies that have created the new economy could within a generation render so much of the population economically superfluous that unemployment rates could reach levels comparable to the Great Depression. One of the most striking features of the new world economy seems to be the prospect of pauperization on a scale not seen since the first industrial revolution.[13]

The aesthetic orientation of the new social order, manifested most obviously in the godlike status of performing artists and professional athletes, corresponds to the triumph of Nietzschean irrationalism in the most recent academic defenses of capitalism discussed earlier. At the level of popular ideology, the most prominent political figure of the new global order personified a vulgar Nietzscheanism: Ronald Reagan, a former movie actor, defined truth as whatever Ronald Reagan wanted truth to be. The degenerate version of the Protestant work ethic that Reagan endlessly preached—that one can succeed against any conceivable obstacle through nothing but hard work—can hardly be anything other than a crude version of the will to power. (The question of whether one is working *productively* or not, which was central to the older Lockean conception of justice, appears to have become irrelevant.) American liberals, chained to such outmoded Kantian notions as "facts," have been powerless to comprehend the dynamics of the new postmodern capitalist world order of images. The ultimate fulfillment of Nietzsche's prophecy seems not to be violent totalitarianism but rather libertarian consumer capitalism.

Given this cultural orientation and the more thoroughgoing breakdown of traditional community and family structures currently taking place, reaction to the social dislocations of the global capitalist economy is unlikely to resemble the organized ideological mass movements of the early- and mid-twentieth century. Although the earlier political movements were the product of social atomization and anomie, they did ultimately require and develop high levels of cohesiveness and organization. The current and probable future situation is more likely to result in the chronic low-level random violence of gangs and terrorists; ideological movements are more likely to take the form of splintered rabbles such as American militia groups. Just as the decentralized high-tech economy makes regulation by national governments more difficult, the very disorganization—and thus unpredictability—of violent responses by that economy's casualties will create severe security problems.[14] The insecurity of the new global economy may represent the culmination of the modern process by which the world's contingency is utterly radicalized.

As my brief discussion has already indicated, this radical contingency results from modernity's partial abandonment of the classical cosmos. If the possibility of human creativity is accepted, then any viable concept of necessity must take this creativity into account. This is precisely what modern objectivism fails to do. If acceptable epistemological limits are conceptualized in impersonal, acontextual terms, then no limits will be found to distinguish acceptable from unacceptable knowledge claims. Similarly, if we assume that limits on human action can only be provided by a fixed principle unaffected by human agency, such as Hobbes's mechanical laws, Kant's categories of the under-standing, and even Marx's scientific analysis of the historical process, then the recognition that reality is at least partly a human creation leads inevitably to nihilism. Nietzsche's conclusion that reality is nothing but a clash of different interpretations can itself be seen as a case of dis-appointed objectivism, since it is based on the recognition that impersonal, objective knowledge is impossible without, however, any consideration that valid knowledge might take any other form.[15]

Similarly, we can see how objectivism and the relativism upon which it is parasitical manifest themselves socially and politically in the tendencies of modern societies toward both technocratic tyranny and moral disintegration. Institutions built on objectivist principles will eventually be perceived as oppressive and dehumanizing, since they will be destructive of fundamental elements of human knowledge and communication, and since a conceptual framework understanding truth and rationality in objectivist terms provides no other alternatives, attempts to challenge the objectivist order will typically take relativist or irrationalist forms.

If we abandon completely the assumption that epistemological and moral limits must take an impersonal, acontextual form, however, it may be possible to speak of a contextual necessity that actually derives from human creative and interpretive capacities. This possibility is implied in recent post-Wittgensteinian philosophy of language and science, and my main task will be to explore it by developing the concept of narrative practice as an alternative to objectivism, specifically by developing the idea of an oral/aural place.

One additional implication of this discussion, incidentally, is that the radical contingency of the biblical picture, which I presented as setting the whole process in motion, may be problematic only when viewed from the perspective of objectivism or essentialism, or, rather, that this picture contains elements of necessity that become obscured by its interpretation in objectivist or essentialist terms. This would seem to be an implication of the discussion of science above, since it will be recalled that at the bottom of modern science lies the confidence in the orderliness of the immanent world, derived from the belief in God's faithfulness. The problem may well lie with the influence that Greek philosophy has had on Christian theology.[16]

In any case, to further clarify this issue it will be helpful to examine the work of several contemporary political theorists who attempt to deal with the contingency implied by the collapse of the premodern cosmos and to discuss the difficulties they encounter. Specifically, I will show that none of these theories is able to articulate a conception of necessity that could establish limits, or defeat relativism, precisely because they are unable fully to escape the objectivist framework of knowledge. Or, to put it another way, none of these theories is able to establish a substitute for the classical cosmos, such as an interpretive principle, that could defeat Nietzsche's claim that reality is a radically contingent clash of subjective interpretations. Examining these theories will further clarify why my project of establishing a non-objectivist conception of necessity might be one fruitful approach to the contemporary question of limits.

Necessity and Contingency in Contemporary Political Theory

I have already discussed in some detail the evolution of modern liberalism. It will be helpful to consider one further example to illustrate the difficulties involved in attempting to establish limits in late modernity. Isaiah Berlin is famous for his discussion of negative and positive liberty. For Berlin, the two conceptions concern themselves with different questions. Negative liberty is concerned with the actual area or space available to the agent for unrestricted movement, and positive liberty is concerned with who or what actually restricts the agent's movement. Berlin argues, of course, that only the negative conception is legitimate, or at least workable, because of the potential for tyranny inherent in the positive conception, which can logically lead to to the idea of forcing someone to be free. In the terminology I have developed so far, it could be said that Berlin's discussion is an attempt to come to grips with the radical contingency of late modern existence. Berlin's critique of positive freedom can be seen as a recognition of the collapse of the classical ordered cosmos with its overarching good for human beings. If reality is not characterized by such an objective good, that is, if there are really only competing goods and indeed competing inter-pretations of the good, then attempts to realize freedom in the positive sense will inevitably result in someone imposing a particular conception of the human good on others who may not even comprehend this conception. The negative conception of freedom can be seen as an attempt to articulate a set of limits, or a conception of necessity, that can coincide with radical contingency. If we cannot find any overarching good for humanity, we can at least declare certain matters private and thus inaccessible to public coercion.

Unfortunately, Berlin's argument self-destructs, because the negative conception of freedom, or rather the distinction between positive and negative conceptions, tacitly assumes that there can be some objective, impersonal measure of the agent's area of unrestricted movement. The distinction between negative and positive liberty, at least as Berlin formulates it, collapses when we consider that the agent and others may disagree about the extent to which he or she actually is restricted; here it becomes a crucial matter *who* is setting the standard of measurement. The idea that there can be an objective, impersonal measure of the extent of the agent's restriction is precisely the product of the "grand metaphysical schemes" of which Berlin is so suspicious. Berlin does not seem to realize that his own radical subjectivism, which denies any fundamental unity to human experience, utterly destroys the objective basis for his distinction. Another way to understand this is to consider Berlin's admonition to "fall back on the ordinary resources of empirical observation and ordinary human knowledge." The obvious question that arises, and that arises from Berlin's own argument, is *whose* version of ordinary knowledge we are supposed to fall back on. To twist one of the phrases Berlin uses, the ordinary experience of an Egyptian peasant is very different from the ordinary experience of an Oxford don. One can also see Berlin's failure fully to appreciate the consequences of the radical contingency with which he is attempting to deal when he argues that only limitations placed by other humans, not natural limitations, should count as restrictions on human freedom. This argument tacitly assumes a natural order independent of human interpretation, which, as we have seen, is a notion incompatible with the subjectivism Berlin assumes to begin with.[17]

What is crucial about Berlin's discussion, for our purposes, is that he develops his negative conception of freedom as an attempt to deal with the radical contingency of the late modern world, but then undermines his own argument by falling back on an objectivist conception of necessity—in this case, some kind of objective measure of the area of an agent's movement. Any conception of necessity that would succeed, given his initial recognition of the extent to which humans interpret the world differently, would have to take this interpretive dimension into account, which Berlin's conception does not do. Indeed, we can also see that Berlin's distinction not only does not solve the problem, it actually blinds him to the real issue, which is the lack of limits in late modernity. As we have seen, it is this, not the notions of community or "collectivism" found in non-liberal political theories, that is responsible for the extreme forms of tyranny experienced in the twentieth century. Premodern politics, although informed by an overarching conception of the human good, never developed totalitarian movements because it lacked any realization that humans could change the natural order.

The failure of Berlin's analysis to escape the objectivist framework can be seen in another way. When liberalism was at its apex, it was itself informed by a grand metaphysical vision of human history—the idea of progress toward a cosmopolitan community of autonomous individuals. Partly in reaction to the deranged manifestations of the progressive ideal that have caused such extensive suffering and destruction in this century, recent liberal theory has retreated to an essentially Hobbesian orientation: it no longer emphasizes the possibilities of progress or liberation, however understood, but rather simply hopes to provide a formal legal framework to enforce mutual forbearance on the part of its citizens. It is unclear, however, how liberalism, stripped of the idea of progress with which it legitimated itself in the nineteenth century, can accomplish even this modest goal. At the sociological level, the negative conception of freedom itself seems tacitly to assume one of the major features of progressive ideology, i.e., that humans can be educated to escape both parochial prejudices and egoistic competitiveness to become tolerant and cooperative cosmopolitans. If the ideal of progress is abandoned, it would seem that intolerance and egoism can be restrained only with substantial coercion. When liberalism abandons the large claims about reality which had set limits to its basic political goals, those goals become absurdly self-contradictory. That is, Berlin and other liberals undermine the idea of negative freedom—turn it into a possible source of considerable coercion—when they attempt to divorce it from the context of the progressive worldview within which it originally made sense. Liberalism has failed to recognize the extent to which its own central concepts are embedded in and even derived from a very specific interpretation of the human condition and thus has failed to understand why any attempt to set limits on human action must deal with the interpretive dimension of human experience.

Perhaps a more striking indication of the difficulties involved in responding to the radical contingency of late modernity can be found in contemporary communitarian theories. Communitarian theorists, as we have seen, claim to eschew any reliance upon universal, ahistorical principles, arguing that such principles are too abstract to be meaningfully applied to any concrete situation. Ethical precepts, or limits on political practice, can only come from concrete historical communities. In this regard the communitarians demonstrate a much better understanding of the late modern situation articulated by Nietzsche than liberals such as Berlin; indeed, in a sense they take Berlin's critique of universal truth claims more seriously than Berlin does himself. Nevertheless, it seems to me that none of the major communitarian theories currently in existence is able to develop a workable conception of limits that could be applied to the political practice of concrete communities.

For example, Michael Walzer and Daniel Bell have both employed the idea of "shared meanings" or "shared understandings." They argue that, contrary to modern liberalism, which sees societies, or at least modern liberal societies, as collections of individuals with conflicting goals, the common vocabulary of any political community articulates certain widely, if not entirely unanimously, shared normative pre-scriptions. Both have attempted to use this insight to articulate a communitarian moral vision for contemporary Western, and especially American, societies.[18]

In one sense, the need for anyone to argue that societies have "shared meanings" shows how the liberal idea of neutrality has confused political debate. It ought to be obvious that any society, virtually by definition, will have a shared vocabulary that shapes the experience of its individual members—even as it may simultaneously place some of those individuals in a subordinate or even marginal position. The crucial question really has to do with the content of those shared meanings and their implications for public order. In this regard, the obvious objection to the idea of grounding public life in the shared meanings of a community is that the idea of a shared meaning offers no ultimate normative standard, no criterion or criteria for distinguishing "good" shared meanings from "bad" shared meanings. How, it is asked, do we deal with a tribe whose shared meanings include ritual cannibalism?

Although such questions are not irrelevant, the really important questions about the idea of shared understandings illustrate the central dilemma of late modernity in a more subtle way. Walzer and Bell have both argued that if a community's shared understandings are identified, they will clarify the nature of the community's basic moral com-mitments, whatever these might be, and at least give the community a better understanding of itself. But one of the most important insights achieved by Nietzschean and post-Nietzschean criticism of objectivism is the extent to which supposedly neutral or unambiguous conceptual categories may mask structures of power and domination. Similarly, it is quite possible that a community's shared understandings might actually *obscure* its basic character.

The most obvious example of this would in fact be the contemporary United States of America. It is a striking fact that the United States, the most individualistic society in the world, probably also has the most widely and thoroughly accepted set of shared understandings, all revolving around the idea of individual freedom. But these shared individualistic understandings, far from clarifying the fundamental structure of American political order, function in such a way as to make Americans themselves blind to the almost tribal homogeneity of American political consciousness, which is so obvious to Europeans or even Canadians. Americans persistently describe their nation as "pluralistic," even though, to take just one example, almost no American could even imagine questioning either the wisdom or the importance of the Constitution. Indeed, it is precisely these shared individualist understandings such as the notion of pluralism that have generated the confused debate about neutrality—they mask themselves to the point that the existence of a society without any shared understandings could actually become an object of serious theoretical discussion.

Eric Voegelin gives another, more general, example of how the shared understanding of pluralism may obscure the basic moral structure of a society. As Voegelin sees it, modern Western societies are better understood not, as pluralist ideology would have it, as collections of individuals with competing worldviews for which some kind of neutral accommodation must be made, but rather as historically stratified structures representing different stages in the deterioration of the medieval Christian worldview: "We are not dealing with human beings who hold this or that opinion as individuals, but with Christians and secularists; not with Christians, but with Catholics and Protestants; not with plain liberals, but with Christian and secular liberals; not with plain secular liberals but with old style liberals of the free-enterprise type and modern liberals of the socialist type; and so forth." The shared vocabulary of pluralism obscures the fact that these supposedly incommensurable worldviews are connected in a very definite way. Hence, a society that understands itself as "pluralistic" will be systematically confused about its own internal tensions and dynamics.[19]

The theories of Bell and Walzer are themselves examples of the possible confusion just described. Both have assumed that if a society has shared meanings, they must be *communitarian* meanings. They have not seriously considered the possibility that a society, such as the United States, might have shared meanings which are *libertarian*, and it could be argued that as a result they fail to understand the nature of American shared understandings.

A rather striking example of this occurs in Bell's dialogue, *Communitarianism and Its Critics*. Bell's "communitarian" interlocuter argues that Americans would not have supported many of the foreign policy adventures of recent administrations if they had realized that such policies actually represented a denial of basic American ideals such as freedom and democracy. As an example, she points out that the Nicaraguan *contras* were not "freedom-fighters" but rather were destroying the Nicaraguan people's hopes for freedom, because they "attacked hospitals and agricultural co-operatives, murdering many peasants along the way, with what seemed to be the general aims of destroying the economic infrastructure and sowing terror in the countryside." Unfortunately, it is undoubtedly the case that many, perhaps a majority, of Americans would regard agricultural coopera- tives as a form of socialism and thus as a threat to freedom, so that destroying such toeholds for the evil empire of world communism would indeed be fighting for freedom. If it were replied that this indicates a confused understanding of socialism, the obvious retort would be that most Americans do indeed share such a muddled understanding.[20]

In a very real sense, Walzer and Bell have not escaped the liberal framework they are attempting to critique. They have taken the liberal notion of pluralism so seriously that they have failed to recognize it as a specific type of (confused and confusing) shared meaning. This leads them to conflate two distinct questions, i.e., whether people in a society agree on anything, and upon what they do in fact agree. They have assumed that if, contrary to the liberal model, there are certain core agreements, then these agreements must indicate the existence of a committment to communal provision of basic human needs. But a set of core agreements may simply indicate, for example, the existence of a community of utilitarian individualists who exclude from full member- ship those who cannot fend for themselves in the market economy. Late twentieth-century America could indeed be understood as a community, but it is a community whose shared understandings establish some rather stringent economic prerequisites for full membership. By failing to see pluralism as itself a particular kind of shared meaning, Walzer and Bell have failed to understand the kind of (utilitarian and/or expressive individualist) community it articulates.

In the terms of our discussion so far, we can say that Walzer and Bell have attempted to use the idea of shared normative understandings as a conception of necessity, i.e., as something that will set limits to the political practice of a community. An examination of a community's shared meanings should at least clarify its basic moral commitments and thus set limits of some kind to the community's actions. But as we have seen, aside from the obvious question of how acceptable other communities might find such moral limits, a set of shared understandings may fail to clarify a society's basic moral structure, or even, in the extreme, fail to indicate clearly the existence of a basic moral structure. There is an important sense in which theorists such as Walzer and Bell, although they do not fall back on an explicitly objectivist conception of knowledge in the manner Berlin does, nevertheless do not entirely escape an objectivist framework, in that they fail to realize how ambiguous and even deceptive a set of shared understandings may be. Hence, the concept of shared meanings cannot (at least by itself) come to grips with the question of limits that is central to late modernity because it cannot answer the question of how a community can evaluate itself, or more specifically, how a community can evaluate its own self-interpretation.

Recognizing this difficulty, Bell eventually argues that what is ultimately needed is indeed some kind of narrative that can render intelligible the evolution of a set of shared meanings. It may be possible to construct a history that shows that one course of evolution in a set of shared understandings represents a gain in understanding, while a different type of change would not. The first evolutionary change could then be regarded as better, and the community would have a way of evaluating its own practice.[21] This possibility leads us to the idea of narrative.

I have already mentioned the attempts of MacIntyre and Stanley Hauerwas to ground ethical and political practice in concrete communal narratives as opposed to universal, ahistorical principles. Hauerwas's moral theology, which explicates the ethical implications of the Christian narrative, contains many brilliant insights and offers a compelling alternative to more conventional forms of moral theology and philosophy. Ultimately, however, the attempt to ground morality in the narratives and practices of a concrete community, although it may avoid the obvious objections that could be made to an essentially static conception of shared meanings, runs into difficulties of its own.

A good example of this occurs in a definitive statement by Hauerwas and David Burrell of the centrality of narrative and the importance of the specifically Christian narrative in ethical reasoning. Hauerwas and Burrell argue very persuasively that conventional modern conceptions of ethical reasoning, focusing on applying abstract universal principles to specific "choices," miss much of what is involved in being a moral agent. By contrast, a narrative can demonstrate why one judges a certain course of action to be better than others by showing the effects specific courses of actions have on people, and indeed by showing the process by which one learns to make judgments about what are more desirable outcomes on a human character. Ethics is not a matter of making "choices," but of living out a narrative that builds character and the capacity for judging character. Here, we appear to have a concrete embodiment of the narrative type of judgment mentioned above—we can construct stories that can illustrate how one particular course of action resulted in an improvement in character (which would be analogous to an increase in understanding), while another one did not.

For Hauerwas and Burrell, then, one judges the relative validity of narratives by the kinds of people they produce. But what then is a better or worse person? Here, they run into serious trouble, for they can only say that a better person is one who has a greater capacity to recognize "the good for humankind." At this crucial point in the argument, they seem to have fallen back on the Aristotelian conception of an overarching, universal good for humanity, which was precisely what they had earlier implied could not be meaningfully described. The connection to Aristotle becomes even more clear when they make the statement, when discussing medicine, that "we need a substantive story that will sustain moral activity in a finite and limited world. . . . The story which accompanies technology—of setting nature aright—results in the clinical anomalies to which we are subjecting others and ourselves in order to avoid the limits of our existence." But much of the recent confusion over what is ethical in medical practice (and in other situations) results from the our discovery of just how much we can control and change "nature." Medical ethics is a simple matter when all but the most minor illnesses mean virtually certain death. "Human limits" are mentioned as if they were an unproblematic given.

In any case, Hauerwas and Burrell go on to offer several criteria of what constitutes a good story. Two of the criteria, which they argue complement each other, again illustrate the unresolved tensions in their argument. They claim that a good story provides us with "room to keep us from having to resort to violence," and that this standard is connected to the criterion that a good story allows for a sense of the tragic. They illustrate the relation between these two criteria with the issue raised above, i.e., the extent to which the (mistaken) modern belief that we can transcend natural limits through technology leads us to act violently toward both ourselves and our environment. The modern story, they argue, lacking any sense of the tragic, cannot provide room to prevent violence. But for some stories, especially those that articulate a finite cosmos, the use of violence can be a virtue. Narrative traditions that have a strong sense of the tragic typically recognize not just the inevitability but indeed the possible appropriateness of violence in human affairs. The disavowal of violence found in the Christian narrative would seem to derive from the perception that human existence is not, at least ultimately, tragic—i.e., that in some way humans cannot fully comprehend, we will finally be delivered from the sinfulness and suffering of earthly existence. Hence, the attempt to derive a basic Christian principle while tacitly relying on the idea of a finite cosmos seems to produce a rather strange claim about how violence and tragedy are connected.

We can see that the crucial problem for Hauerwas and Burrell is that at certain key points in the argument, they fall back on precisely the kind of universal principle that they had previously argued was untenable. Hence, their argument fails really to come to grips with the implications of their own critique of modern objectivist approaches to morality. Although their employment of narrative concepts illuminates aspects of ethical life obscured by conventional accounts of ethical reasoning, they have really only shifted to a different level the question we encountered earlier in the discussion of shared meanings, i.e., what ultimate standard of judgment can we apply to a particular human practice? This question was precisely what the concept of narrative was supposed to render irrelevant by providing a contextual standard for judging changes within human practices. But, as we have seen, Hauerwas and Burrell do not accomplish, or at least do not fully accomplish, this task. Latent objectivist elements, in the form of unproblematic (and also unspecified) "natural limits" and an apparently self-evident "good for humankind" still lurk in the structure of the argument and indeed end up carrying much of its burden.[22]

MacIntyre seems to have recognized more clearly than Hauerwas and Burrell the implications of the breakdown of the classical cosmos, as his discussion of the moral virtues and their setting in the context of a narrative is explicitly conceived not only as an alternative to modern objectivist approaches to ethical reasoning but also as a substitute for Aristotle's finite cosmos, or as MacIntyre refers to it, his "metaphysical biology." I will examine MacIntyre in some detail here because his explication of narrative and related concepts will be central to my later discussion. Ultimately, I will want to put this concept on a different footing than he does, and, in so doing, begin to derive concrete implications for politics from it.

MacIntyre argues that all premodern moral reasoning was teleological in nature, with the telos for a person's moral actions given by a narrative tradition encompassing the society in which he or she lived and providing exemplars for individual behavior, thus inculcating the virtues necessary for the individual person to attain a degree of fulfillment and for the society to preserve itself. Modernity has attempted to abstract moral questions from this social context and in so doing has lost the teleology necessary for coherent moral reasoning. What must be done, as MacIntyre sees it, is to revive narrative traditions through local communities struggling against the extant Weberian order or possible future Nietzschean disorder and thus provide a new grounding for moral discourse. The structure of such narrative traditions must be such that they will exemplify and inculcate the virtues necessary to sustain those practices that create and sustain human communities.

There are four key concepts in what MacIntyre sees as the essential structure of moral reasoning and ethical practice: virtue, practice, narrative, and tradition. Or, rather, as MacIntyre puts it, the key concept is that of a virtue, which requires for its intelligibility the conceptual background provided by the concepts of practice, narrative, and tradition; these are actually stages in the logical development of the concept. Let us examine each one and their relationship.

MacIntyre begins by saying that, as a first approximation, "a virtue is an acquired human quality the possession and exercise of which tends to enable us to achieve those goods which are internal to practices and the lack of which effectively prevents us from achieving any such goods."[23] By a practice, MacIntyre means "any coherent and complex form of socially established cooperative human activity through which goods internal to that form of activity are realized in the course of trying to achieve those standards of excellence which are appropriate to, and partially definitive of, that form of activity, with the result that human powers to achieve excellence, and human conceptions of the ends and goods involved, are systematically extended."[24]

A practice then consists of a community of people undertaking an activity in which they attempt to achieve goals defined by and defining the activity, according to standards of excellence partly definitive of and partly defined by that activity. No goals or standards are properly external to the practice. It is in a sense self-contained; indeed, it looks something like Aristotle's teleology. (MacIntyre in fact sees himself as articulating the most important aspects of a tradition of moral reasoning of which Aristotle is the most important representative, although Aristotle's natural teleology is in certain respects different from the narrative teleology more typical of the tradition.) What is particularly important about this idea, however, and what distinguishes it from the natural teleology of Aristotle, is that "practices never have a goal or goals fixed for all time." Rather, "the goals themselves are transmuted by the history of the activity." Past successes result in new present understandings of what the goals of the practice are.[25] This is why practices, particularly those dealing with building and sustaining human communities, must be informed by, or enclosed within, a narrative.

A narrative, in turn, is that which gives intelligibility and accountability to the actions of a person. It is a story with a particular meaning, one peculiar to the person who is its subject, but one that must imply responsibility to other persons. In terms of the virtues, then, a narrative will unify them by bringing together relevant practices into a quest for the good, rather than simply a number of separate and possibly contradictory goods which are the goals of different practices. And finally, the narratives of individual human beings are drawn together by a tradition, for individuals must begin their quest for the good from a starting point defined not alone but by the community and tradition into which they are born, and must engage in that quest with others. A tradition is not an attempt to uphold the past against the future, but rather it draws upon the past to define and redefine the goals of the future. It will be partly constituted by an ongoing discussion about just what the tradition is.[26]

Thus, for MacIntyre, successful moral reasoning and practice takes place within a tradition enclosing a narrative or narratives that inform a number of practices, themselves successful or unsuccessful depending on the possession and exercise of the relevant virtues. Further, the tradition will be modified by the vicissitudes of the narratives that make it up, which in turn will be extended by the success of the practices they inform, which themselves will also be progressively changed. All three elements that make up the context of a virtue have the same dynamic structure. In referring to this structure henceforth, I will use the term *narrative practice*, in order to avoid an awkward phrase such as "tradition-informed narrative practice," and at the same time to retain the historical sense which might be lost by simply talking about a "practice."

For reasons that will become clear as the discussion proceeds, I believe that MacIntyre's idea of a narrative practice is essential to constructing a political theory to inform ethical communities which can construct a new public realm for postindustrial and ultimately post-bourgeois societies. Perhaps the most important such reason is that MacIntyre's formulation, unlike the others discussed so far, does seem to have thoroughly avoided explicitly or tacitly incorporating any objectivist elements. What this means, however, is that it is extremely unclear how MacIntyre would respond to the claim that what I have called a narrative practice is relativistic or historicistic. Although the question of an ultimate standard of morality cannot arise for someone attempting to critique MacIntyre on his own grounds, since his presentation is consistently contextual, other questions can arise that he does not address. Specifically, it is not hard to frame at least three major objections to the concept of a narrative practice. First, how do we adjudicate among apparently incommensurable practices or narrative traditions? Second, and really just the other side of the first problem, how do we gain critical distance from the practice or narrative of which we find ourselves a part? Finally, what substantive content can MacIntyre supply to this abstract description of a narrative practice? In terms of our discussion so far, we could say that the problem with MacIntyre's conception of a narrative practice is that it does not appear to contain any elements of necessity; the direction and goals of the narrative practice are potentially radically contingent, because of its dynamic, changing character. To put it another way, although MacIntyre's idea of a narrative practice escapes objectivist categories and does not tacitly rely on a natural order unaffected by human agency, it is not clear whether it really constitutes a substitute for Aristotle's closed cosmos, or his metaphysical biology. Or, as J. Budziszewski points out, MacIntyre's expurgation of Aristotle's metaphysical biology from moral theory seems to require its replacement with a "metaphysical history";[27] it is not clear how he would avoid the same indeterminacy we saw in Marx and Nietzsche.

MacIntyre has attempted to answer these questions about narrative, not with a metaphysical history, but with more narratives.[28] Essentially, he has attempted to argue, in keeping with the idea we discussed earlier, that some narratives are more plausible than others because they can be seen as bringing about an increase in understanding relative to their rivals. He has not, however, attempted systematically to analyze further the structure of what I have called a narrative practice as elucidated in *After Virtue*. My project could be described as an attempt to do this in order to see if any elements of necessity can be found in, or derived from, this structure.

As I have already mentioned, I believe that such an analysis will yield a conception of necessity in the form of a speech-based concept of place. Specifically, I will show how MacIntyre's discussion of narrative practice needs such a concept to be complete on its own terms. In so doing, I will modify MacIntyre's conception of a narrative practice in a manner that will eliminate the need for the kind of historical teleology which it may presently imply, replacing such a teleology with speech-based places of necessity. These oral/aural places will set limits on the actions of both individuals and communities and provide substantive content to the idea of a narrative practice. That is, the places inherent in the speech act will the provide the non-objectivist conception of necessity which I have argued is necessary to fully escape the objectivist/relativist dichotomy and make a communitarian political theory workable.

My project then is to develop a non-objectivist conception of necessity applicable to late modern political life from an analysis of what I have called a narrative practice. In order to accomplish this, however, it will be necessary to understand the objectivist/relativist dualism from which we are trying to escape. It is essential to be very clear about what pitfalls to avoid when constructing the concept of place. The first task to be undertaken, then, is a careful explication of the nature of objectivism.

2

SCIENTIFIC PRACTICE
AND ITS IMPLICIT CRITIQUE OF OBJECTIVISM

In a very real sense, the central problem of modern philosophy—the justification of knowledge—articulates the ambiguous nature of modernity discussed in the previous chapter. On the one hand, this problem is a manifestation of the desire to generalize the spectacular successes of modern science to all aspects of life. To early modernity, it seemed that if political and social practice could emulate whatever it is that makes science work, the public and private pathologies recurrent throughout history could be eliminated or at least greatly ameliorated. And to early modernity, it seemed that the crucial aspect of science was the attainment of reliable knowledge. Certainly modern philosophy has taken, usually explicitly and always implicitly, science as its paradigm of attaining true knowledge. If we ask, however, why this seemed so important, that is, why reliable knowledge should become so central a problem, we immediately encounter the radical contingency of modernity; alongside the tremendous optimism of early modernity regarding the possibilities inherent in science lurks a suspicion that there really is no basis for knowledge. However we approach modernity, it seems that a central problem is how scientific knowledge can continue to grow when our attempts to discover a foundation for such knowledge seem increasingly less successful. I have already mentioned briefly recent developments in the philosophy of science and language. In this chapter I shall discuss the matter in more detail in order to construct a basis for establishing limits for political practice.

We have already seen that the empiricism of Hobbes could not demonstrate the existence of physical laws external to the subject. A similar, or perhaps complementary, impasse occurred in the rationalist philosophy that followed from Descartes; just as empiricism could not satisfactorily account for order in the empirical world, rationalism could not account for the possibility of empirical knowledge, because it could not logically get beyond that which we know innately or *a priori*.

Kant attempted to get around both these difficulties by arguing that the subject unavoidably projects a conceptual framework onto the world it experiences, but that this framework contains the basic categories, such as causation, with which we understand and therefore can be confidently relied upon to give us adequate knowledge of the world as we experience it. The breakdown of this conception, the realization that what Kant had taken as *a priori* categories of the understanding were simply hypostasized elements of Newtonian cosmology, led to a thoroughgoing subjectivism in continental thinking; the conceptual framework projected onto the world by the subject could be completely indeterminate. In the terminology developed earlier, Kant's epistemology could not prevent the world as we experience it from becoming radically contingent; thus, science ultimately could not be given any privileged position as a means of attaining reliable knowledge.

While one line of continental thought moved in the direction of discrediting all knowledge claims, including even those of science, a different post-Kantian program more familiar to English-speaking people took over the task of explicating scientific knowledge and thus providing an exemplar for all legitimate knowledge. This was positivism. In one sense, positivism took as its starting point the Kantian bifurcation of consciousness into noumenal and phenomenal realms. We cannot know the noumenal realm, reality as it actually is, as we can know the phenomenal realm; since the noumenal realm is the territory of traditional metaphysics, this amounts to a sharp distinction between metaphysical and empirical statements, with only the latter counting as true or even (in some versions of positivism) meaningful. True knowledge then can be obtained by ruthlessly eradicating all metaphysical elements from the language and thus the methods of science. If this could be done, scientific theories could be proven by the application of the proper methods to reality; this would allow theories to be built from statements that could ultimately be reduced to data of sense experience.

The positivist program thus could be seen as a somewhat more sophisticated version of empiricism, and, in fact, it suffered the same fate as its predecessor, i.e., it was shown to be incoherent on its own grounds. It first proved impossible to demonstrate how, i.e., by what method, a scientific theory could actually be "proven" or even shown to be "probable"; it could not be tested for all possible cases to which it might apply and there was no strictly logical way to generalize from a limited number of cases. The positivist program of developing a rigorous inductive logic failed. Similarly, the attempt to construct a neutral "observation language" which would provide the building blocks for strictly empirical scientific theories or statements ran aground, since, as critics of positivism demonstrated, even the most banal knowledge claims or observations contain elements of subjective interpretation. Positivism eventually issued forth in a noncognitivism parallelling that of post-Nietzschean thought.

Even before the positivist program suffered its final demise, conventionalist philosophers of science such as Pierre Duhem and, later, Karl Popper, while accepting the positivist dichotomy between empirical and metaphysical statements and the general objectivist conception of legitimate knowledge, realized that an inductive logic could never be constructed and that facts were inseparable from, and indeed partly formed by, theories. For the conventionalists, theories could at best be only falsified, not proven. Thus, the conventionalists focused on the methods for deducing hypotheses from theories and for testing such hypotheses. But again, since the strict separation between metaphysical and empirical statements could not be maintained, that is, since all scientific experiments, or all empirical "facts," ultimately are shaped by and are inextricably intertwined with the vocabulary and conceptual framework of the knower, and, further, since the vocabulary and conceptual framework themselves inevitably contain assumptions of which the knower is not aware, then strictly speaking, no theory could even be falsified.

As a result, the conventionalists were forced to admit that the apparent truth or falsity of any scientific theory rested upon certain conventional decisions made by the community of scientists. Duhem, for example, argued that the acceptance of scientific theories rested upon their simplicity, while Popper and some of his followers attempted to enumerate a set of standards governing what kinds of conventional decisions would be allowed about, for example, the manner in which theories could be modified or augmented. These strategies seemed either to allow a very large arbitrary element to exist in scientific method, as in the case of Duhem's standard of simplicity, which threatened to reduce science to aesthetics, or else, as in the case of Popper, to establish impossibly rigorous standards, given actual scientific practice. Thus, the conventionalist approach apparently failed to come to grips with the implications of its own critique of positivism.

The failure of objectivist (whether positivist or conventionalist) philosophy of science did not, however, mean that the last hope of grounding knowledge had been destroyed. The work of the conventionalists helped set the stage for more recent philosophers of science such as Stephen Toulmin, Michael Polanyi, Norwood Hanson, and Thomas S. Kuhn, who have been referred to as "revisionists." The revisionists, by showing the untenability of understanding knowledge only in terms of the knowing subject's relation to the objects of knowledge, have shifted attention to the broader context of scientific knowledge, which includes the community and tradition of which the scientist becomes a part. This in turn has shifted our understanding of rationality away from the narrow confines of certifying factual knowledge and toward communicative competence in specific contexts.

In this chapter, I want to examine the work of one of the revisionist philosophers of science, Michael Polanyi (1891–1976). By explicating Polanyi's understanding of how we attain scientific knowledge, which he takes as exemplary of all knowledge, I hope to point out what the main features of the objectivist conception of knowledge are. That is, I will use Polanyi's discussion of scientific knowing to show what is wrong with, or missing from, the objectivist paradigm. Doing this will provide guidelines as to what should be avoided in attempting to derive a conception of necessity, and thus of place, from a consideration of our acts of communication and their context. This is important because, as noted earlier, the crucial difficulty with such an endeavor is that while few political theorists today still hold overtly objectivist views, subtle manifestations of objectivism still affect our thinking, so that particular care must be taken to be aware of such manifestations. Additionally, and most fundamentally, Polanyi's description of knowledge will provide the basis for explicating the actual details of this concept of necessity; certain of the concepts developed therein will be particularly useful in developing the logic of communication central to my thesis.

It might be objected here that by taking scientific knowledge as paradigmatic of all knowledge, Polanyi is engaged in a reductionist move similar to that of the positivists. In fact, however, a full explication of scientific knowledge will, according to Polanyi, ultimately require a discussion of human rationality in all its facets, including, as noted earlier, communicative competence in the context of various practices. Also, I should point out that by taking Polanyi as my starting point, I do not mean to imply that I think he has said the last word on the issues at hand. Rather, I am using his work because it is representative of the work of the revisionists and because, as mentioned earlier, some of his formulations will be particularly helpful for some of the concepts I want to develop.

Intellectual Passions and Scientific Knowing

Polanyi's starting point is to show that all knowledge is *personal*. The ideal of "objective" knowledge, in the sense that objective means impersonal, is unattainable. Knowledge cannot be detached from the knower. All forms of knowledge contain an irreducible element of personal appraisal of orderliness, rationality, wholeness, etc. An example involving probability will illustrate this. In *Personal Knowledge*, his major work, Polanyi tells how (at the time he was writing) the train station at Abergele, just past the border between England and Wales, had "Welcome to Wales by British Railways" inscribed on the lawn with white pebbles. Someone passing by the station might ask whether this could have happened by chance. If we calculate the probability of the pebbles being arranged this way by sheer chance, it would be so small that we must certainly conclude that someone had done this on purpose. But if the pebbles were simply scattered all over the lawn, we would not likely ask if this was due to chance or purpose, even though the probability of this particular arrangement would still be fantastically low. The reason for this is that we always make personal appraisals of orderliness, so that in the first case the question of purposeful activity came up, while in the second it did not, even though in the second case the probability of occurrence of the particular existing arrangement was also extremely low.[1] What makes the message at the train station interesting, or even intelligible as something distinct from its surroundings, and thus a possible object of knowledge, is not the probability of its occurrence, but our personal recognition of the the message in English.

Again, no matter how formalized a scientific procedure may be, there is always an element of personal appraisal or judgment left over. This ability to make personal judgments about the correct use of instruments, acceptable margins of error, and so forth, is what is taught in scientific training, which proceeds not by giving students explicit, exhaustively formalized rules of procedure and then turning them loose in the laboratory, but by example and supervision of the students' practice, which in turn attempts to emulate the given examples.[2] This personal element is why, for Polanyi, there can be no real distinction between the logic of discovery and the logic of justification. The logic of justification—how one would convince anyone of the validity of one's personal discoveries—is a description of the logic of discovery.

In saying that all knowledge is personal, Polanyi is of course saying at one level what has emerged from the work of other revisionist philosophers of science, i.e., that all "facts" are partly formed by theories, that is by the conceptual and perceptual frameworks of the knower; but by calling attention to the personal element, he avoids falling into the trap of yet another set of Kantian-like abstractions, and, in fact, has established a concrete starting point for further reflection.

If all scientific knowing and all scientific practice involves elements of personal appraisal (implying that *all* knowing must involve elements of personal appraisal), how are these personal appraisals made? What generates them? Polanyi argues that the source of our standards of order and meaning is a temporal practice, a groping toward rationality and order which is rooted in our most primordial forms of sentience and motility, and is shared with more primitive organisms. Knowledge, and indeed, more fundamentally, perception, are gained through this process. This process, or practice, in turn, is best described as one of problem solving. A large part of the text of *Personal Knowledge* is taken up with discussions of various learning experiments conducted on both animals and humans, and Polanyi concludes from these that the fundamental orientation of all living things is toward solving problems generated by their interaction with their environment. Notice that I do not say "solving problems presented by their environment," or something of the sort, but rather "solving problems *generated* by their *interaction* with their environment." The difference is crucial, since the latter formulation retains the irreducible element of personal appraisal that is crucial to Polanyi's epistemology, as well as indicating that the objects of our knowledge are not something thrown over against us but something in which we participate.[3]

Polanyi categorizes learning processes into several types and observes that, since even the most primitive level of learning involves attempts to act systematically until an order congruent with the systematic behavior emerges, "the whole process clearly shows the animal's capacity to be intrigued by a situation, to pursue consistently the intimation of a hidden possibility for bringing it under control, and to discover in the pursuit of this aim an orderly context concealed behind its puzzling appearances."[4] A similar, though more complicated and articulate process takes place even in the most sophisticated types of human learning, as for example when a medical student learns X-ray diagnosis,[5] or in solving mathematical problems.[6] Additionally, it would appear that other human orientations, such as wonder or angst, are derivative from the more basic orientation of problem solving, and can have analogs in animal behavior.[7]

Polanyi elucidates the passionate nature of human knowing by observing that problem solving in animals is based on drive satisfaction, and this primordial orientation is still massively present in much human problem solving: "To a disembodied intellect, entirely incapable of lust, pain or comfort, most of our vocabulary would be incomprehensible."[8] But human problem solving, although rooted in primitive drives, can go far beyond these to the point where delight is taken in problem-solving for its own sake; this is the source of our higher intellectual powers and results in our appreciation of intellectual beauty, that is, our appreciation of the heuristic value of our attempts to solve puzzles, of their intimation of as yet unknown aspects of reality. The standards by which the scientific community judges the worth of scientific enterprises are generated by the passionate nature of scientific inquiry.[9] Specifically, this is why abstract theory is valued more highly than sense experience—its abstract nature can give greater insights into hitherto unknown or even unsuspected aspects of reality: "When we claim greater objectivity for the Copernican theory," writes Polanyi,

> we do imply that its excellence is, not a matter of personal taste on our part, but an inherent quality deserving universal acceptance by rational creatures. We abandon the cruder anthropocentrism of our senses—but only in favour of a more ambitious anthropocentrism of our reason. In doing so, we claim the capacity to formulate ideas which command respect in their own right, by their very rationality, and which have in this sense an objective standing.[10]

Polanyi's language here may seem confusing at first, but it actually clarifies the nature of personal knowing. Our most primitive forms of problem solving are based on primordial drives and the direct and very fallible experience of our senses; as our problem solving becomes more sophisticated, it relies more on the abstract theory generated by our higher rational powers and thus increasingly ceases to be grounded in fallible and subjective sense experience, becoming instead more firmly grounded in our appreciation of the beauty of a form of activity that can (although it does not always) allow us much more far-reaching insights into the nature of a puzzle and the implications of its solution, thus making this form of activity more universal and therefore more objective. The crucial difference between a rat working through a maze to get some food and a scientist developing a theory is that the scientist has a greater understanding of what he or she is doing in his or her problem-solving efforts and finds beauty in those efforts precisely because they have a life of their own, transcending the mere satisfaction of primitive drives (although, as already noted, the rat does have *some* limited appreciation of what it is doing). But again, the irreducible personal aspect of knowing is emphasized when it is understood that the beauty of which Polanyi speaks here is not in "nature," but in our interaction with reality. And, in turn, this conception of intellectual beauty thoroughly eschews any kind of mind-body dualism, since it emphasizes that even our most abstract intellectual powers are ultimately rooted in our most primitive forms of sentience and motility, which have the capability of disclosing (although only to a limited degree) hitherto unknown aspects of reality. Additionally, we should note carefully what Polanyi means by equating objectivity with universality. My immediate sense experience is relatively subjective because only I experience it directly. But when I set forth an abstract theory, more firmly grounded in appreciation of problem-solving abilities than mere sense experience, it can be accessible to other people, and thus can be more universal, or objective. Notice here that what is objective is still personal, and indeed is given its objectivity by the very persons to whom it is accessible. Indeed, to the extent that our attempts to communicate our problem-solving attempts are grounded in an appreciation of our problem-solving abilities, they are more accessible than individual sense experience because they can even (in some cases) be accessible to animals.[11] Finally, it should also be noted that Polanyi's formulation does not imply an unlimited capacity to solve problems, since it recognizes that we are finite, limited, fallible beings. It is true that the idea of problem or puzzle solving does imply that a solution in some sense exists to every situation that arises, but it does not imply that we, as finite beings, can always know precisely what that solution is, or even that the idea of a "solution," as we typically understand it, is the proper way to think about all problems.

This discussion points to the first critique of objectivism that emerges from Polanyi's explication of scientific knowing. Objectivism attempts to do away with the essential personal element of knowledge. As we have seen, this is not possible, and the idea of impersonal knowledge not only badly distorts our understanding of the knowing process but also creates confusion in our other intellectual endeavours, since these invariably depend on explicit or implicit epistemologies. Any attempt to describe human knowledge, even if based on highly "objective" knowledge such as is obtained in mathematics and physics, must take into account the ubiquitous and irreducible personal element involved.

Given our tendency to think in objectivist categories, the question that tends to arise at this stage is how, if our knowledge and our evaluations of that knowledge is always personal, we escape mere subjectivity. This question seems particularly urgent given that Polanyi seems to ground knowledge aesthetically. But, as we will see, this aesthetic dimension is only the most superficial aspect of the knowing process, and is ultimately grounded in conceptions of responsibility. We have in fact already seen hints of how we avoid subjectivism when we saw that Polanyi regards our puzzle-solving efforts as superior or inferior depending on the degree to which they are able to intimate hitherto unknown aspects of reality. This aspect of the knowing process will now be further elucidated by an explication of Polanyi's conception of tacit knowledge.

The Tacit Structure of Knowing

I have stated several times that Polanyi regards the way and the extent to which a problem-solving process intimates hidden aspects of reality as the measure of its beauty and worth. It would seem to follow from this that the problem-solving process itself, and, derivatively, our valuations of various problem-solving attempts, are based on some kind of faith or trust in reality. This is indeed the case, and Polanyi discusses this in considerable detail.[12] I will return to this discussion later in this chapter, but here I want to focus on the basis of that faith, and why such a faith would seem reasonable rather than blind or arbitrary. The basis of our faith in our contact with, or participation in, reality and in our puzzle-solving projects lies in the actual structure of the knowing process, which Polanyi describes as having a *tacit* foundation.[13]

Polanyi wants to show that the process of knowing is such that, after we know something explicitly, we recognize that we must have somehow "known" it tacitly beforehand. To do this, he argues that all knowing is analogous to the kind of knowing involved in perception and the use of tools. In the case of perception, Polanyi accepts the findings of gestalt psychology that show that the perception of a coherent object is accomplished by relying on a subsidiary awareness of various clues as to the nature of the object being focused upon. That is, "the appearance of a thing at the centre of my attention depends on clues to which I am not directly attending."[14] Some of these clues cannot be experienced in themselves, such as the contraction of one's eye muscles; others, such as the things one sees out of the corner of one's eyes, could be observed directly if one wanted to. It is these clues, on which we do not focus our attention, that allow us to perceive as something intelligible the thing on which we are focusing.[15]

Similarly, when we use tools, there is a very real sense in which we make them a part of our body. When we are using a hammer, we do not (at least after we have learned how to use it properly) feel that the handle has struck our palm when we hit the nail but that the hammer has struck the nail. This is because we are attending from the feeling of the hammer in the palm of our hand to the head hitting the nail. The feeling of the hammer in our hand is, in Polanyi's terms, what we are subsidiarily (or proximally) aware of; the head hitting the nail is what we are focally (or distally) aware of. We attend *from* our subsidiary awareness *to* our focal awareness.[16] We are not aware of subsidiary things in the same way that we are aware of focal things; there is a sense in which we do not seem to be aware of them at all. But we must rely on subsidiary awareness in order to have any focal awareness whatsoever. That is, we could not make sense of the world if we just looked at things in themselves, out of any context; we must attend from the relevant context to the object of awareness. Similarly, if we change our focal awareness from the whole to the particulars of which we had previously been subsidiarily aware, we lose the sense of the whole. If we focus on the feeling of the hammer in the palm of our hand, we will not be able to use the hammer properly.

This is tacit knowledge. We attend *from* things that we tacitly know but are not explicitly aware of *to* things we do explicitly know, and can only explicitly know thanks to the tacit knowledge embodied in our subsidiary awareness. Tacit knowledge integrates the context of our knowing act with the thing being known to give it meaning as something explicitly known. All knowledge must be tacit or based on tacit knowledge. It is at this level that attempts to exhaustively systematize or formalize knowledge break down. I have earlier said that Polanyi finds systematic attempts to solve puzzles in even the most primitive learning, which might seem to imply exhaustive formalization. But this systematic activity is itself rooted in the mysterious and inarticulate generation of a whole situation from its constituent particulars.

This, of course, sounds very much like some of what Wittgenstein has to say. He also regards knowing as a matter of attending from a context to the thing known. For example:

> "I noticed that he was out of humour." Is this a report about his behaviour or his state of mind? ("The sky looks threatening": is this about the present or the future?) Both; not side-by-side, however, but about the one *via* the other.[17]

Indeed, Wittgenstein's discussion of one's sensations when touching an object with a stick is identical in import to a similar discussion by Polanyi as well as to the example of the hammer already mentioned.[18]

Wittgenstein is concerned with this problem mainly with regard to language, of course. Much of our philosophical discussion simply becomes meaningless if we look *at* words, rather than attend from their context to their meaning. We create insoluble problems by dragging words out of their normal use in a language game and considering them in contexts where they do not belong and thus have no meaning. Applied to the problem of knowledge generally, this is the second major failing found in objectivism: it attempts to understand knowledge as abstracted from the relevant context. Polanyi's analysis shows, on the contrary, that knowledge can only be attained by relying on the context of the knowing act, and therefore a proper description of the knowing process must include this crucial aspect.

A particularly important manifestation of this aspect of objectivism is what is usually referred to as language realism, i.e., the idea that reality is a large but finite text and that language gets its meaning by corresponding (at least when it is purged of the sloppiness and vagueness of everyday speech and usage) to this text, or to put it differently, that each word has a specific, contextless "meaning-in-itself." It is language realism, of course, that Wittgenstein is particularly concerned to combat in the *Philosophical Investigations*. Language-realist thinking seems to be the source of the confusion encountered in positivist philosophy of science whereby the conceptual vocabulary of physics is mistaken for a description of what physicists are actually doing when they are doing physics. The vocabulary of physics is wrenched from its context in scientific practice and hypostasized into a description of scientific practice itself. This of course would be a particular case of the more general problem in modern thought of mistaking the vocabulary of classical mechanics for a description of "reality" as it "actually is," rather than understanding this vocabulary as a set of abstractions useful for understanding certain features of relatively large, relatively slow-moving bodies. Such misplaced concretion derives from abstracting things from their proper contexts.

A third aspect of objectivism that comes to light here is that its descriptions of knowledge are invariably dualistic. This is true in two senses. The first sense is that objectivism ignores the actual context of the knowing act, concentrating only on the "subject" and the "object." We might say that Polanyi has replaced the subject-object dualism with a triad of subject, object, and context (although it should be added that this is potentially very misleading language). The second sense is that, to the extent that objectivism understands the knower as proceeding without any tacit assumptions, i.e., as having explicit knowledge of everything that he or she is doing, it thinks in terms of a mind-body dualism where the "mind" is somehow abstracted from the body and its situatedness in the context of knowledge. Again, Polanyi avoids this problem by careful consideration of the role our rootedness in various contexts plays in our acts of knowing.

If we examine further Polanyi's discussion of tacit knowledge and particularly the problem of formalization, we can gain some further insights into the failings characteristic of objectivism. Polanyi argues that the exact nature of tacit knowing can never be formalized because, first of all, attempting to focus on what was previously subsidiary will either destroy its meaning (if we look directly at it) or else will simply make something else tacit, if we attend from a new subsidiary awareness to what was previously tacit; and secondly, the description of what happens when tacit knowing takes place is not tacit knowledge. He describes experiments where films were taken of people riding bicycles and then run in slow motion to discover just how bicycle riders keep their balance. It turns out that a fairly complicated series of corrections (which can be put in terms of mathematical formulas) are made by the rider as the bicycle starts to tip too far to the right or to the left. But knowing this does not mean that the people who conducted the experiment now have the relevant tacit knowledge of how a bicycle is ridden; they have an explicit description of what happens when someone uses tacit knowledge to keep his or her balance on a bicycle (which in turn required the researchers to use tacit knowledge of their own). This example also illustrates an important point in Polanyi to which we will return: tacit knowledge means knowing more than one can say. Most people who ride bicycles have no knowledge of the experiments conducted or their results, but they can still ride a bicycle. And attempting to ride a bicycle by following the explicit rules determined by the experimenters would hardly work, since no one could make the complicated calculations necessary in the time available to correct the motion of the bicycle.[19]

Polanyi wants to argue that scientific knowledge, and all knowledge, is structured like perception and tool-using. That is, it is either tacit, or, if explicit, it is based on tacit knowledge. Science does not work by applying a set "method" to collected data; rather, scientific intuition leads the scientist to attend from the particulars of his or her subsidiary awareness to a new insight that integrates the data into a theory. "The efforts of perception are evoked by scattered features of raw experience suggesting the presence of a hidden pattern which will make sense of the experience. Such a suggestion, if true, is itself knowledge, the kind of foreknowledge we call a good problem."[20] Similarly, "all [scientific] research starts by a process of collecting clues that intrigue the inquiring mind, clues that will largely be like the peripheric clues of perception, not noticed or not even noticeable in themselves. And a good problem is half a discovery."[21] Polanyi illustrates this with a large number of examples, including Einstein's discovery of relativity.[22]

From here, Polanyi describes the actual structure of a scientific discovery (or an act of knowing generally): scientists have to rely on the accepted interpretive framework of science as a set of general clues for their inquiries, and they rely on these clues as "the presence of hidden knowledge."[23] That is, if, or to the extent that, the accepted interpretive framework of science is true, then by knowing it, scientists already "know" things yet to be discovered. The discovery of hitherto unexpected things through this reliance on these clues is also the verification of the original interpretive framework. Nothing else can verify it. Polanyi puts it this way:

> We make sense of experience by relying on clues of which we are often aware only as pointers to their hidden meaning; this meaning is an aspect of reality which as such can reveal itself in an indeterminate range of future discoveries. This is, in fact, my definition of external reality: reality is something that attracts our attention by clues which harass and beguile our minds into getting ever closer to it, and which, since it owes this attractive power to its independent existence, can always manifest itself in still unexpected ways. If we have grasped a true and deep-seated aspect of reality, then its future manifestations will be unexpected confirmations of our present knowledge of it. It is because of our anticipation of such hidden truths that scientific knowledge is accepted, and it is their presence in the body of accepted science that keeps it alive and at work in our minds.[24]

Scientific inquiry (or reflection, or, indeed, potentially all purposeful human activities) can make explicit what was once tacit, although in so doing it still relies on other tacit knowledge.

The crucial role played in this conception of scientific knowing by the fact that we know more than we can say, or that our tacit knowing is derived from potentially existing hidden knowledge, can explain at least three important things. First, it accounts for the primacy of theoretical science and the superiority of theory over sense experience, since it is in abstract theory that we can make the greatest use of our tacit powers to discover hitherto unexpected things. Intuition is a more powerful tool than perception since it can draw on a broader range of clues. Second, and as a necessary counter to any inducement toward regarding the superiority of theory as evidence of a mind-body dualism, it accounts for why we can have confidence in theory as bearing on the same reality that we experience through our senses, since our tacit knowing powers remain rooted in the most primitive forms of experience where the evidence of the senses predominates. This is also the fundamental basis of the faith we can have in the personal aspect of our knowing. Although we establish our standards of knowledge ourselves, our acts of establishing those standards are always guided by the primordial interaction with reality that generates our tacit knowing. Our self-established standards are fallible but not arbitrary. Finally, it may give some clues about solving the problem raised by Kuhn in his discussion of incommensurable paradigms. The ability of the old paradigm to generate an unexpected discovery (the new paradigm) shows that it did contain some truth, but that this truth has been superceded by the greater truth of the new paradigm—assuming that the new paradigm can itself generate unexpected discoveries.[25] The problem of apparently incommensurable paradigms is, as we have already seen, extremely important for any discussion of communicative practices in the context of political theory, and I shall rely heavily on Polanyi's formulations when I approach this question later.[26]

I should emphasize at this point that Polanyi's conception of tacit knowing does not imply the existence of Platonic Forms or Aristotelian essences or something of the sort, as might be inferred from his claim that explicit knowledge is tacitly "known" beforehand. The crucial link with reality is a process, or practice, in time, that generates knowledge through interaction with reality. It is this process that is missing from accounts of knowledge explicitly or tacitly informed by language realism; or rather in these accounts the process of tacit knowing is conflated with what is being known. A reminder from Wittgenstein will be helpful here:

> We predicate of the thing what lies in the method of representing it. Impressed by the possibility of a comparison, we think we are perceiving a state of affairs of the highest generality.[27]

Polanyi does not fall into this trap. Indeed, this aspect of Polanyi's description of knowledge points to the fourth major problem with objectivism: it understands knowledge in a static fashion. Objectivist descriptions of knowledge tend to consider only the accomplished feat of knowing, not the actual process of knowing,[28] something most obviously manifested in the way positivism typically considered only completed systems of physical theory, rather than considering developing systems or the actual history of older systems;[29] this failure is what leads to the idea that scientific practice can be exhaustively explicated in terms of an abstract, impersonal, eternally valid (and in this sense static) method.

At this point the reader may be somewhat dismayed, since it appears that the only test of the validity of our present knowledge is its ability to lead us to new and unexpected knowledge, itself ultimately untestable unless and until it produces more new and unexpected knowledge . . . a kind of infinite regress in reverse. In other words, the implication of Polanyi's epistemology is that there can be no certain knowledge, at least in the sense that we normally think of certain knowledge, i.e., as something exhaustively specifiable.[30] This is indeed the case, but it by no means implies that there can be no knowledge. In fact, in one sense it is this very uncertainty that allows knowledge to grow; our awareness that we are constantly relying upon pieces of an as yet unsolved puzzle is part of what fuels our intellectual passions.

Somewhat more generally, it will be seen that when Polanyi says that we know more than we can say, and say more than we know, or that we rely on intimations of things we do not yet explicitly know, he is saying that our scientific theories and even our everyday utterances are overdetermined. This is true, but it by no means follows that this over-determination is irrational or chaotic; indeed, it is our tacitly-grounded faith that it is not that allows us to pursue knowledge. It will immediately be clear that Polanyi is actually making a very large ontological claim here. I shall not discuss this in the context of Polanyi's thought but rather will return to it in the discussion of the logic of the speech act, where it can be dealt with more fruitfully.[31] I shall only mention here that the claim Polanyi is making can be expressed by the idea that unintelligibility is parasitical upon intelligibility, or that intelligibility is more fundamental than unintelligibility, and that this is paradigmatically demonstrated by the speech act.

In this regard it may be helpful to reconsider Descartes's program of systematic skepticism in light of Polanyi's theory of tacit knowing. The real problem is not so much that Descartes thought he could doubt everything until he found something impossible to doubt, since he recognized that he must have some kind of prior ideas of "thinking" and "existing"; rather the problem lies in his assumption that these ideas were somehow "clear and distinct" and that this should be the standard for all knowledge. It is this conception of acceptable knowledge that has wreaked havoc in modern thought, not universal doubt, which is impossible anyway. "Universal doubt" does not make explicit what was once tacit, as might be inferred from Descartes's description of what he was doing; it simply applies a certain (erroneous) set of tacit beliefs to explicit problems. (Polanyi actually argues, again relying crucially on the idea of tacit knowledge, that doubt is in fact a form of belief.[32]) This is why Polanyi refers to his program as "post-critical": rather than attempting to know through universal skepticism, an impossibility, he attempts to understand knowing by examining our inarticulate but powerful tacit abilities. It should be noted here that this does not mean that Polanyi thinks we should accept uncritically whatever beliefs we might happen to hold (indeed, this is what he accuses critical philosophy of doing with its ideas of clear and distinct knowledge and universal doubt); rather, we need to examine carefully how it is that we do in fact rely upon a host of unknown and even unknowable assumptions in order to obtain knowledge.

This discussion leads us to the fifth problem area for objectivism, i.e., its presumption or goal of universal skepticism. As we have seen, this is not really possible, is certainly not a useful heuristic device, and indicates a rather naive understanding of our orientation in the world. Indeed, we can see that this problem is related to the abstract, dualistic nature of objectivist thought which I earlier elucidated, since only by (explicitly or tacitly) conceiving oneself as an abstract mind removed from one's bodily location in the world could one seriously consider universal skepticism to be possible.

A further consideration of the matter of systematic skepticism and certain, thoroughly explicit procedure and knowledge is in order here. If science really works the way Polanyi says it does, how can scientists gain knowledge—i.e., do science—when they hold (as many, if not most, do) precisely the kind of objectivist misunderstandings of knowledge that Polanyi attacks? Polanyi in fact argues that such beliefs have caused serious problems in the biological sciences and even more so in the social sciences,[33] but what is particularly interesting is that he is able to use his conception of tacit knowledge to give an ingenious explanation of how physical scientists (and, to the extent that they are actually doing science properly, biologists and social scientists) can continue to do science successfully while holding erroneous views as to how it works: when scientists read or espouse an incorrect objectivist or positivist description of science, they *tacitly* supply the missing details, just as they practice science by relying on tacit knowledge not found in any description of "scientific method." This situation is analogous to people who give directions around their own neighborhood to strangers and mislead the people being directed by giving only a partial explanation while tacitly supplying the missing details to themselves.[34]

I will give two further applications of Polanyi's conception of tacit knowing (as well as the rearrangement of basic concepts that it entails) in order to clarify his implicit critique of objectivism. The first is his discussion of the problem of universals. This is of course a crucial problem, since it bears directly on the question of whether we can ever agree on the validity of competing knowledge claims. Polanyi argues that the term "man" is not just a name or label we apply to a set of things through some kind of habitual association, as in nominalism; nor is it an "essence" of some kind that must be determined. Rather, "man" is a concept generated for focal awareness by the subsidiary awareness we have of all men we have ever seen. "In speaking of man in general we are not attending to any kind of man, but relying on our subsidiary awareness of individual men, for attending to their joint meaning. This meaning is a comprehensive entity, and its knowledge is wiped out by attending to its particulars in themselves."[35]

Doubtless this formulation would strike a language realist as somehow begging the question, since in order to have an awareness of an individual man, we must have known what constituted a "man" in general to start with. (This might even seem to be what Polanyi is saying if his notion of tacit knowledge is misunderstood.) The cause of this misunderstanding, of course, is ignoring what Polanyi recognizes as crucial: that knowing takes place in time. Our recognition of any individual man and our generation of the universal "man" are both complicated tacit sorting-out processes that go on in time, and are never entirely complete, either in terms of our learning as children or in terms of our routine recognition when in full command of our native language. Again, Wittgenstein is most helpful in stating the problem succinctly:

A wish seems already to know what will or would satisfy it; a proposition, a thought, what makes it true—even when that thing is not there at all! Whence this *determining* of what is not yet there? This despotic demand? ("The hardness of the logical must.")[36]

This example again illustrates the static, abstract, and dualistic nature of objectivist thinking, this time as it is manifested in the language-realist understanding of universals, whether it takes an essentialist or nominalist form. Either of these alternatives ignores the dynamic nature of universal formation and attempts to consider the universal in abstraction from its context (or the subject and the universal object abstracted from the context that generates the universal for the subject). Indeed, we can also see how the two traditional alternatives are impersonal, because they ignore the concrete person whose interactions with reality form the universal.

Another example of Polanyi's idea of tacit knowledge will be put to use later when developing concepts directly relevant to political theory.[37] Here, Polanyi is in part attempting to combat reductionist views of knowledge and life generally. It is not possible, he observes, to explain the workings of a machine in terms of the principles of physics and chemistry only. This is because a machine works according to operational principles that are not part of the conceptual repertoire of physics or chemistry. "The class of objects which could conceivably represent any particular machine would form, in the light of pure science—which ignores their operational principle—an altogether chaotic ensemble."[38] Physics or chemistry might give some causes of why a machine failed to work, after it had been determined, according to its operational principles, that it had failed to work, but they would not explain how the machine worked or failed to work. This seems rather obvious when it is explained in this manner, but it can help, when combined with the concept of tacit knowledge, to explain how reductionist explanations of every sort can get a foothold.

When we think that we can explain the workings of a machine in terms of physics and chemistry, we are relying on a tacit conception of a machine (that is, something that works according to certain purposeful operational principles), gained through experience with machines as machines. Our "explanation" of the machine solely in terms of physical and chemical principles can only appear to make sense to us because we are relying on our tacit knowledge of a machine as a machine to give coherence to our explanation. Here, our focal awareness is on our apparent explanation of the machine's workings in terms of physical and chemical principles but it depends on our subsidiary awareness of what a machine is (as well as other things) in order to appear to make sense. If the awareness of what a machine is were cut out of our subsidiary awareness, our focal awareness of our explanation could never be generated.[39]

Polanyi extends this analysis to higher levels of reality:

> The position just reached shows the impossibility of behaviourism. It follows from it that we can identify tangible manifestations of mental processes only by first recognizing the mind at work in them; that in fact a rational pattern of behaviour must be comprehended as a whole, before we can set out to analyse it; and finally that if we did succeed, *per impossible*, in keeping track of the elements of mental behaviour without reference to mind, these particulars observed in themselves, would remain meaningless, and experiments conducted with these meaningless fragments would be meaningless. The actual practice of behaviourist experimental psychology is rescued from this fate, by tacitly relying on the mental interpretation of its observations, which are then translated into an objectivist language.[40]

If behaviorists ever actually looked *at* behavioral phenomena in themselves, as they claim to do, they could make no sense of them. They can only appear to make sense of such phenomena by attending from the whole of rational behavior that is part of their context to the phenomena themselves, and then constructing theories that tacitly rely on the interpretive framework so provided.

This application of the principle of tacit knowing may seem a bit confusing because the operational principles of the machine and the whole of rational behavior are doing double duty. They are initially what one is focally aware of, attending to them from various particulars that make them up, but later become part of the subsidiary awareness that makes the focal awareness of the explanations in question appear to make sense. What is important is that without them, the reductionist accounts of machine operations or human behavior, which claim to be doing away with them, will be impossible. Also, it is again important to realize that we do not have our conception of a machine as a machine (or rational behavior as rational behavior) in an *a priori* fashion; it is something generated tacitly through actual encounters with many machines (or acts of rational behavior).

I will conclude this section by reiterating what I believe to be the most important aspect of tacit knowing, or to put it differently, the most important failing of objectivism. As has been emphasized throughout the discussion, tacit knowing is an process that remains fundamentally dependent upon and enmeshed with the context of the knowing act; the most basic feature of Polanyi's notion of tacit knowledge is our necessary acritical reliance upon the context of our knowing acts. Objectivism's single greatest failing, then, may be that it attempts to abstract knowledge from its relevant context. This abstraction could be understood as the basic precondition of the other features of objectivism—its impersonal, dualistic, skeptical, and static conception of knowledge (and as we shall see, its lack of awareness of the communal context of knowledge)—since, as we have seen, each of the other features depends upon an abstraction of the completed body of knowledge from the context of its discovery.

The contextual aspect of tacit knowledge leads to another consideration. In terms of our broader purposes in this study, we might say that, given the contextual and teleological features of tacit knowledge, it could be described as a kind of practice, in Alasdair MacIntyre's sense, or at least that it could be said that it is both rooted in and is the basis for various practices. This feature of knowing thus leads us to the final aspect of Polanyi's thought that I would like briefly to discuss. This is what he calls conviviality, or the web of practices based on and grounding tacit knowing that make articulate communication possible. Here, we return to the role of faith in the knowing process, and in so doing, emerge from a description of knowledge that still moves close to the orbit of a subject-centered conception of rationality to one which expands our understanding of rationality to something more like communicative competence.

Convivial Practices and the Structure of Articulate Culture

"Articulate systems which foster and satisfy an intellectual passion," says Polanyi, "can survive only with the support of a society which respects the values affirmed by those passions, and a society has a cultural life only to the extent to which it acknowledges and fulfills the obligation to lend its support to the cultivation of these passions."[41] By "society" Polanyi here means the broader society, including its political, economic, etc. institutions, but he could also mean simply the scientific community. In either case the crucial elements of lending support to the cultivation of intellectual passions are those of faith and authority. And again, tacit knowing is inextricably involved in both.

Like other revisionist philosophers of science, Polanyi recognizes the importance of authority in science. Specifically, for Polanyi, the authority structures of the scientific community rely on overlapping competences. Each scientist pursues a problem of interest to himself or herself, and submits his or her findings to the authority of those working in closely related matters for acceptance or rejection, which will in turn determine whether or not changes in the prevailing orthodoxy will take place. Both the individual scientist's work and the judgment made upon it by prevailing opinion are guided by three basic professional standards: sufficient degree of plausibility, scientific value (which in turn consists of accuracy, systematic importance, and intrinsic interest), and originality. The first two standards tend to enforce conformity, while the third encourages innovation; the result is a creative tension between tradition and dissent. Scientists in training are "socialized," so to speak, into the professional standards of science. Although in any given area there will be quite likely be a small number of highly esteemed authorities, no area of science is dominated by a complete monopoly of authority, and no area becomes isolated from the rest of science, because there is enough overlap between areas that a particular area will also be supervised in part by authorities from other, related, areas. Thus, uniform professional standards can prevail throughout science, and authority is dispersed in the sense that a given scientist will both supervise other scientists and be supervised by other scientists.[42] Of course, this picture is somewhat idealized; actual scientific authority can result in harsh discipline and can certainly make mistakes, but it is still essential—science is inconceivable without it.[43]

The role of faith in Polanyi's discussion of science and community is a dual one. In the case of the relationship of the larger society to the scientific community, faith means granting autonomy to the scientific community. This is based not on the idea that science necessarily has an immanent logic of its own, but on a recognition that authority is necessary for the preservation of culture generally and that we all rely on various kinds of authorities for our knowledge of everyday things and more profound things, both of which are in turn based on our own understanding of cultural excellence and worth. We allow autonomy to cultural authorities, and particularly scientific authorities, because we appreciate the value, or the beauty (in the sense this was used in discussing intellectual beauty—problem solving that transcends the mere satisfaction of primitive drives and is done for its own sake), of what they are doing, even though we do not fully understand it.

This aspect of Polanyi's thought may seem problematic, since it seems to imply a notion of epistemological privilege inconsistent with other aspects of his argument. I will in fact return to this issue later[44] and modify somewhat Polanyi's formulation.

In any case, this faith in turn rests on the kind of faith that sustains the scientific community, and is thus rooted in and necessary for tacit knowing. We submit to authority because we can observe that the authority is doing at a more sophisticated level what we are doing in our everyday (problem-solving) activities: relying on an authoritative framework to make discoveries that validate the truth of that framework, and which will in turn generate new discoveries that will validate the previous discoveries, and so on. The web of problem-solving activities that we are constantly engaged in, relying on our tacit knowing powers, is the basis for the faith required for our participation in other, more sophisticated problem-solving activities, which must begin with submission to authority—an act based on and structured like tacit knowing.[45] Our submission to authority thus parallels our submission to the relevant context in an act of perception, except of course that the former is a more conscious action, and that since the authority is an actual person or persons, the dynamic structure of the knowing process means that we can reach the stage of questioning and even surpassing the relevant authority in a particular endeavor. Of course, this picture is idealized again; cultural authority is always required to use coercion, and the whole structure is in danger of disintegrating if we begin to lose our ability to trust our tacit knowing powers, i.e., if we insist on exhaustively formalized procedures for our everyday and scientific practices.

By elucidating the communal and communicative nature of the knowing process, Polanyi has finally grounded the original aesthetic basis of knowledge in a more solid conception of personal responsibility based on faith, since we can only have an appreciation of intellectual beauty (or at least an undistorted appreciation of it) if we both responsibly submit to the authority of others and act responsibly in our own authoritative capacities within the web of problem-solving activities that make up our convivial existence. And since any conception of truth that we can have will always depend on the proper functioning of these convivial problem-solving activities, truth is inextricably bound up with faithfulness to our responsibilities in these settings. And finally, the faith and faithfulness necessary for this communicative understanding of knowledge are not arbitrary or blind because they in turn are grounded in and form the grounding for the tacit structure of the knowing process, which leads us to believe that the past successes of our problem-solving activities point to further future successes.

To summarize the structure, or rather, process, of knowledge as Polanyi sees it, then, we can say that our problem-solving activities are driven by our intellectual passions, by our appreciation of the beauty of our problem-solving activities; these in turn are channelled and ordered by our tacit use of the accepted framework of knowledge in the relevant area of endeavor; and this in turn is sustained and modified by the overall community (scientific or otherwise) held together by faithfulness to one's calling to solve problems, which finally is again necessary to have and to appreciate intellectual passions.

We might say here that Polanyi has actually elucidated a kind of "inductive logic." Note, however, two important aspects of this logic. First, this logic cannot be exhaustively formalized, resting as it does on our ultimately inarticulate tacit powers. We might actually describe it as a kind of "hidden" or "moving" teleology, since in Polanyi's description, we always move toward goals we only tacitly know; we "induce" knowledge from the various clues that we encounter and simultaneously generate a new tacitly known goal, one taking shape even before we have completed "inducing" the previous one. We might even say that Polanyi's basic intention is not epistemological, in the sense of explicating the "structure" of knowledge, but rather ontological, in the sense of articulating the orientation of trust and loyalty that makes knowledge possible.

Second, unlike abstract, formalized deductive logic (or the inductive logic that positivism attempted to develop), this logic can only be understood in terms of a very broad conception of human rationality, which extends to the capacity to learn communal practices appropriate to specific contexts. Indeed, the reason why Polanyi takes scientific knowledge as his exemplar of human knowledge generally is not because it is necessarily more "exact" or "methodical," but because scientific communities most closely approximate the idealized knowing community that Polanyi constructs in his theory (although, of course, scientific communities do fall short of this ideal).

This discussion finally identifies the sixth objectivist mistake that I will mention, i.e., that it ignores the inescapable communal and communicative dimension of knowledge. Needless to say, such an omission would have an important effect on attempts to develop normative political prescriptions.

Having described the basic aspects of Polanyi's philosophy of science, which necessarily expanded to all facets of human knowing, I will finally recapitulate the critique of objectivism that has emerged. From our explication of Polanyi's theory of knowledge, we can distill six main features of objectivist epistemology, which are also six crucial failings: objectivism understands knowledge as impersonal, failing to take into account the irreducible personal element in knowledge; it depicts knowledge in an abstract fashion, omitting the context that allows knowledge to be attained at all; it is dualistic, in that it thinks only in terms of "subject" and "object" and implicitly regards the knowing subject as a disembodied mind; it is static, concentrating only on completed knowledge rather than actual acts of knowing; it adheres to universal skepticism as a heuristic device, which amounts to a tacit use of certain erroneous assumptions about the knower's place in the world; and it fails to include the communal context of the knowing process. These, then, would be the pitfalls we must avoid in developing a concept of necessity that can save the idea of a narrative practice from charges of relativism, since this can only be done by escaping the objectivist framework of thought.

Before I begin this task, however, one important question must be considered. If objectivism is so manifestly inadequate as a description of science or knowledge generally, why has it exerted such a hold on the modern Western mind? Why have we had to wait until the late twentieth century for revisionist philosphers of science to expose its failings? The basic answer that I would put forth is that there are some very powerful experiential sources of objectivist conceptual categories, both as they appear in the formulations of modern philosophers and in everyday thought patterns. A full discussion of all such sources would obviously be beyond the scope of this work, but I will examine one very subtle and pervasive source, i.e., the phenomenological, perceptual, and psychological effects of literacy. By comparing aspects of cognitive and communicative processes in literate and oral cultures, we can see how literacy can be a powerful factor encouraging objectivist thinking, and we can also obtain some clues about the approach needed to escape objectivist thinking in our discussion of political practice. This will be my task in the next chapter.

3

THE WRITTEN WORD AS AN
EXPERIENTIAL SOURCE OF OBJECTIVISM

Although philosophers have occasionally discussed the effects of different communications media on the human mind, most famously in Plato's critique of writing, the Western philosophical tradition has not in general given much sustained attention to such issues. This may be at least partly due to the modern objectivist paradigm, which assumes that the subject can abstract itself from the context of knowledge. In any case, it has not been until this century, at least in the English-speaking world, that the differences between oral and literate cultures have been systematically investigated. Further, although the literature on the differences between literate and nonliterate thought processes has very large implications for political theory as well as philosophy and theology, it has received very little attention from writers in these fields.[1] Thus, my discussion of this literature can have applications beyond my specific use of it here, both epistemologically and politically.

This literature is best understood in the historical context of its development. The earliest work was actually done by classics scholars focusing on Homeric poetry. Although before the twentieth century there were scattered and vague recognitions that Homer's poems may have been the products of an oral culture, this idea did not receive a systematic explication until the work of Milman Parry (1902–35). Parry's argument, in briefest form, is that the distinctive features of Homeric poetry are due to the limitations placed on it by oral methods of composition. Specifically, Homer's poems consist of repeated standardized formulas organized around similarly standardized themes. For Parry, the crucial aspect of Homeric poetry was "the dependence of the choice of words and word-forms on the shape of the hexameter line." Obviously, all poetry composed in meter will exhibit this characteristic to some extent, and earlier criticism had noticed some instances of it in Homer; but Parry was the first to argue that this dependence on meter necessitated a thoroughly formulaic approach in Homer and to demonstrate the extent to which the Homeric poems were formulaic. Earlier criticism had missed this point because it attributed to Homer a kind of "creativity" that, as we shall see, is really only possible in highly literate cultures. Subsequent work by Parry and his student Albert B. Lord elaborated these ideas. Parry and Lord studied illiterate epic singers in isolated areas of Yugoslavia and found that their poetry followed patterns similar to those of Homer.[2] Another classicist, Eric A. Havelock, has investigated in great detail the implications for social structures and education (and thus thought processes) of oral or partly oral cultures as opposed to more fully literate cultures. He has particularly emphasized that the formulaic aspects of oral poetry are closely tied to mnemonic considerations, i.e., to the lack of permanent information storage devices in oral cultures. Another one of Havelock's most important theses is that Plato's philosophy is to a great extent an attempt to articulate the conceptual language and educational apparatus appropriate to an interiorized literacy.[3] I shall return to this matter later in this chapter.

Havelock's book *Preface to Plato*, which began the investigations noted above, appeared in 1963. It was one of several works to appear in the late 1950s and early 1960s that can now be regarded as seminal works in the study of oral-literate polarities. Another crucially important work was Walter J. Ong's *Ramus, Method, and the Decay of Dialogue*, which appeared in 1958. Ong argued in part that the structure of the "logic," i.e., the program or system for classifying and ordering knowledge, of the sixteeth-century educational reformer Peter Ramus was dictated by the conceptual and perceptual shifts brought about by the establishment of print literacy.[4] Ong has since become the most widely known and respected scholar studying problems related to orality and literacy.

An article published in 1959 by a psychiatrist, J. C. Carothers, "Culture, Psychiatry, and the Written Word," pointed to the significant differences in types of psychiatric disorder found in literate and non-literate populations. Based on comparisons of rural African populations with European populations, Carothers generalized that nonliterate people suffering from psychological confusion tend to direct their reactions outward, so that affective disorder takes the form of mania, as in "going berserk" or "running amok," while literate people tend to direct such reactions inwardly, being much more likely to display depressive syndromes or obsessional neurosis, which are rarely encountered among nonliterates. Carothers's discussion of how these manifestations of psychological disorder relate to the predominant modes of communication in oral and literate cultures represented another important early development in this field.[5] Another article, published in 1963 by two anthropologists, Jack Goody and Ian Watt, entitled "The Consequences of Literacy," which discussed the effects of literacy on both psychological and social organization, proved to be the springboard for considerable further research along these lines.[6] Additionally, *Singer of Tales* (1960),[7] in which Lord, whom we mentioned above, continued the studies begun by Parry in Yugoslavia, was another influential work from this period.

Two other books from this period did not treat oral-literate polarities explicitly but did discuss related matters and have influenced subsequent research. One was Thorlief Boman's *Hebrew Thought Compared with Greek*, which first appeared in English translation in 1961 and which argued that Hebrew thought tended to draw its models of reality from aural experience while Greek thought tended to rely more heavily upon visual experience.[8] The other was Claude Levi-Strauss's *The Savage Mind* (published in English in 1966), which, in attempting to link the structuralistic "logic" of tribal myth to spoken language, also unintentionally drew attention to the polarities between orality and literacy, although not so much for the structuralist school itself as for scholars in other areas.[9]

Finally, at a more popular, journalistic level, Marshall McLuhan's *The Gutenberg Galaxy* (1962) discussed some of the effects of print literacy and argued that the development of electronic means of communication such as radio and television would bring about an era of renewed orality, as different from the modern "typographic" era as the latter was from earlier, largely oral cultures.[10] More scholarly writers such as Ong have urged that McLuhan's claims are rather exaggerated and misleading, but that his basic insight is not entirely erroneous. I shall discuss this issue below.

More recently, a second generation of scholars has urged that the claims of Havelock, Goody, and others need to be qualified, since these earliest writers tended to emphasize quite sharply the differences between oral and literate cultures and occasionally came dangerously close to a deterministic model of the effects of literacy. More recent scholarship has given considerable attention to the ways in which oral and literate modes of communication interact with each other and with their overall social context.[11]

Havelock, in a move similar to McLuhan's, has speculated that the sudden outburst of scholarship on oral-literate differences was due to the effects of two generations of radio, which affected the balance of

sense perception among literate Westerners enough to make them aware
of some of the earlier changes brought about by writing and particularly
by print literacy.[12] Whatever validity there is to this idea (or to the larger
thesis, associated with McLuhan, that electronic media of communication will bring about a revival of orality), it is the case that since the early
1960s there has been a veritable explosion of studies on various aspects
of orality and literacy. The field has matured to the point where certain
fairly basic conclusions can be regarded as reasonably reliable and thus
can be appropriated by philosophers and political theorists for application to matters in their own disciplines. I believe such applications can
yield extremely fruitful results.

Before I begin a detailed discussion, I should mention that my
discussion will be quite simplified. Specifically, I have drawn mainly on
the work of the first generation of scholars in this area, represented by
Parry, Lord, Havelock, Goody, and especially Ong, whose work in part
has synthesized the main early lines of research, partly because it will
keep the discussion to a manageable length, and partly because the less
complex model of the earlier writers will bring out most clearly my main
points. What follows, then, should be read with several caveats in mind.
First, as I have already mentioned, I do not want to argue that literacy is
the *only* source of objectivism. Obviously there are many factors
contributing to the development of objectivist consciousness. To take just
one example, numerous twentieth-century theorists, ranging from
Michel Foucault to Eric Voegelin, have argued that modern objectivism
is ultimately the product of a particular psychology, although these
commentators differ widely on its nature. While I have no necessary
reason to quarrel with this general thesis, or with certain other
explications of the origins of objectivism, attempting to examine all such
possible influences would obviously be beyond the scope of my project.
Literacy, however, can be regarded as an important source because it
affects our thought processes in very subtle ways at very fundamental
levels. Indeed, examining the effects of literacy can make clearer the
ways in which objectivism is not merely a theoretical abstraction but
rather a concrete, everyday, lived orientation. Second, I am not arguing
that there is an inevitable chain of causation from literacy to objectivist
thinking; literacy only makes objectivism *probable*. That is, literacy creates
an experiential framework in which objectivist modes of thought
become more likely. The arguments that follow are not intended to be
interpreted deterministically. Finally, the fact that I will emphasize some
of the ways in which literacy can restrict our imaginations should not be
taken as an indication that I want to romanticize oral cultures or to

advocate anything so absurd as returning to a nonliterate state. My purpose is to point out some potential limitations imposed on our thinking by literacy, so that we can be more aware of these limitations and use the knowledge thereof as a starting point for further reflection.

With these qualifications in mind, then, let us examine more closely some of the basic findings of the relevant scholars.

Some Salient Characteristics of Oral Communication

I have already indicated that literacy tends to superordinate visual experience over oral/aural experience and in so doing can cause us to think in the kinds of categories characteristic of objectivism. In fact, this is a simplification. Literate people do not use their eyes more than nonliterate people; people in "primitive" cultures are generally much better at visually detecting details than highly civilized people. What is different is that writing, and particularly printing, links a particular kind of visual experience to verbalization and communication, a situation quite different from what prevails in oral cultures. Specifically, for the literate person, the relative stasis of the written or printed word—its status as an object in three-dimensional space—becomes paradigmatic for visual experience, so that through vision the dynamism of the lifeworld can be stopped and subjected to detailed description and analysis. Only literate people can conceive the lifeworld as a kind of "snapshot" and abstract elements of this world from their context and analyze them. Nonliterate people cannot abstract themselves from the lifeworld's dynamism, which results in the apparently paradoxical situation that, although they usually are very good at noticing visual details, they have a very difficult time giving accurate verbal descriptions of visual phenomena. Hence the fundamental difference between the oral and literate noetic situations is the centrality of a particular mode of visual experience for literate perception, communication, and thought processes.[13]

Because of the limitations on visual experience peculiar to the nonliterate, the crucial feature of an oral culture is the centrality of sound to all thought and communication. Sound is irreducibly dynamic; although it is possible to conceive other kinds of perception, especially vision, in static terms, this is quite impossible with sound. This is because the dynamism of sound (and specifically the spoken word) is not that of an object moving through three-dimensional space but rather the dynamism of continually passing into and out of existence. An oral culture can hardly conceive of words as labels of some sort, since spoken words are not "things" that can be picked up and "attached" to other things; a word must be an event or an action. Further, sound for oral peoples is dynamic also in the sense that it is linked to power: it must be driven by power from a source of some kind, which is why words (i.e., dynamic actions, events) themselves are understood to have great, even magical, power.[14] Another fundamental implication of sound-based communication is that, since words are always produced by a concrete person, oral cultures generally conceive the world, including nature, in personal terms. At the same time, this feature of sound-based communication means that oral cultures will be highly communal, with more highly externalized, less introspective personality types.[15]

Scholars in this area all agree that it is difficult for a literate person to appreciate how different the oral lifeworld is from the world of literacy. Walter Ong points out that

> [T]he purely oral tradition or primary orality is not easy to conceive of accurately and meaningfully. Writing makes "words" appear similar to things because we think of words as the visible marks signalling words to decoders: we can see and touch such inscribed "words" in texts and books. Written words are residue. Oral tradition has no such residue or deposit. . . . Though words are grounded in oral speech, writing tyranically locks them into a visual field forever. A literate person, asked to think of the word "nevertheless," will normally (and I strongly suspect always) have some image, at least vague, of the spelled-out word and be quite unable ever to think of the word "nevertheless" for, let us say, 60 seconds without adverting to any lettering but only to the sound. This is to say, a literate person cannot fully recover a sense of what the word is to purely oral people.[16]

The dynamic nature of sound has perhaps its most fundamental effect in that, lacking any way of storing information outside of actually existent persons, oral cultures must rely on memory and direct communication to organize existence. Thus, the thought processes of oral cultures will be structured by these features. Speaking, and thus thinking, in oral cultures must always be closely related to actual existential contexts, will tend to be rhythmically oriented, and will tend to be highly formulaic in content, something we have already briefly noted in our discussion of Parry's investigation of Homer. All of these features aid memory.[17]

The problem of oral memory is a useful place again to emphasize how difficult it is for literates to get a grip on the psychodynamics of orality. The prodigous memory of oral cultures is legendary among literates, and many literate people have been told that oral poets can recite epic poems word-for-word exactly as they learned them. In fact, as the studies of Parry and Lord showed, the performances of oral poets always contain variations, though rarely drastic ones.[18] Also, in tests measuring ability to memorize lists, nonliterate people actually did *worse* than literates.[19] Misconceptions about oral memory arise from literates projecting onto oral cultures the literate method of verbatim memorization from a text. Oral people can scarcely memorize verbatim, since there is no "text" from which to memorize. Rather, the oral memory gets its scope and power from the skillful use of various mnemonic devices, most of which are not only seldom used by literates but would actually regarded as poor speaking or writing style.[20]

More specifically, Ong has noted what he believes are nine important characteristics of an oral mentality which derive from the basic features of sound noted above. They can usefully be divided into two groups. The first five are primarily related to the problem of memory that we have discussed already, while the last four are more directly associated with the phenomenological properties of speech and hearing. The effects of the personal, communal orientation of oral cultures appear in both groups. A brief discussion of these features can provide essential background for a solid understanding of how literacy tends to induce objectivist thinking.

First, then, oral expression tends to be additive rather than subordinative; there is typically no attempt analytically to break up a series of actions or events into hierarchies of importance indicated by subordinate clauses. Events are related one after the other in succession, because the hierarchies and divisions which must be indicated by linguistic structure in written communication can be indicated by the existential contexts that surround oral communication. To illustrate this we can examine two English translations of the creation narrative in Genesis. The first is from the Douay version (1610), itself a product of a culture with literacy but still heavily oriented to oral modes of communication (a situation that, as we will see, is typical of cultures with writing but no printing or else of cultures in the early stages of print literacy):

> In the beginning God created heaven and earth. And the earth was void and empty, and darkness was upon the face of the deep; and the spirit of God moved over the waters. And God said: Be light made. And light was made. And God saw the light that it was

good; and he divided the light from the darkness. And he called the light Day, and the darkness Night; and there was evening and morning one day.

The second is *The New American Bible* (1970), produced by a highly literate culture:

In the beginning, when God created the heavens and the earth, the earth was a formless wasteland, and darkness covered the abyss, while a mighty wind swept over the waters. Then God said, "Let there be light," and there was light. God saw how good the light was. God then separated the light from the darkness. God called the light "day" and the darkness he called "night." Thus evening came, and morning followed—the first day.

The Douay version, as Ong remarks, "renders the Hebrew *we* or *wa* ('and') simply as 'and.' The New American renders it 'and,' 'when,' 'then,' 'thus,' or 'while,' to provide a flow of narration with the analytic, reasoned subordination that characterizes writing." The first version is more like the additive Hebrew original, and might be regarded by highly literate people as unacceptable or at least inferior style.[21]

The second feature of oral cultures noted by Ong is that oral communication tends to be aggregative rather than analytic; because of the demands of memory, oral expression makes prominent use of formulas that aggregate or cluster elements. Ong observes that "oral folk prefer, especially in formal discourse, not the soldier but the brave soldier, not the princess but the beautiful princess; not the oak but the sturdy oak. Oral expression thus carries a load of epithets and formulary baggage which high literacy rejects as cumbersome and tiresomely redundant because of its aggregative weight." This is partly the source of the formulaic epithets in Homer. Expressions such as "running-dog lackeys of the capitalists," which sound ludicrous when employed by college-educated Westerners, would be typical products of an oral or largely oral culture with its need to aid memory.[22]

Since one cannot "look back" at an uttered expression the way one can with a written or printed line of words, oral expression is typically redundant, thus allowing both speaker and listener to keep track of what is being said. Ong observes that such redundancy is in a sense more natural to thought and speech than the "sparse, linear" writing style cultivated by high literates, and thus the latter actually puts a strain on the psyche. This strain is ameliorated in part by the fact that writing is itself a slow process, allowing the writer to reorganize his or her mind's more natural, redundant processes. In cultures where literacy has not yet been fully interiorized, literates will often display this redundancy even in their writing.[23]

A fourth feature of oral cultures is that, since they must expend a huge amount of time and energy remembering things, they will tend to be conservative or traditionalist. Only a culture with at least some literacy could expect or even value a great deal of intellectual innovation. The capacity of literate cultures for innovation actually arises from the conservative features of writing. Ong points out that since the text takes on the functions of memory, the mind is freed for greater speculation and innovation.[24]

Goody and Watt observe that oral cultures are traditionalistic in another way: when change does occur, the oral tradition is altered to take such change into account, and the now outmoded elements of the tradition are simply forgotten, meaning that oral peoples have no way of realizing how their current cultural practices differ from those of the past; oral peoples will tend to think that current arrangements are those of time immemorial. Another way of putting this is that objective history is not possible without written records.[25] Ong refers to this as the homeostatic characteristic of oral cultures.[26]

Moving into the second set of features, those most closely associated with the phenomenological properties of speech and hearing, a sixth feature of oral cultures is that they are, as Ong puts it, "close to the human lifeworld." That is, since they cannot develop elaborate abstract or analytical categories to structure knowledge (because they cannot distance themselves from the dynamism of the lifeworld), they must conceptualize knowledge in terms of concrete human activities. Two good examples of this occur in the *Iliad*. In Book II, Homer presents a "list" of ships, rulers, and territories that is in fact not a list but rather locates the relevant information in a context of human action. Similarly, in Book I, navigation procedures are located in a narrative of specific acts. As we shall see shortly, the capacity wrought by literacy to abstract knowledge from the human lifeworld can be tremendously enabling, but it can also produce destructive conceptual confusion in certain contexts.[27]

Closely linked to the preceeding feature of oral cultures is their agonistic tone. As noted above, nonliterate cultures cannot abstract knowledge from the dynamic lifeworld, and since the lifeworld is often the scene of struggle, such cultures tend to situate knowledge in a context of struggle. As a specific example, the strong tendency of oral cultures to think in personal terms (i.e., terms drawn from the lifeworld experience of language) means that when something goes wrong, it will typically be assumed that some concrete person is responsible for it. Thus, oral cultures tend to think in polarized terms revolving around heroes and villains, good guys and bad guys, with both elaborate, highly stylized praise and invective.[28]

A distinction between orality and literacy that relates very clearly to the problem of objectivism is that, as Ong puts it "for an oral culture learning or knowing means achieving close, empathetic, communal identification with the known." The visual aspect of writing tends to separate the knower from the known, or the "subject" from the "object." This kind of distancing, as we have noted, is not possible to any great extent in oral cultures. I will discuss this aspect of oral-literate polarity in more detail shortly.[29]

The final feature of oral cultures noted by Ong, and again one important for future discussions of objectivism, is that nonliterate people tend to think situationally rather than abstractly. A classic study by A. R. Luria of peasants in the Soviet Union illustrates this well. In one case, subjects were presented with drawings of four objects, such as a hammer, saw, log, and hatchet, of which one fitted into a different category than the other three, and asked to group them. Although the subjects with some reading ability were able to group the objects "correctly," i.e., according to abstract conceptual categories, the illiterate peasants attempted to group the objects according to how one would use them in actual lifeworld situations. In the above example, the illiterate subjects were baffled, since all the items seemed to go together, i.e., one might chop the log with the hatchet, saw it with the saw, etc. Separating the log from the tools made no sense, since then there would be nothing on which to use the tools. Similarly, Luria's illiterate subjects resisted giving abstract definitions of such objects as trees, instead expressing surprise that anyone should ask such bizarre questions as "What is a tree?" This important characteristic of oral thought processes again indicates the importance of action for communication based on sound.[30]

An important corollary of this point is that, since they think situationally, not abstracting from particular contexts, oral people are unconcerned with what would strike a literate person as inconsistencies or even contradictions in oral formulas, epithets, sayings, etc. Thus the "beautiful princess" and "brave soldier" we encountered earlier can be replaced by the (equally stylized) "unhappy princess" or "braggart soldier" in different contexts. Since any given formula is only encountered in a given context, contradictory formulas (contradictory, when abstracted from their proper context by a literate observer) can equally well be a part of the repertoire of a particular oral culture.[31]

Having briefly discussed some of the most important features of oral consciousness, I want now to explicate the transformations that occur with literacy. As I do this, I will refer to the discussion of objectivism in the preceeding chapter. Later, I shall illustrate the conclusions drawn with examples from philosophy and political theory. This will give us some clues about how we might go about escaping the subtle manifestations of objectivism that drag us toward relativism or irrationalism and what this would imply for politics.

Aspects of Literate Consciousness

To understand how literacy restructures thought processes it will be necessary to examine in more detail different forms of literate and postliterate media of communication. I have already said that it is a simplification to say that literacy superordinates visual experience over oral/aural experience; the crucial aspect of this superordination is the way a particular aspect of vision is linked with verbalization. But even this simplifies, since different types of literate media link vision and verbalization differently, or to different degrees. Early forms of writing, such as cuneiform or hieroglyphics, which employ picture-symbols, do this only to a limited extent. Pictographic writing systems such as this are not the same thing as mere pictures, because a given picture could mean many things or many words, whereas writing systems "determine the exact words that a reader can generate from the text." But these writing systems still retain a great deal of the sound-dimension of words because they must represent each word with a picture of some concrete thing or event that exists or occurs in the oral/aural lifeworld, meaning that the meaning of the word can only be understood by fairly direct reference to its existential context, which in turn means that words will still tend to be understood as events rather than signs or referents.[32]

The really crucial change in this regard comes with the invention of the alphabet, or, to be more exact, the Greek alphabet, which contains vowels as well as consonants. Since each letter represents only one sound (or at most a few related sounds), rather than entire words, the crucial connection with the oral/aural lifeworld is broken, or, more correctly, drastically attenuated; a written word as written word has no obvious connection to anything in the lifeworld. With its connection to existential events broken, an alphabetically written word becomes a set of abstract symbols in static, quasi-permanent space, rather than a dynamic event. The context that is so important to oral communication and still relevant to pictographic writing and even syllabaries and the Semitic alphabet, which does not indicate vowels in the same way as the Greek alphabet does, and thus leaves the identity of a given written word somewhat ambiguous and therefore dependent on existential context, tends to recede greatly into the tacit or even unconscious background.

Once this happens, several of the distinguishing features of oral cultures previously noted will tend to fade away. Knowing will no longer mean empathetic participation with the known but a relative distancing of oneself from the known, and with the lively, often combative lifeworld receding into the background, situational thinking will tend to be replaced by abstract thinking, modes of expression will be less closely linked to the lifeworld and more oriented toward abstractions, and the agonistic tone of oral cultures may become more irenic, corresponding to the neutrality of visual space. At the same time, separated from actually existent persons and locked into abstract visual space, words themselves can tend to take on a life of their own in a way they cannot in an oral culture. Specifically, with literacy comes the possibility of language realism, i.e., the idea that reality is in some way a large but finite "text," and that language gets its meaning by somehow "corresponding" to this text. Such a correspondence or referential understanding of language would be quite unimaginable in an oral culture.[33]

Ong gives a very useful illustration of the spatializing effects of the alphabet. The alphabet implies that words are present all at once, rather than in a dynamic fashion, that they "can be cut up into little pieces, which can even be written forwards and pronounced backwards: 'p-a-r-t' can be pronounced 'trap.'" He continues: "If you put the word 'part' on a sound tape and reverse the tape, you do not get 'trap,' but a completely different sound, neither 'part' nor 'trap.'"[34] The game of asking someone to "say 'part' backwards" would be unintelligible and unimaginable without alphabetic literacy. Thus, with the alphabet comes a crucial step in bringing about the spatialization of language barely begun with pictographic writing.

Another way to illustrate this point is to examine the claim sometimes made in deconstructive criticism that words "move around" in that they do not unambiguously refer to or correspond to one thing. This claim may seem at first to contradict the idea that literacy allows people to take the relative stasis of the written word as a paradigm for visual experience. Clearly, however, to speak of words as "moving around" is to conceive of a word as an object in three-dimensional space, and the dynamism invoked is one of visual space, which is quite different from the dynamism of the oral/aural world, where words are sound events in time that are always passing into and out of existence. Hence, the claim that words move around or that they "carry" an indeterminacy of meaning is parasitical upon the relative stasis of the written word and the resulting capacity to conceive of a word as an object in three-dimensional space.

The effects of literacy remain relatively limited, however, as long as writing remains the most advanced method of communication. There are several reasons for this. First, literacy itself will continue to be relatively limited. In societies where pictographic writing systems are employed, very few people can learn to read and write because of the huge amount of time and effort necessary to learn these complicated systems. The alphabet makes reading and writing much easier to learn, but as long as reading material remains in relatively short supply because it must all be produced by the slow process of writing, much of the population will remain nonliterate and thus still tied to the oral world. Further, the literate elements of the population will remain in contact with illiterates and thus in contact with the oral mentality. Also, the scarceness of written resources means that literates will in many situations still use oral methods of dealing with the world (for example, oral memory devices) rather than using writing for such purposes. Indeed, in a society with writing but no printing, literates retain much of the oral orientation even while using writing. Since written manuscripts are frequently difficult to read, reading is normally done aloud, so it can be done slowly enough to decipher the text. Silent reading has only been generally cultivated since the advent of printing, with its uniform and easily readable texts. (We are all familiar with Augustine's wonderment at Ambrose's habit of reading silently.) And of course reading aloud does not allow one to spatialize and decontextualize words as thoroughly as silent reading does. The retention of oral thought processes in a literate culture is referred to by Ong and others as "oral residue," and can be found even today in (socially or geographically) isolated areas of the most modern societies.[35]

Printing, then, is the final step necessary for the complete triumph of a literate mentality, and for reasons we have to some extent just indicated. It makes reading material readily available, thus encouraging universal literacy and more general use of literate artifacts. This in turn can allow greater accumulation of information through such things as encyclopedias. The uniformity of printed items makes indexes possible, meaning that information can be found faster. (Indexes would make little sense if only written manuscripts were available, since all the labor of creating an index would have to be repeated for every single book produced.) The accumulation of information made possible by printing is the crucial step in destroying the mnemonically-oriented features of an oral or partly oral culture. Knowledge can be remembered (or rather, stored) even when it is abstracted from its existential context, so the additive and aggregative characteristics of oral speech forms become simply redundant, and the redundancy of speech itself can seem burdensome. With the mind freed from the burdens of memory, intellectual innovation becomes highly valued, and a conservative attitude toward knowledge and information may even be regarded as immoral. Also, print will accelerate the tendency of writing to break down the homeostatic character of oral or residually oral cultures by revealing an objective history in the stored information that accumulates. All of these prominent features of oral cultures will tend to vanish as print literacy spreads.

In terms of the perceptual effects discussed earlier, the uniformity of print also makes silent reading much easier and its elimination of personal idiosyncrasies (i.e., different writing styles) from the text decontextualizes words more relentlessly than ever, thus intensifying the crucial effects of literacy already mentioned. The spatialization of language, begun by pictographic writing and accelerated by the alphabet, takes a quantum jump with printing. In terms of the history of Western culture, then, although classical Greece shows the definite effects of a significant level of alphabetic literacy, it is not until after the invention of the printing press—indeed, some considerable time after this, as a significant oral residue remains with even the most educated classes until the eighteenth century—that literacy exerts its full force on the Western mind.[36]

By the nineteenth century, Western culture, or at least its dominant elements, had become thoroughly visualist in orientation, due mainly to its almost exclusive reliance on writing and especially printing as means of communication. In the later nineteenth and twentieth centuries, however, a number of technological innovations—telephone, radio, and television being the most notable—have occured that may have increased the extent to which Western societies rely on hearing for communication. This has prompted certain commentators, most notably McLuhan, to argue that we are entering a new age of "secondary" orality, which will recapture many of the elements of earlier "primary" oral cultures.

As mentioned above, other writers have considerable doubts about this proposition, for a number of reasons. First of all, the new sound-oriented media of communication themselves are products of a literate culture and require literacy, and visual constructs generally, to make them work. Indeed, many of the new electronic media, such as the computer, are not sound-oriented but work mainly through print and graphics. Second, the new types of electronic media actually increase our use of print and stored information, so that oral memory, such a crucial feature of primary oral cultures, becomes even less important to us. Third, the new electronic media seem to increase the tendency of printing and visualist orientations to neutralize the lifeworld. For example, the kind of openly agonistic orientation found in earlier political debates would be entirely unacceptable in present-day televised presidential debates. Ong argues that the electronic media of this century have actually amplified to new levels our visual orientation.[37] Indeed, there is beginning to develop a literature that argues that television, far from increasing our oral orientation, as McLuhan thought, dramatically intensifies our visual orientation and is bringing about what might be best described as a postliterate visual culture of images. Although it is true that television, unlike large-screen motion pictures, requires sound to be effective, it works mainly through rapid-action images; there is little sustained or elaborate conversation in most television programming.[38] I shall discuss this matter in more detail shortly.

Despite the criticisms of McLuhan's thesis adumbrated above, most of the writers in this area do agree that during this century there has been a partial revival of an oral orientation, and that this could be a springboard for a more thoroughgoing reorientation, although this would be a vastly more difficult and complicated task than is implied by McLuhan's work. An example from recent trends in philosophy might illustrate this to some extent. If we accept, for the moment, my thesis that objectivism is to an important degree the result of a literate/visualist orientation, we might say that the decreasing popularity in the post–World War II period of the most blatant forms of objectivism (such as positivism) might be partly due to the increasing effects of orally oriented media of communication, while the focus on narrative by recent ethicists such as Alasdair MacIntyre and Stanley Hauerwas, and the attempt to use the speech act as an ethical paradigm by Jürgen Habermas and others, plus the general recognition of the importance of context for knowledge, may indicate a partial recovery of oral consciousness. Indeed, it could even be argued that fields such as philosophy of science and political theory have recently evidenced a shift away from a philosophical paradigm of argumentation toward a rhetorical one—that is, from an ideal of exhaustive demonstration to a model of plausibility. On the other hand, the persistence of more subtle manifestations of objectivism (which I shall discuss shortly) would tend to corroborate the claim that the new electronic media have only partly revived orality and may have actually intensified certain aspects of a literate/visual orientation.

Having established the extent to which various communications media push us in the direction of a literate orientation, let us now examine the important features of such an orientation. As I have already explained, I want to argue that literacy is an important source of objectivist thinking, so I will discuss its effects in terms of the characteristics of objectivism noted in the previous chapter.

We have seen that objectivism attempts to understand human knowledge in impersonal terms. One of the most important features of literacy is that it allows people to think impersonally. As we have seen, oral people inevitably understand the world (including nature) in personal terms, since for them communication is always tied to an actually existent, and present, person. Writing dissolves the immediate link between a person and his or her words and thus allows the reader to understand words, and thus reality generally, in an impersonal fashion.[39]

Two important points should be noted here. First, in keeping with the discussion above, the extent to which people can think impersonally will be linked to the extent to which they have interiorized literacy, which of course is not an either/or matter. Cultures with writing but not printing will still have a tendency to personify nature, although perhaps not to the same degree as entirely oral cultures. Second, the ability to think impersonally is in many ways very enabling. For example, it would be quite impossible to do science without the ability to understand nature impersonally, at least to some extent. Conceiving things impersonally only becomes a liability in certain contexts—most notably, for our purposes, when we are attempting to understand our processes of knowing. Here an impersonal framework can possibly cause us to commit the error discussed in the previous chapter of mistaking the impersonal vocabulary of physical science for an actual description of what the scientist is doing when he or she does science. The ambiguousness of this aspect of the shift to literate consciousness is, as we will see, typical of most of the changes wrought by literacy.

Another important feature of objectivism is that it tends to conceive of knowledge as abstracted from context. As with the capacity to think impersonally, this ability to understand knowledge abstractly is dependent upon literacy. We have seen that oral cultures, for a variety of reasons, must locate knowledge in the context of narratives, formulaic sayings, etc. Only with writing (and especially printing) can knowledge be abstracted from these contexts and converted into the forms of (relatively) context-neutral lists, tables, etc., which could never be remembered in oral form.[40] Again, this can produce many benefits. Aside from the obvious problems related to the need to carry knowledge in the memory of actually existent persons (as opposed to books, etc.) relatively little knowledge can be accumulated when it must be accompanied by the necessary narrative and formulaic mnemonic baggage, since this baggage itself requires memory use. On the other hand, the capacity to abstract things from context, can, if taken too far, result in an utter fragmentation of knowledge and thus of the world. The literate world has a tendency to become a jumble of mutually unconnected, reductively conceived "facts." Perhaps even more fundamentally, it is important to remember that knowledge made abstract by writing is only relatively abstract, since it must be ultimately connected to its existential context to be intelligible. And this is where the process of abstraction can be very disabling, since it will become quite possible, if one's vocabulary has been formed by intense immersion in the relatively decontextualized knowledge of a literate culture, to forget, when reflecting upon our processes of thinking and knowing, that knowing takes place in a context. We have already mentioned a specific example of this particular pitfall, the (explicit or tacit) language realism that results when one starts to imagine that words have a life of their own, something that can only happen to a literate person.

A good example of how subtle and pervasive this aspect of literate consciousness can be is given by Goody. Anthropologists frequently attempt to understand the cosmologies and other beliefs of "primitive" peoples by means of tables that show correspondences between various elements of the tribal worldview. As Goody points out, however, tables are literate artifacts; they spatialize knowledge and turn words into referents in ways that are quite foreign to the nonliterate mind. Their use is thus likely to be misleading at best.[41] The anthropologists here are suffering from a problem common to all literate people: literacy so deeply imprints certain patterns in our thinking that we normally find them entirely "natural" and can scarcely imagine anyone not thinking in these ways.

A third feature of objectivist accounts of knowledge is that they are dualistic. This is the case in two senses: first, in that they understand knowledge in terms of a subject-object dichotomy; and second, in that they (at least tacitly) understand the knower as a disincarnate mind. Both of these are associated with literacy, and in fact, like the abstraction previously discussed, are related to the ability to decontextualize knowledge that literacy brings. It is certainly only with literacy that a strong distinction can be made between the subject and the object, i.e., that the knower can be relatively abstracted from what is being known. This is partly because hearing cannot distance one from phenomena the way vision can. When one hears, one always experiences oneself at the center of events, whereas vision puts one at the periphery. It is also, as we have seen, partly, or additionally, because only with literacy does one acquire the habit of abstracting oneself from the world's dynamism to focus on static phenomena.[42] (Recall that oral people can be very perceptive visually, but have not connected vision with verbalization and thus cannot give accurate or articulate visual-spatial descriptions of objects.)

Some distinction between knower, known, and context is essential for any form of analytical thinking, since what is to be analyzed must be in some way separated from the analyst and the context in order to be broken up, taken apart, etc., and this distinction is much more easily made when one can rely upon visual experience linked to verbalization.[43] The problem is that when literacy has become deeply interiorized, we will tend both to perceive this separation in exaggerated measure and to generalize it to all of our experience, thus thinking in terms of a subject-object dichotomy, since so much of our vocabulary will be drawn from relatively decontextualized visual experience. This same decontextualization contributes to a tendency to think in terms of a mind-body dualism, since the somatic elements of language, so important in primary oral communication, tend to fade far into the background when one's vocabulary becomes highly abstract.[44]

To put this aspect of literate consciousness in proper context, recall that Michael Polanyi attempts to discuss knowing as a kind of participation in or with what is being known, and argues that we tend to miss this and think in subject-object terms, because we forget about the overall context of which we are subsidiarily aware. We can see how the decontextualization of knowledge brought about by literacy could make this happen; that is, we can see that this decontextualization can make us forget that our relative abstraction from what we are analyzing is itself dependent on the overall context, which includes both us and the objects of our analysis.

A fourth feature of objectivism discussed earlier is that it tends to understand knowledge in static terms. Here, the connection with literacy and static visual experience as opposed to the dynamism of hearing seems obvious. But in fact the connection is more subtle and more profound, since, as we have seen, although vision can be understood statically, whereas hearing cannot, visual experience is by no means always static. There is much dynamism and change in our everyday visual experience. Our tendency to automatically think of vision as static is itself partly a product of taking the written or printed word, locked as it is into a semipermanent place in space, as the paradigm of something seen. Thus, literacy not only superordinates visual experience and links it to verbalization but actually superordinates a particular moment of visual experience.

Additionally, print literacy tends to promote a static sense of closure. "The printed text," says Ong,

> is supposed to represent the words of an author in definitive or 'final' form. . . . Once a letterpress forme is closed, locked up . . . the text does not accommodate changes (erasures, insertions) so readily as do written texts. By contrast, manuscripts, with their glosses or marginal comments (which often got worked into the text in subsequent copies) were in dialogue with the world outside their own borders. . . . The sense of closure or completeness enforced by print is at times grossly physical. A newspaper's pages are normally all filled . . . just as its lines of type are normally all justified. . . . Print is curiously intolerant of physical incompleteness. It can convey the impression, unintentionally and subtly, but very really, that the material the text deals with is similarly complete or self-consistent.[45]

The textbook, which tends to present the subject matter in a given field as a fixed body of knowledge, is a product of printing.[46] The sense of closure discussed here by Ong may have been at work in the tendency of positivist philosophy of science to take as its model of science not the ongoing work of scientists at the leading edge of various disciplines but rather the essentially static, fixed, closed body of knowledge making up classical mechanics. As with other aspects of literate consciousness, for some purposes a static framework is quite useful, even necessary. But for other purposes, especially those dealing with dynamic human activities such as knowing, a vocabulary heavily weighted toward stasis can cause serious conceptual confusion, as the example just recalled from our earlier discussion illustrates.

The tendency to think in terms of a universal skepticism, and to understand knowledge as being produced by such skepticism, is another feature of objectivism that we have discussed. Again, such universal skepticism is possible only with literacy. As we have seen, nonliterate people think in concrete, situational terms. Watt and Goody observe that people in oral cultures can certainly express doubt, but only with regard to highly specific events, knowledge claims, etc. Doubt is always contained within a concrete context. Only literate people can doubt everything, or rather, convince themselves that they could doubt or have doubted everything. The crucial factor here appears to be the way in which the decontextualization brought about by literacy homogenizes knowledge. For the oral person, doubt regarding one context cannot be generalized to others, while for the literate, specific doubt can spread throughout the homogeneous space of abstractions he or she uses for analysis.[47] It is scarcely accidental that Descartes understood all space as homogeneous extension. Of course, the ultimate connection of all knowledge and thought with concrete existence in the lifeworld is why only the illusion of having attained a universally skeptical stance is possible, and not universal doubt itself.

Finally, we have observed that objectivism ignores the communal context of knowledge. In terms of the consequences of literacy, this is to some extent another example of the general decontextualization of knowledge that can take place. But literacy does have additional effects that can much more specifically result in highly individualistic orientations and self-understandings. For example, the breaking of the word's connection with other actually existent persons can make literate people more aware of themselves as individuals.[48] Additionally, the capacity to think abstractly, i.e., non-situationally, is what allows introspection; one can only analyze oneself as oneself by (partly) abstracting oneself from the specific lifeworld situations in which one always finds oneself. Luria's illiterate subjects, mentioned earlier, typically had difficulty with articulate self-analysis, normally deferring to the community for an evaluation of their own characters.[49] Ong points out that the introspective characters typical of the modern novel are possible only in a culture that has interiorized literacy. Oral cultures tend toward the unselfconscious "type" or "flat" characters found in, for example, Homer.[50] Finally, Ong and others have pointed out that certain aspects of literacy can have somewhat indirect effects on the development of individualism. The cultivation of silent reading, for example, required larger homes with individual rooms and thus contributed significantly to the bourgeois idea of privacy, something largely unknown to earlier cultures.[51] Or again, there can be little sense of private ownership of words or of plagiarism—the violation of such privacy—in an oral culture, since everyone draws upon a common stock of stories, sayings, etc.[52] Of course, it is important to recognize that the differentiation of the individual from the group has had many salutary effects. But if taken too far or if misunderstood, as in objectivist accounts of knowing (not to mention liberal political theory), it can be thoroughly destructive.

From the above discussion, we can see that there are many parallels, or points of congruence, between the important features of literate consciousness and the basic characteristics of objectivism. Of course, such correlational evidence is not in itself enough to sustain the point I want to make here. What is needed is not exactly a causal explanation, since we are attempting to escape such objectivist modes of thought, but rather an explanation that demonstrates that literacy can create a context or configuration where objectivist thinking becomes more probable. I believe I can provide this by considering what I believe to be the crucial aspect of the transformations brought about by literacy: this is the tendency to perceive the world and ourselves abstractly, i.e., cut off from the existential context necessary for meaning. If we briefly reconsider the above discussion, we can see that this feature of literate consciousness seems to be the basic factor in generating objectivist orientations. The abstraction of the word from the context of an existent speaker in the dynamic lifeworld is what can bring about impersonal thinking and abstract, context-neutral knowledge. Also, the ability to abstract ourselves and our knowledge from a given context is what allows us to think in terms of subject-object or mind-body dualisms, to generalize skepticism to universal proportions, and to perceive ourselves as being capable of knowledge apart from a community of knowers. Additionally, the tendency to think in static terms ultimately rests upon the ability wrought by literacy to abstract phenomena from the world's dynamism. This abstraction itself, of course, comes from taking the static written word as an epistemological paradigm. We might say that the stasis of the written word, as opposed to the dynamism of sound, is the most basic phenomenological aspect of literate consciousness, while the capacity for abstraction, made possible by the written word's stasis, is the most fundamental conceptual aspect of the literate mind. This capacity for abstraction, it seems, can create a context where the failings characteristic of objectivism can appear. As we have already seen, many of the most important results of literacy can be quite beneficial, but can become destructive if misused. The capacity for abstraction created by literacy can result in a context where such misapplication can result. In the previous chapter we saw that excessive abstraction seemed to be the most important single characteristic of objectivism. To some extent, it seems, objectivism is the result of unwittingly misusing the capacity for abstraction brought about by literacy. This capacity for abstraction, then, seems to be the crucial link between literacy and objectivism. Although this capacity is of course tremendously enabling, it can, if employed uncritically, lead to serious conceptual confusion in certain endeavors.

In sum, then, I believe we can draw the conclusion that literacy has contributed significantly to the objectivist understanding of knowledge (and thus to conceptual confusion in other endeavors explicitly or implicitly based upon our prevailing epistemological ideas). As I have already urged, it would be quite incorrect to understand literacy as the only source of objectivist thinking, or to fail to recognize the many benefits of literacy. But we can now see some ways in which literacy may have contributed significantly to some of our current theoretical and practical dilemmas. Also, we can see that the effects of literacy typically operate at an extremely subtle level, i.e., in terms of our vocabulary, perceptual frameworks, and even in the actual shaping of what we understand as consciousness. Thus, we must be prepared to reform some of the most basic elements of our thinking.

With regard to the effects on consciousness of the new electronic media, especially television, the available evidence seems to strengthen, or perhaps extend, my thesis. Briefly, it appears that a postliterate visual orientation offers the worst of all possible words—that is, it embodies the worst aspects of both oral and literate cultures. Neil Postman argues that as passively received images replace the text that the reader must actively examine, analytical capacities decrease. At the same time, however, the capacity of television to present a rapid succession of drastically different images intensifies the literate tendency toward abstraction from the world and fragmentation of the world. People in a postliterate visual culture lose the capacity for analytical thought brought about by literacy while retaining—indeed, enlarging—the literate tendency to see the world in fragmented, reductionistic terms. The crucial factor in bringing about this situation is that the electronic media of communication, beginning with the telegraph and culminating with television, drastically increase the decontextualization of knowledge characteristic of literacy. In a pre-electronic print culture, knowledge, although abstracted from context in the ways we have discussed earlier, can only be transported at a speed at which humans can move—that is the speed of horseback, or later the railroad. Hence, some of the original existential context of the knowledge will be retained because of the slow pace of its diffusion. But with the telegraph and later electronic devices, knowledge can move around the world at the speed of light and thus be almost completely torn from its original existential context. If the decontex-tualization of knowledge begins with pictographic writing, is accelerated by writing, and takes a quantum jump with printing, it gets completely out of control with the new electronic media. Although some abstraction is required for analysis, this extreme decontextualization reduces the world to a jumble of disconnected quanta of information and thus destroys the connective context necessary for analysis.[53]

Similarly, Joshua Meyrowitz argues that television decontextualizes not just knowledge but also social interactions. In premodern cultures, the social places and behaviors of individuals and especially groups were differentiated by separate spatial locations: people worked in one place and worshipped in another, different social classes lived and worked in different types of buildings or different parts of the same building, and so forth. In nineteenth- and early twentieth-century literate cultures, different levels of reading skill and different reading interests further differentiated children from adults, men from women, and different social classes and professions by presenting social situations in different ways for different audiences. Television, by contrast, inevitably presents a given social situation in the same way for all viewers, thus wrenching social roles and behaviors from context: individuals see other people, especially authority figures, acting in ways they otherwise would not see, thus changing their perceptions of how they relate to others, and especially changing their perceptions of others' roles. A particularly striking example is that TV shows such as "Father Knows Best" and "Leave it to Beaver," which superficially appear to glorify earlier patriarchal bourgeois culture, in fact unwittingly subvert that culture by showing parents debating how to control their children or even how to hide weaknesses from them, something children would not see in real life (except by accident) and would not read about in children's books. The confusion about social roles of the last three or so decades can be at least partly attributed to the way television breaks down the spatial and literary boundaries that allowed those roles to function.[54]

Additionally, whereas the telegraph operates through printed language, which promotes, as we have seen, relatively impersonal, dis-passionate analysis, television operates mainly through visual images, which encourage direct, highly emotional responses.[55] McLuhan's thesis that the new electronic media would bring about a renewed orality seems to have been based on the perception that people were losing analytical skills while simultaneously becoming more emotional, some-thing that implied a similarity with oral cultures, but it failed to recognize the tremendous decontextualization of knowledge inherent in the electronic media. We might say that if a literate culture is objectivist or rationalist, a postliterate visual culture, consisting of a chaos of unconnected emotive images and decontextualized social behavior, is relativist or irrationalist.[56] These findings actually strengthen my thesis. Just as relativism is derivative of objectivism, the new electronic media are derivative of literacy. The developing postliterate relativist orientation can be seen as the logical culmination of the earlier literate objectivist orientation. The ultimate problem remains understanding objectivism and elaborating non-objectivist modes of thought which can allow us to escape the relativism into which we are rapidly sliding.

In any case, in order both to make the implications of literacy more concrete and to demonstrate what might be entailed in an orally oriented reorganization of our thought, I will discuss some of the ways in which literacy has affected philosophical discourse itself.

Literate Objectivism and the Western Philosophical Tradition

As mentioned above, Eric Havelock has analyzed Plato as part of a broader investigation of the effects of literacy on Greek culture. Havelock's basic thesis is that Plato's philosophy is an attempt to articulate the conceptual vocabulary and educational apparatus appropriate to an interiorized literacy. His starting point is Plato's attack on poetry. Havelock argues that poetry as described by Plato corresponds to the characteristic features of oral cultures that we described above. That is, the poetic world attacked by Plato is the active, personal, concrete, formulaic, participatory lifeworld of orality, while Plato represents the static, impersonal, abstract, analytic, detached world of literacy. For example, the "dream" state excoriated by Plato corresponds to the trancelike state achieved by poets and audience alike during oral recitation of poetry. Havelock points out that poetry was the fundamental educational medium for early Greek culture; most if not all knowledge was remembered in poetic form. Thus, the poetic or oral state of mind was the ruling mindset, that is, the mindset of the "many." If the analytic thought made possible by literacy was to develop its potential, it would have to eliminate the retarding effects of the old oral mentality. Hence, a new vocabulary, centered around concepts rather than actions, and a new method of education, based on analytic argumentation rather than formulaic repetition, would be needed, and Plato attempts to develop these in the *Republic*.

Havelock's book has been subject to much criticism, but from the knowledge recently discovered about oral cultures and the effects of literacy, we could plausibly maintain that he has explicated one dimension of the overall environment in which Plato worked, i.e., a situation where literacy was beginning to become widely interiorized at the expense of the older oral culture. Certainly, Havelock's discussions of Plato's conceptual innovations are very suggestive. Here I will briefly discuss two of the important points he makes.

We have already seen that oral people think in contextual, situational terms, and that an important consequence of this is that inconsistencies in formulaic sayings and the like are not noticed, or rather, are not considered a cause for concern, since oral thought does not generalize across contexts, at least not to the extent that literate thought does. For literate people, the kinds of apparent contradictions or inconsistencies found in an oral culture's store of wisdom violate a most fundamental requirement of the literate mindset, i.e., consistency, which is generated by the tendency to abstract knowledge out of contexts and generalize it across contexts. Thus, when Plato critiques the inconsistency, plurality, and inexactness of *doxa*, "opinion," as opposed to the consistency, uniformity, and exactitude of truth arrived at philosophically, he is, as Havelock sees it, articulating a developing literate consciousness in opposition to the oral mentality.[57]

Similarly, Plato needs to develop a vocabulary of formal abstraction to replace the concrete event- or action-oriented vocabulary of the old oral culture. Specifically, he must, as Havelock sees it, elucidate entities that are noncorporeal and timeless, so that they can be generalized across contexts and will not be tied to particular times and places, as the units of Homeric discourse apparently are. From this arise the Forms. Of course Plato does not actually escape time and space (since this is impossible), and in his attempt to explain the Forms he relies on language that has strong visual connotations. As Havelock says, "the Form of bed undeniably suggests visual relationships—an ideal geometry of a bed—even at the highest level, and so on down the scale of intellection to the poet's imperfect visualisation. . . . Repeatedly, in striving for a language which shall describe that new level of mental activity which we style abstract, [Plato] tends to relapse into metaphors of vision, when it would have been less misleading to rely always on idioms which stress the critical effort of analysis and synthesis."[58] From our discussion of the effects of literacy, we can readily understand that Plato would have been particularly susceptible to visual metaphors.

As we have mentioned, Plato himself criticized writing. But this hardly contradicts Havelock's thesis. One can certainly be unaware of one's own assumptions, especially if they are as tacit as many important aspects of a literate mentality are. Thus, one could critique writing, deeming it inferior to speech, even as one was profoundly affected by the subtle effects of literacy. Actually, as might be expected from our earlier discussion of how elements of an oral mentality linger residually in earlier stages of literacy, Plato himself does exhibit important oral residue. Specifically, he still understands words as having a kind of fundamental power, just as oral people do, and unlike modern philosophers—but his understanding of a word is of course that of a literate person.

Finally, it is important to see that Havelock's interpretation of Plato contains an important truth even if it fails to get at Plato's "real" intentions or focuses on only part of the relevant historical context. When Havelock analyzes various features of Plato's thought, e.g., the Forms, as products of an emerging literate consciousness, he employs conventional interpretations of Plato. His innovation consists in his thesis about the origins of the Forms in literate consciousness, not in any new idea about what Plato meant by the Forms. Whether or not such interpretations are what Plato really intended, they are the way literate people have understood him. Thus, we can say that, whatever Plato meant, the conventional interpretations of him show the effects of literacy on our thinking. What could be regarded, then, as the foundation of objectivist thinking, is, one way or another, at least partly the product of literacy.

In terms of the modern development of objectivist thinking, Ong discusses how a visualist orientation plays a crucial role in Kant's thinking. Kant's understanding of intellectual knowledge in terms of phenomena displays a visual orientation, since *phainomenon*, "appearance," is derived from *phainein*, "to show," "expose to sight." As a result, says Ong,

> the essential Kantian problem thus connects with Kant's use of the sensorium. If intellection or understanding is conceived of by using a model from the field of vision, the phenomenon-noumenon problem automatically emerges from the model, the problem whether apprehension can get beyond surfaces. It can never get to an interior as an interior, but must always treat it somehow as an exterior. If understanding is conceived of by analogy with sight alone . . . rather than by analogy also with hearing . . . understanding is ipso facto condemned to dealing with surfaces which have a "beyond" it can never attain to.[59]

Hearing, on the other hand, can give access to interiors as such. According to Ong, it "reveals the interior without the necessity of physical invasion." We can tap a wall to discover where it is hollow inside, but to discover this by sight, we would have to open up the wall, make the inside an outside, and destroy its interiority as such. "Sound reveals interiors," says Ong,

> because its nature is determined by interior relationships. The sound of a violin is determined by the interior structure of its strings, of its bridge, and of the wood in its soundboard, by the shape of the interior cavity in the body of the violin, and other interior conditions. Filled with concrete or water, the violin would sound different.[60]

We shall return to the matter of the interiority of sound later,[61] as it will be important for some of the concepts to be developed. For the moment, the important point is the extent to which the problem of relativism or irrationalism, based as it is upon the doubts cast by Kant on our ability to get beyond the framework we project onto the world, is dependent upon the kind of uncritical visualist orientation promoted by literacy.

The implication of literacy in the Kantian problem of knowledge can form a starting point for an examination of the subtle effects of literacy in contemporary attempts to escape objectivism. I have noted earlier that literacy can induce objectivism in subtle forms and that we may actually be thinking in objectivist terms precisely when we think we have escaped such an orientation. Nowhere, according to Ong, is this more true than in the work of Jacques Derrida and the deconstructionists. Derrida's work attacks objectivism as it manifests itself in what he calls "logocentrism," which corresponds closely to what I have termed language realism. Derrida and other deconstructionists argue that the written (or printed) text breaks down logocentrism by showing the extent to which words do not unambiguously correspond to or refer to objects of some sort, since words in a text can take on many meanings or have many implications. Logocentrism itself, however, is, according to Derrida, derived from "phonocentrism," which takes the spoken word as in some way fundamental and in some way corresponding or referring to objects. The Western philosophical tradition has made a fundamental error in debasing writing compared to speech, because a focus on writing can break up such a referential conception of language in the manner described above. As Ong points out however, "recent work on the orality-literacy contrasts . . . complicate[s] the roots of phonocentrism and logocentrism beyond the textualists' [i.e., deconstructionists'] account."[62] Specifically, as we have seen, the description of the spoken word given by Derrida is one that only a literate person would hold; nonliterate people attribute fundamental importance to spoken words, but they understand them as events or actions, not as referents of some sort. What Derrida calls phonocentrism results from projecting a literate language realism onto the spoken word. That is, his criticism of the Western philosophical tradition for taking the spoken, rather than the written, word as a model misses the point because the philosophical tradition was actually taking the written word as a model and imputing its properties to the spoken word. Derrida critiques the philosophical tradition for focusing on the spoken word because it supposedly escapes the ambiguities of the written word. While it is true that words spoken from one person to another are typically less ambiguous than words written for no one in particular,[63] the notion that words could somehow correspond unambiguously to fixed objects is, as we have seen, very much a product of a literate consciousness and would be quite foreign, if not unintelligible, to the oral imagination. The philosophical tradition understood the spoken word as privileged over the written word precisely because it imputed to it the qualities of the written word. Logocentrism causes phonocentrism, not the other way around, as Derrida thinks. As Ong puts it, "it would appear that the [deconstructionist] critique of textuality . . . is still itself curiously text-bound. . . . [It] derives its appeal in part from historically unreflective, uncritical literacy."[64] What this means is that the deconstructionists have succumbed to objectivism just as they have thought they had escaped it. We can see this in another way if we consider the deconstructionist notion that because language is not characterized by ultimately unambiguous reference, there must be an irreducible random or chaotic or ironic element to it. This conclusion only follows if one has already tacitly made the objectivist assumption that either language must contain some kind of exact correspondence with reality *or* else it ultimately fails to have meaning. But if one drops this assumption, there are other possibilities. Language can have ultimate meaning without having some kind of translucent "correspondence" with "reality."

In terms of successfully escaping from objectivism, it might be worthwhile briefly to examine the relationship to orality of two recent philosophers, both of whom are crucial to this study, i.e., Polanyi and Wittgenstein. It has undoubtedly occurred to the reader during the discussion of oral and literate thought processes that Polanyi's description of knowledge seems to draw upon motifs that we would properly associate with an oral/aural orientation. This is in fact an argument that William H. Poteat makes. Poteat observes that Polanyi's formulations tend to conflate logical categories, which we normally understand as atemporal, and causal categories, which we typically take to be temporal. What Polanyi is attempting to do with this somewhat awkward vocabulary, says Poteat, is to convey a sense of the world's being ordered temporally, as it would be understood from an oral/aural paradigm, rather than being ordered atemporally, as it would be seen from a visual standpoint. The result is the dynamic teleology, or inductive logic, that we discussed in the previous chapter.[65]

Similarly, it could be argued that Wittgenstein, or rather the later Wittgenstein, might be understood as having achieved a partial recovery of a more oral orientation. Certainly the most important aspect of Wittgenstein's later thought is his insistence that words and utterances must always be kept in context to be properly understood. The importance of context for an oral orientation and the tendency of a literate/visualist orientation to abstract things from context have been major themes in our discussion. Indeed, Wittgenstein's method of proceeding, through a series of examples and questions rather than through an abstract statement of what he wanted to get at, is more in keeping with an oral orientation than with a literate/visual one. Additionally, although he does not say much about experiential or sensory sources of the objectivist orientation he was attacking, his procedure, which attempts to slowly eradicate the objectivist mindset through repeated examples, seems to indicate that he realized how deeply rooted and subtle this orientation is. In this regard, our discussion of literacy can also help us see why Wittgenstein is frequently misunderstood as some kind of proto-deconstructionist. Such a reading is precisely what one would expect if studying him fails to defeat the language realist mindset that all literate people tend to have: if language does not "correspond" to something, then it cannot have meaning.

There is also some anecdotal evidence that Wittgenstein may have partly recaptured an oral orientation. It is well known that he abandoned the theory of linguistic meaning detailed in the *Tractatus Logico-Philosophicus* (itself an obvious example of an extreme visual orientation), after teaching schoolchildren. His contact with people just learning to read may have made him more aware of the contextual features of knowledge that are easily missed by highly literate adults. Similarly, I earlier mentioned Boman's work, which argued that the Hebrews were primarily oriented toward sound while the Greeks were more oriented toward vision. Wittgenstein is reported to have said to M.O.C. Drury that "your religious ideas have always seemed to me more Greek than biblical. Whereas my thoughts are one hundred per cent Hebraic."[66] It is at least conceivable that Wittgenstein's later understanding of language embodied some of the Hebraic oral orientation.

To summarize our discussion to this point we can say, then, that the relative stasis of the written or printed word provides the phenomenological basis for the conceptual capacity to understand ourselves and the world in highly abstract terms. This capacity can be very enabling, but with it also lurk very subtle dangers. Specifically, this tendency toward abstraction seems to be an extremely important source of objectivist modes of thought and thus indicates that a literate-visual orientation can be understood as a prime culprit in our current epistemological and political disorientation. A recovery of certain aspects of orality may be a possible therapeutic device.

The discussion of objectivism and its experiential sources therefore suggests two possible approaches to the problem of escaping the objectivist/relativist dilemma. At one level, we might attempt to develop a non-objectivist concept of necessity by a phenomenology of the speech act, or at least certain aspects of it, and at an explicitly political level, we might investigate how we could incorporate elements of an oral/aural orientation into our political vocabulary. I shall in fact attempt both of these approaches, first developing the concept of necessity and then using it to inform my discussion of what a more speech-based political vocabulary would sound like. The first task, then, is to explore certain aspects of the speech act.

4

Beyond Objectivism:
The Logic of the Speech Act

Our discussion so far has carried us over a considerable range of philosophical terrain. It is now time to pull this diverse material together and to construct one of the concepts that will be central to the rest of the argument. In the first chapter I argued that what we need is a non-objectivist conception of necessity to reorder our radically contingent world. Or more specifically, in terms of ethical and political questions, we need a non-objectivist conception of necessity to solve the problems of incommensurability and critical distance with regard to narrative practices of which we are a part. In the next two chapters I used Michael Polanyi's discussion of scientific knowing to elucidate some of the salient features of objectivism and then discussed how the superordination of visual experience that accompanies literacy can be a very powerful and subtle source of these features in our thought processes. Defeating the tendency we have to think in terms of an objectivist/relativist dichotomy would require an examination of speech and hearing and an application of the results of this examination to our political vocabulary. In this chapter, then, I will discuss the work of several writers who have undertaken such an examination. The result will be a preliminary or rudimentary formulation of a non-objectivist conception of necessity. Specifically, we will be able to say by the end of this chapter that we have a concrete standard by which to judge ethical and political actions: whether or not a given speaker in a given context was faithful to his or her words. This formulation will in turn be elaborated in the next chapter. First, however, we need to derive this initial result from a consideration of necessity and contingency in light of our discussion so far.

Necessity and Contingency in Visual and Aural Contexts

William H. Poteat has explicitly undertaken an investigation of the concepts of necessity and contingency in terms of our basic sensory orientations. Taking as his guiding principle the idea that all of the concepts we think with are generated out of our concrete mindbodily[1] existence in the world, he has first argued that the concepts of necessity and contingency that we normally use are largely derived from the second-order account of our visual experience that emerges with the diffusion of literacy and then has discussed what these concepts might be like if we derive them from an account of our oral/aural experience. The result is that the concepts we get from such a consideration are broader and in important ways more useful than the ones we get from visual experience, and that specifically, necessity and contingency are not mutually exclusive: we can derive a conception of necessity that can coexist even with absolute contingency. Let us examine these findings.

Poteat begins by observing an important difference between vision and hearing that we have already discussed in our investigation of the differences between oral and literate orientations. With vision it is possible in a sense to bracket out time, or to conceive of a visual event as occurring in such a brief lapse of time as to be timeless and thus in a sense eternal. Of course we can never actually bracket out time; all seeing does take place in a temporal context. But we can abstractly imagine a visual experience taking place in an infinitesimal period of time such that it is virtually indistinguishable from no passage of time. In this instance, we can imagine instantaneous visual comprehension of an ordered, coherent picture, even though in our actual daily activities we would never experience anything quite like it. If we imagine ourselves looking at, say, a painting, and if we imaginatively "stop" the "time" of the actual dynamic process of seeing, we can, Poteat says,

> remark another, perhaps the unique, feature of the visual field before my fixed gaze: its dynamism notwithstanding, every "part" of that determinate surface, bounded by the frame of my open eyelids, is at once sensuously and simultaneously co-present with every other "part." And when I take one further step back from my "actual" seeing, that is, when I abstract myself one remove from my seeing, already limited by our prescribed conditions, I gain the unique power of sight, prescinded from the dynamism that characterizes "actual" seeing: the power to see in an instant without temporal density an at once finite, static, and eternal spatial configuration whose "parts" are determinate and sensuously simultaneously co-present in (visual) space with each other and with the totality that they jointly comprise.[2]

With vision, therefore, we can imagine a coherent ordered whole (virtually) independent of time. Hans Jonas, who has performed a similar analysis, observes that this experience is the source of such dichotomies as being-becoming, eternity-time, essence-existence, and even theory-practice.[3] And, as we have seen, the ability to imagine such an abstract, (nearly) timeless frame of reference is itself brought about by literacy, which enables people relatively to abstract themselves from the world's dynamism.

If we examine hearing, on the other hand, we discover that we cannot imagine such an abstraction, at least not in any way that would yield a coherent perception of anything but raw sound. Whereas we can take in a coherent visual picture in such a short time that we can and generally do abstractly imagine this occurring in no time, we cannot do this with hearing. We would need some short but extended time period to recognize a coherent, motival sound activity, such as part of a melody or a spoken word. If we tried abstractly to compress this time period down to the infinitesimal passage of time we imagined in the visual case, we could hear at best only a noise, not a coherent, recognizable melody or word. Says Poteat:

> Could anything be heard in the ["timeless"] world depicted here . . . ? The instants that provide the conditions for the existence of the simultaneously co-present particulars in the scene before me in our picture have among them only the relations of instantaneous co-presence and (visual) spatial contiguity. Of any of these we may say that it is above or below, to the left or to the right of some other. Such a "conceptual" matrix provides no "logical" place for a tone—or even just for a sound to appear. If we are to have sounds, we shall have to restore to the picture the conceptual resources for introducing real temporal succession. . . . The "time" through which a tone is distended, giving it life, is a temporal succession, whether during the span of a whole note, quarter note, sixteenth, or whatnot. . . . [4]

What this analysis shows is that while vision and hearing are both temporal, vision can be understood in relative abstraction from time while hearing cannot. Thus, if we think in heavily visual terms, we are more likely to lose a sense of the world's temporality; or to put it another way, we are more likely to understand the world's order and coherence in essentially static, three-dimensional spatial terms. This is a conclusion central to the discussion of orality and literacy in the previous chapter, and we may suspect that the almost universal tendency of the Western philosophical tradition to assume that any ultimate order to the world must be unchanging is at least in part a result of such a literate/visual orientation.[5] Certainly the above discussion complements the argument made in the previous chapter that a literate/visual orientation can subtly promote an objectivist approach which understands knowledge and order as essentially static, i.e., abstracted from the world's dynamism, and indicates that one way to defeat objectivist thinking, especially in the more subtle manifestations in which it appears, may be to develop conceptions of order that derive from dynamic oral/aural models.

To this end, then, let us examine what necessity and contingency might be like in visual and oral/aural models. Poteat begins by examining the etymologies of the words "necessary" and "contingent." Like language philosophers such as J. L. Austin, Poteat believes that etymologies reveal the way in which words are generated from concrete mindbodily activities. Necessary and necessity come from the Latin *cedere* and *ne*. *Cedere* means to go, to proceed, to go away, withdraw, give ground, retire, while *ne* is the original Latin particle of negation, so that *necedere* then means not to go, not to proceed, not to go away, not to withdraw, not to give ground, not to retire, and by transference, to be unavoidable, inevitable. For contingent, we have the Latin verb *contingere*, which means, in transitive form, to touch, to touch with, to border on, to reach, and by transference to concern, to affect; in its intransitive form it means to happen, to befall (usually of good luck).[6]

Recalling our earlier use of the terms necessary and contingent, i.e., that necessary means derivable and contingent means underivable, we can see that a necessary occurrence, one that is unavoidable or that does not "withdraw from" a cause or a source of order, can be understood as derivable from the cause or source of order, such as the events in Aristotle's closed cosmos are (although, as we shall see, there may well be other ways to understand necessity). The case of contingency is more complicated. The reason for this is that we use the word contingent in two somewhat different ways. In one typical usage, contingent means "dependent upon," as in "Our activities tomorrow are contingent upon the weather." This meaning is actually similar to the way we use necessity (a point I shall return to later), and we can see that it seems to derive from the transitive form of *contingere* (that is, to touch, to touch with, to border on, to reach). In the other typical usage, contingent means something more like an uncontrollable chance event, unpredictable or underivable from what has gone before, as in "I am keeping $500 in the bank in case of any future contingencies." Here, it seems more closely related to the intransitive form of *contingere*, i.e., to happen or to befall, and also closer to our initial use of the word as something underivable. It is this second use of the word that I will be mainly concerned with here, although I will eventually return to the first meaning as well.

If we apply these etymologies to the visual model we earlier discussed, we can see that necessity, that which does not go, does not give ground, does not retire, and contingency, that which happens, befalls, or reaches, will be mutually exclusive. Poteat says:

> Necessity allows—at least while subject to the picture of sight— *only* for that sense of "time" within which a thing "unchangingly" endures and that is indistinguishable from eternity, while contingency precisely *requires* those senses of time in which motility, change, style, motif, and intention—perhaps even novelty—may appear. And we can see, too, that this contrast derives from our picture of seeing, since it is uniquely in this picture that the "time" that is eternity stands out opposed to all the others. The relations among the particulars of my visual field are the very opposite of contingent. Being simultaneously (visually) co-present, they are in a necessary relation to one another, that is, in the relation of not withdrawing from one another, not retiring from one another: in short, in the relation of being unmovingly, unchangingly present with one another, in the sense of 'present with' associated with visible things.[7]

That is, if we think in terms of our visual model, derived from literacy, necessary relations must be in some way static and unchanging, because this is the only way their particulars can avoid moving away from each other. Necessity will mean in this picture only that which endures "unchangingly" in eternity.

If we think largely in terms of this model then, change and movement become quite problematic, and we will tend eventually to conclude that either the world is ultimately all necessary, either somehow determined or at least with possibilities eternally fixed by eternal essences of some kind, or else—if no such eternal essences exist— the world is radically contingent, underivable, chaotic, with no ultimate order to it. In the first instance, any change that takes place is not really novel change, since it can be derived from the eternally given necessary order of reality, and in the second instance the existence of truly novel change implies that there can be no necessary order to the world, since such change falls outside of any ultimately fixed, eternal order. This is the problem identified in the first chapter: our world has become radically contingent with the destruction of the necessity of Aristotle's closed cosmos.

What might necessity and contingency be like if we think of them in terms of sound, then? Poteat considers two cases, music and speech. In the case of music, there is certainly a sense in which we can talk about necessity and contingency coinciding. As we listen to a piece of music, the notes that we are about to hear are certainly contingent, in several senses. Most obviously, the person(s) performing the music may fail to sound the relevant notes. More importantly, the first time we hear a piece of music, we do not know which notes will follow the ones we have heard; the resolution of a chord as we hear it is contingent. More generally, a given piece of music may be resolved in a number of ways when being composed. In these ways and others, the notes in a piece of heard music are contingent: they happen in a way that is not exhaustively derivable from what has gone before. At the same time, Poteat argues, a piece of music is also subject to a kind of necessity. Specifically, a piece of music is always subject to a motif, such as the eight-tone scale, which establishes in some way the range of possibilities open to that piece of music. That is, in terms of the etymology of necessary discussed earlier, the motifs encountered in music make the various notes necessary in that they ultimately will not move away from or will not withdraw from, the form introduced by the motifs. "The relations of the earlier and the later [notes]," says Poteat, "are not those of cause and effect, [but] nevertheless the constituent notes of the heard music, *as susceptible of resolution in time into a finite whole* . . . are bound together, not by *necessity* such as obtains in a dead slice of (visual) space, but by a *motif*: a lively temporal configuration, habitable by the mindbody, the particulars of which happen in time (as does also the configuration taken as a whole), but the occurrences of whose particulars are neither causally related nor mutually radically underivable. . . . "[8]

To take the most extreme example, we could imagine a piece of music that played every conceivable combination of notes allowed by the eight-tone scale, with an upward and downward range of octaves determined by the highest and lowest note audible by at least one pair of human ears. Although this peculiar piece of music would take an extremely long time to play, all of its possibilities would be given by the eight-tone scale and in this sense it does not move away from the motif of this scale. As noted above, the necessity here is not one of causation; it would be odd to speak of the eight-tone scale causing the piece of music.

Rather it sets limits to what can occur in the piece of music, and in this sense ensures that the particulars of the piece of music will not move away from or withdraw from an ordered whole of some kind.[9] Note that we have here isolated another possible meaning of necessity, that is, a set of limits to particular occurrences. This conception of necessity is more flexible than the visually-based conception of particulars being exhaustively derivable. Thus, in the case of the temporal phenomenon of music, necessity and contingency can coexist.

If we examine our example more closely, however, we will see that this musical case really only contains relative contingencies. All the possibilities, even in the piece of music that plays all the possible combinations of notes in the eight-tone scale, while certainly temporal, are given, eternally, by the motif of the eight-tone scale. That is, although a particular note is not exhaustively derivable from what has gone before, all the possible combinations of notes are exhaustively derivable from the eight-tone scale.[10] The situation is analogous to Aristotle's cosmos. Although movement and change take place, that is, although, from a given viewpoint, contingencies occur, these are only relative because all the possibilities of movement and change are given in the eternal essences or potentialities of natural beings. Similarly, all the changes and movements that may take place in a piece of music are eternally given by the motifs that inform it. A musical model such as the one discussed here would still be incapable of dealing with the situation described in the biblical picture of reality, where the world has infinite possibilities. In order to deal with the problem of absolute contingency, we must turn to the speech act.

Absolute Contingency and the Speech Act

Before I discuss the speech act in this context, it will be helpful to clarify what is meant by absolute contingency. Poteat points out that, strictly speaking, an absolutely contingent occurrence, if we take this to mean "a pure, radically underivable, therefore motifless, hence meaningless happening," is only abstractly conceivable. This is because "existentially, a radical novelty or an 'absolutely' random occurrence, *to be remarked as such*, must after all fall within the sense-giving and sense-reading matrix of my lively mindbody, and as such, *if remarked*, appears as a radical *other-than* of this matrix of meaning and intentionality."[11] That is to say, a truly absolutely contingent occurrence would not be noticed by us, since in order to qualify as such, it would have to fall outside the limits of our capacity to perceive. Or, to put it in terminology used earlier, there is a fundamental sense in which unintelligibility is parasitical upon intelligibility; any attempt to describe or even remark an unintelligible occurrence must do so in terms of things and occurrences that are intelligible.

If we did abstractly imagine an absolutely contingent occurrence, however, a crucially important feature does emerge: such an occurrence must in some sense be unique, without antecedents, disconnected.[12] If it in some way was derivable from, i.e., was necessarily related to, previous occurrences, it would not be absolutely contingent. At this point we might notice an interesting feature of such an occurrence, which is that it in a sense complements the picture of necessity derived from vision. For the visual model, contingency and change are not possible; all the particulars of an occurrence are simultaneously co-present. Hence, if we attempt to understand contingency using this model, we will get a conception of abrupt, total, disconnected change, as if the world were a series of snapshots flashed before our eyes, with each instantaneous picture potentially or conceivably completely unrelated to the previous one or to subsequent ones. This seems to be the problem discussed above, where if we conceive necessity in static, visual terms, change and contingency become highly problematic, either not really real or else total and absolute. Also, the discussion of the relations between particulars in our static visual model above indicates that one might be tacitly conceiving the world in this way to have the doubts about causation that Hume did: in a given snapshot, the particulars are eternally fixed in their given relations to each other, while in the next one they are eternally fixed in a different set of relations; nowhere in this static model can one "see" causation occurring.[13] Again, then, we can see how our current perception of the world as radically contingent is dependent upon a heavily visual orientation; we realize that there is much change in our world but we cannot grasp how such change could be necessary, that is, connected or motival.

Now, what of the meaning of necessity and contingency in the context of a speech act? I will begin by stating Poteat's basic formulation and then backtrack to an earlier stage in the discussion to elucidate it. Poteat wants to say that

> as the actually existent speaker at the center of this speech event, I am under the sway of the motifs of the natural melodiousness of the human voice in speech; of the motifs of the syntax, grammar, and semantics, that appear in what I and my fellow speakers *do* and are, in speaking, *given to doing*; of the motifs of my general

intentional orientation from out of my mindbodily being toward the world; and of those of the particular intentions to say what on this occasion I want to say. . . . But the heart of actual speech is the *radically* contingent, *absolutely* novel, and underivable act of owning up to these my very particular words—*and this is so no matter how often it is done.* . . . Authentic speech is the act of owning my own words *before you.*[14]

That is, a given speech act is subject to various types of necessity, but its core is the absolutely contingent act of the speaker being faithful to his or her words. It is this conception that must be unpacked.

The best way to approach this task is to apply Polanyi's conception of tacit knowledge earlier discussed. According to this, any act of perception or cognition must acritically or tacitly rely upon the context of the act in order to generate the actual object of perception or knowledge. Now, if we consider the relation of the act of perception, tool-using, or whatever, to the context, we can in fact say that the act is absolutely contingent but still subject to necessity. It is, to begin with, absolutely contingent because it is underivable from its context, that is, since, precisely because we acritically rely upon the context, we cannot derive the act, as it happens, from its context. We could only do this if we somehow critically or explicitly relied upon the context and so could analyze the generation of the act from the context as it happens. But this we cannot do. Another way to understand this is to recall the point made earlier, i.e., that an absolutely contingent occurrence would not be noticed by us, since it would fall outside the limits of our capacity to perceive. This is precisely what happens in our tacit generation of a whole entity from its constituent parts in an act of perception, tool-using, etc. The act of generation, while it is the basis of perceiving, cannot itself be perceived by us; it is beyond the limits of our capacity to perceive. In this sense it is absolutely contingent. At the same time, however, the act in question is subject to necessity (indeed, an absolute necessity), precisely because we must acritically rely upon the context to generate the object of perception or cognition, that is, because we cannot move away from, withdraw from, or retire from, the relevant context. Without the context, the act of perception or tool-using cannot take place.

To clarify this, and in particular to clarify the meaning of necessity here, I think it will be helpful to reconsider Polanyi's discussion of the operational principles of a machine. Although the physico-chemical makeup of the machine sets limits to what the machine can do, and can be used to explain why a machine failed to work, the machine's operational principles, or the machine as a machine, cannot be derived from its physico-chemical makeup. There is a logical and ontological gap between the machine's physico-chemical makeup and its operational principles. In terms of necessity and contingency, we can say that, with regard to its physico-chemical makeup, the machine as machine is absolutely contingent; its operational principles cannot be derived from the physico-chemical makeup of the machine. At the same time, the machine as machine is subject to necessity from its physico-chemical makeup, not in the sense that it can be derived from such makeup (since, as we have just seen, it cannot), but in the sense that its physico-chemical makeup sets limits to what it may do. This model is analogous to the model of our acritical reliance upon a context to generate an act of perception, tool-using, knowledge, etc. Therefore, it makes clearer part of what I meant when I said that these acts are subject to necessity from their contexts: the contexts set limits to what may be generated from them; not just anything may be generated from a particular context. This is a concrete manifestation of the acts' being subject to necessity in that they cannot move away from their contexts.

We can at this point fruitfully consider the usage of contingent (given in the statement, "Our activities tomorrow are contingent upon the weather") which I earlier mentioned but have since ignored. In speaking of a machine, we would say that the machine as a machine, or the operational principles of the machine, are contingent upon its physico-chemical makeup in that this makeup sets limits to what the machine may do or whether it will work. This sense of contingent seems similar to what we mean by necessary. In fact, this meaning of contingent contains elements of both the other meaning of contingent, just discussed, and of necessary, in the sense of setting limits, in that to say that the operation of the machine is contingent upon its physico-chemical makeup is to say that it may or may not happen (contingency in our second sense) depending upon whether the limits established by its physico-chemical makeup, that is, its necessary conditions, are breached or not. The machine depends upon its physico-chemical characteristics but is not derivable from them. Hence, it is not surprising that the etymology of contingent is close to that of necessary; there are important ways in which necessity and contingency coincide. We only understand them as opposites when we understand necessity in visual terms, as implying "exhaustively derivable from."

As I have already indicated in the discussion of orality and literacy, this crucial aspect of our acts of knowing can be obscured by an excessively visual orientation. Specifically, we can see that if we attempt to understand such acts with the static visual model developed above, we will miss the fundamental feature of our acritical reliance upon the context to generate our knowledge, since the temporal aspect of this generation can be readily bracketed out. We will tend to abstract ourselves from the context and thus understand the act of perception, cognition, etc., as a case of an object's being eternally beheld by an eternal, static subject, rather than dynamically generated from the subject's interaction with the context. Or to put it another way, we will have a strong tendency unwittingly to understand the act as a static "state" of some kind. This problem is analogous to the tendency of literate people to understand words as things rather than as actions or events. We abstract the word or act from its temporal context and regard it as a "thing" that can be exhaustively described. Yet another way to put this is that the failure to recognize the logical gap betwen act and context, which is created by the acritical reliance upon the context, could result from the literate habit of reducing all occurrences to things in abstract, homogeneous space. (This also accounts for the tendency to reduce the machine to its physico-chemical makeup.) On the other hand, if we apply a model where hearing and the temporality of sound are central, we can more readily appreciate this acritical reliance.

Now let us return to the speech act. In this case, as in the case of perception, both speaker and listener must acritically rely upon or trust the overall context of the speech act in several senses. Obviously, they must rely upon shared language, knowledge, etc. More fundamentally, however, the listener must, as he is listening, acritically trust the speaker's act of speaking; he cannot, in the context of taking in the other's words as intelligible speech, doubt what the speaker is saying, or rather, doubt that the speaker is at some level speaking intelligibly, even though he may dismiss the entire utterence as nonsense or fraudulent immediately upon discerning the meaning—or even if he intends to do so before even hearing the utterance. Similarly, the speaker, as she is speaking, must speak her words as words with the intention of being intelligible: even if she wants to lie or be ironic, her attempt to do so must acritically attempt to be intelligible to the listener, because if she fails in this, her irony or falsehood cannot have the effect wanted. This is true even in the case where one person speaks to another in a language the hearer does not understand: the speaker's utterance is still intelligible as an utterance in a foreign language, and the speaker must have acritically attempted to be intelligible, at some level, to the listener— even if the use of a foreign language was a deliberate attempt to confuse the listener. Just as, generally speaking, unintelligibility is parasitical upon intelligibility, in the speech act, even the grossest unfaithfulness is parasitical upon a more fundamental and unavoidable faithfulness. Or, to put it in a more direct analogy, an attempt to speak to another in an unintelligible fashion is itself only possible within a context of intelligibility—that of doing something recognizable or intelligible as speaking unintelligibly; and similarly, to find another's speech unintelligible is itself possible only in a context of intelligibility—that of finding something recognizable or intelligible as speaking unintelligibly.

As we have already seen, Polanyi makes a similar point when he argues that doubt is always embedded in a framework of tacit belief and acceptance. Lack of trust or faith is possible only in a larger context of more fundamental trust and faith. Wittgenstein illustrates this point well in *On Certainty*:

> If someone doubted whether the earth had existed a hundred years ago, I should not understand, for *this* reason: I would not know what such a person would still allow to be counted as evidence and what not.[15]

Wittgenstein is observing here that the vocabulary necessary to express doubts about the existence, or prior existence, of the earth contains elements that themselves presuppose the earth's prior existence in order to be intelligible in a language game. Using these elements of language to attempt to doubt what they presuppose makes the utterance (relatively) unintelligible, that is, intelligible only as a joke or something of the sort.

If we develop this insight in terms of our earlier discussion, this unavoidable faithfulness of the speech act makes it both absolutely contingent but still subject to necessity. If we must acritically rely upon the context of the speech act in order to speak, then the speech act itself, as it happens, is absolutely contingent, because, as it happens, it is underivable from the context. As with an act of perception, it could only be derivable if we somehow critically or explicitly relied upon the context and as a result could analyze the generation of the speech act from the context as it happened. But, again, we cannot do this. The speech act, or actually, the faithfulness of the speech act, is absolutely underivable, as our acts of perception are absolutely underivable. Likewise, in the case of necessity, we can see that the speaker and hearer cannot move away from, withdraw from, or retire from the context of the speech act, precisely because of the unavoidable intelligibility of the speech act. The faithfulness of the speech act is necessary even as it is underivable. In this phenomenological context this is an absolute kind of necessity: we simply cannot withdraw from the context, even if we think we can and imagine ourselves as doing so. At other levels, this necessity becomes more complicated, as we will see. But, from this analysis, we can say that necessity can coexist with absolute contingency, meaning that we have a concrete basis for setting limits on our actions.

We can also briefly note here what we mentioned in our discussion of the machine, i.e., that contingency in the sense of "depending upon" also characterizes this situation. Our speech acts are not derivable from their context; in this sense they are absolutely contingent. But they also depend upon the context, in that in order to happen they must conform to certain limits, i.e., necessary conditions, established by the context. Another way to put this is to say that the speech act is both contingent as underivable from its conditions and subject to necessity as dependent upon these conditions. In the "generic" speech act of this phenomenological context, the necessary condition is that the speech acts must be in some fundamental way intelligible. In other contexts, as we have mentioned, other or additional necessary conditions will obtain.

At this point, it may be asked why, if this coexistence of necessity and absolute contingency is characteristic of all our acts of perception, tool-using, and knowledge generally, and in fact is a general circumstance of reality as we experience it (as in the examples dealing with machines and biology), I have used the speech act to illustrate it. There are two main reasons for this. First, since the speech act is the experience or action most closely and directly linked to the dynamism of sound as we experience it, it is the paradigm least likely to succumb to the problems, which we have already discussed, inherent in a visualist approach. Second, since the speech act is typically, or paradigmatically, a communal activity, it will produce the paradigm most readily translatable into an ethical or political context. We can construct concepts appropriate for political practice in a way that would be difficult, if not impossible, using perception or similar human activities as a model.

Our next problem is in fact to take our phenomenological model of the speech act and put it in a form suitable for ethical and political questions. This is what will finally take us back to Poteat's initial formulation. Before elaborating the concept, however, I want to discuss three objections that might be made to the formulation so far.

First, it might be objected that there is something peculiar about applying the etymological formulation of necessity—not to move away from—to an oral/aural phenomenon. It would seem that this formulation is really only applicable to visual phenomena, as in the first model we discussed, since it is, after all, a spatial concept. In fact, however, both Poteat and Walter Ong, whom we discussed in the previous chapter, argue that it is quite legitimate to talk about oral/aural space. Ong observes that "we can apprehend space in terms of sound and echoes," so that "space thus apprehended has qualities of its own. It is not spread out in front of us as a field of vision but diffused around us." Since sound can be apprehended from any direction, the hearer experiences himself or herself as being situated at the center of an acoustic field, instead of in front of it, as with vision. He continues:

> Being in the midst of reality is curiously personalizing in impli-cation, since acoustic space is in a way a vast interior in the center of which the listener finds himself together with his interlocutors. The oral-aural individual thus does not find himself simply situated somewhere in neutral, visual-tactile, Copernican space. Rather he finds himself in a kind of vast interiority.

> Because of its association with sound, acoustic space implies presence far more than does visual space. . . . Noises one hears, for example in a woods at night, register in the imagination as presences—person-like manifestations—far more than do move-ments which one merely sees. In this sense acoustic space is precisely not "pure" space. It is essentially inhabited space.[16]

Jonas has noted that it is possible to speak of acoustic space, as Ong does above, but then dismisses this idea as a metaphor. "Real space," he says, "is a principle of co-temporaneous, discrete plurality irrespective of qualitative difference."[17] Clearly, Jonas is understanding space in terms of the visual model earlier discussed, and by "real space" he means what Ong is calling "'pure' space." But the "inhabited space" discussed by Ong is more than a metaphor; indeed, Poteat, using Polanyi's principle of our necessary acritical reliance upon context, argues that our notions of space are parasitical upon notions of place, i.e., that our concept of "pure" space is parasitical upon our experience of "inhabited" space. He observes that we generally understand space as "primordially that within which objects are enabled to be the particular objects which they are and the medium within which these objects are distinctly separate." Opposed to this, he argues, space is "primordially that by means of which I orient myself, or, more exactly, by means of which I am oriented from within my body. To such a view my orientation to my body as an object or from my body as an object among objects to others is derivative." Space then is "primordially a pre-reflective vectorial orientation, and this precisely is my body in its pre-reflective integration into a world." In other words, our conception of space as the medium "out there," in front of us, where different objects are distinctly separate, is parasitical upon our primordial bodily orientation in the world, our basic habitation in the world. "It is within an oriented *whence* that primordial spatiality lies, and it is from within this *whence* that all orientation derives. If there is no such orientation from within a pre-reflective *whence*, then there is and can be no reflective orientation." This is to say that space is dependent upon place—the place of our bodies in the world. "Existentially, as the concrete person I am, *extension* is not first of all space, but rather is *place*. . . . Place is the *where* of my body . . . and is the condition of my having any 'relations' whatsoever."[18] The place which Poteat speaks of here is the same thing as the inhabited space of which Ong speaks. If we accept Ong's claim that this inhabited space is best revealed, or experienced, through sound, it appears that not only can we legitimately speak of oral/aural space, but that this is even more fundamental than "pure" visual space, which requires this primordial habitation in order to be conceptualized.[19] Hence, it is surely legitimate to speak of "not moving away" from the context in a speech act; we shall examine more closely what this might mean shortly.

A second possible objection, one that would be raised from a Heideggerian or post-Heideggerian perspective, is that the account given here of a speech act assumes that language itself is somehow unproblematic, that the words are taken to somehow correspond to meanings exactly, or that the indeterminateness of language is ignored. The account given here is well aware, however, that language is not an unambiguous correspondence; indeed, it is based on this insight. But it is also well aware, and is based on, the idea that the overdetermination inherent in any speech act is itself rooted in intelligibility. The assumption that such overdetermination is somehow fundamentally unintelligible, or at least has an irreducibly unintelligible element to it, or, to put it differently, that intelligibility is parasitical upon unintelligibility as well as vice-versa, is, as we have seen, itself a form of disappointed or tacit language realism; it makes the language realist assumption that either language ultimately corresponds to reality in some sense or that if language does not so correspond, it must have an irreducibly unintelligible element or aspect to it, and simply chooses the latter option over the former.

As a specific example, we can take Heidegger's assertion that

we do not merely speak *the* language—we speak *by way of* it. We can do so only because (or to the extent to which) we have already listened to language. What do we hear there? We hear language speaking.[20]

In one sense, Heidegger is correct when he says we speak by way of language. But he then understands this to mean that language exists in some way independent of us. This, however, is ultimately to conceive of language in a language realist manner, i.e., as some kind of large text. I believe Wittgenstein is attacking this problem when he says:

> Suppose it were asked: "*When* do you know how to play chess? All the time? Or just while you are making a move? And the *whole* of chess during each move?"[21]

We can only ask such a question if we conceive of "knowing how to play chess" as a static body of knowledge, rather than as an active practice. The question arises when we wonder where the "knowledge"—conceived as some kind of "thing" in our heads, or somewhere—goes when we are not making a move or not playing chess. Illustrated in this manner by the problem of "knowing how to play chess," the error seems obvious enough. The mistake becomes more subtle, however, when we talk in terms of large abstractions like "language." Here we can—thanks to our literate conception of a word as something with a life of its own—quite innocently conceive "language" in the same way as the above questions understood "knowing how to play chess," i.e., as something with a life of its own, independent of our actions, which can be off doing all sorts of strange, mysterious, and deceptive things when we are not actively using it.

The third objection that might be raised is that, after having stressed the untenability of ahistorical essentialist formulations of necessity (such as those found in Aristotle or natural right theory), and after having stressed the importance of a dynamic framework of practice, narrative, and tradition, I have proceeded to articulate a universal, neutral, ahistorical notion of necessity in what I have termed the "generic" speech act. But this is not the case. Although the discussion attempts to articulate an aspect of experience common to all humans, the articulation itself is highly specific and in no way pretends to be something that all humans would find accessible. To take one obvious example of how this is so, the analysis depended on the meanings and etymologies of English words; in another language a different type of analysis might have to be performed. More profoundly, this articulation is one that is likely to make sense only to highly literate, analytically-oriented people who, however, have been able to retain or regain enough of an oral/aural orientation to appreciate the differences between vision and sound. For people with an even more thoroughgoing visual orientation, some different approach might be required. And for people with a more substantial oral/aural orientation, the formulation developed here might seen awkward and cumbersome if not actually bizarre and meaningless. Indeed, for most people, certainly for highly oral people, an infinitely more edifying formulation of the idea that intelligibility is more fundamental than unintelligibility would be found in Genesis:

God said "Let there be light," and there was light. . . . And God saw that it was good.

Different articulations of common human experience, or indeed different articulations that there *is* common human experience, will be appropriate for different traditions or even at different times within the same tradition. What my analysis does imply, however, is that these different articulations will be, or rather, can be made, intelligible to each other. The problem with this third objection is that it takes the particular articulation of the experience developed here to be "literally" the experience "in itself"; that is, it commits a visually-oriented error.

Speech-Based Necessity and Politics

To return to the main line of the argument then, how can we put the concepts just derived into a form applicable to ethical and political questions? As might be suspected, since the context of the speech act is so important, we can only fully explicate the concept of necessity by considering the appropriate ethical and political contexts of particular speech acts, which for our discussion here means from within Alasdair MacIntyre's concept of a narrative practice. This is what I will do in the next chapter. We can, however, give a preliminary formulation here. The starting point is again the unavoidable faithfulness of the speech act. We have seen that, for the speech act as speech act, we must unavoidably remain faithful to, that is, not move away from, the context of the act. Our question becomes, how do we know what constitutes moving or not moving away? In keeping with our earlier formulations, we would reply that it is the context itself, or, more precisely, it would be the different motifs relevant to the context in question, that indicate what would constitute moving away from or withdrawing from the context, that is, what would constitute being unfaithful to one's words.

At this point the term "motif," which was earlier used in an obvious application to music, may need some clarification. Again, this is something that will happen as we proceed, but we can give a preliminary definition. The O.E.D. gives as part of its definition of "motif," "in literary composition: A type of incident, a particular situation, an ethical problem or the the like, which may be treated in a work of imagination. Also in *Folklore*, a recurrent character, event, situation, or theme." It is also an obsolete form of motive, which etymologically is derived from move and thus is related to movement.[22] Basically, I will want to develop the notion of an event or perhaps a movement, although this will require careful elaboration. For the moment, it will be adequate to understand a motif to mean something like a theme or, referring to its older usage, a motive.

In the context we have already discussed, that of an unspecified "generic" speech act, the motif (the theme or motive) that makes the speech act subject to necessity (that is, that indicates what constitutes moving away from the context) is a mutual attempt to be intelligible— even if this attempt is itself the basis for (a derivative) unintelligibility. In this situation, the mutual attempt to be intelligible is unavoidable, so this motif or motive provides an absolute necessity. In an ethical or political context, the motifs that would supply elements of necessity and thus indicate what would constitute an attempt to withdraw from the context would be the events or motives relevant to the narrative practice. That is, in a given context, we can say many things (indeed, an infinite number of possible things), but only some of them will be appropriate, and thus will not constitute moving away from, or withdrawing from, or abstracting ourselves from, the relevant context. What is appropriate will be given by the relevant motifs; they set limits to what may be faithfully said. At the same time, all that can be said cannot be exhaustively derived from these motifs; whether or not the speech act will be appropriate or faithful is still absolutely contingent. Another way to put this is that the necessity here is not absolute, as it was with the "generic" speech act, where we must at some bedrock level be intelligible; rather, the motifs of the given practice, narrative, or tradition, like the motifs associated with music, set limits to actions, or, to put it differently, indicate what would be appropriate or inappropriate, faithful or unfaithful, valid or abstracted speech acts. Unlike the motifs associated with music, however, these motifs will not determine all the possibilities of the speech acts. This conception of necessity still coexists with an element of absolute contingency. In our earlier discussion, an absolutely contingent occurrence had to be in some way unique. If we consider the speech act, we observe that every speech act, taken in its overall historical context, is unique; although speech acts abstracted from their overall contexts can, of course, be classified in a variety of ways, a given speech act, in its historical context, is unique precisely because every particular context is unique. Hence, every act of faithfulness is ultimately unique and underivable. Only the paradigmatic personal speaker could be guaranteed to be always faithful. Finite and fallible humans can and do, at any time, fail to be faithful.[23]

Stating the matter this way, of course, brings us back to Poteat's orginal formulation. Indeed, what we have said here is congruent with the biblical understanding of humankind as the covenanting animal. What is specifically human on this view is not, or at least not primarily, our capacity for abstract rational thought or aesthetic creativity, but our capacity to be faithful to our words before another person. Our words create a world, but it is our faithfulness to those words that orders that world. We are creators in that we speak a world into existence, but we are also creatures in that we cannot speak any world we want into existence. The creativity of speech is fundamentally different from aesthetic creativity in that it is limited by the necessity of responsibility. It is similar to the Aristotelian paradigm of humanity as the political animal, but broader in that it does not restrict the scope of politics with a notion of a fixed natural order itself beyond politics or of a subpolitical realm such as the household. All human activities are potentially political in that all human activities involve attempts to be faithful to others. Debate over the faithfulness of actions would be central to traditions informed by such a conception of necessity.

The formulation I have developed here can illuminate a paradox in the biblical worldview discussed by Reinhold Niebuhr. Niehbur points out that the biblical idea of original sin seems to be illogical because it claims that "man sins inevitably and by a fateful necessity but that he is nevertheless to be held responsible for actions which are prompted by an ineluctable fate."[24] He then goes on to argue that this conception, although illogical, is indeed supported by human experience, something that he thinks demonstrates the limits of logic. Based on our discussion so far, we could say that the biblical idea of original sin is illogical perhaps only from the standpoint of a visually-based logic; it might make perfect sense in terms of the speech-based logic developed here. Specifically, if we define sin, as Niebuhr does, as the attempt by humans to deny their finitude and become God, that is, to abstract themselves from their context of finitude, we can see that, in the context of all human existence or the life of any particular human being, this would be an inevitable outcome of the human condition as both creator and creature, but nevertheless something that could, at any particular moment, that is, in any particular context, be avoided.

Our formulation can also give us some clues about the resolution of an issue raised in the first chapter. There, I argued that although the radical contingency of the biblical worldview destroyed the classical cosmos and made modern nihilism possible, the real culprit in destroying any possible limits, or any understanding of necessity, for human actions was the modern objectivist conception of acceptable knowledge. I suggested that the biblical understanding of reality may contain elements of necessity that have been obscured by the objectivist model. The analysis of this chapter has shown that a kind of necessity can coexist with even radical contingency, and that this necessity resides in the capacity of speakers to be faithful to their words, which is of course the central theme in the biblical stories.

Before we begin to explicate in more detail what the motifs of necessity relevant to political practice would look like, it will be helpful to observe several important points about the concept of necessity we have developed here. First, it may have occurred to the reader that what I have called a motif sounds something like Austin's notion of a felicity, i.e., that which is a necessary condition for the successful or appropriate performance of a speech act. A speech act can only accomplish what it is supposed to accomplish if all the relevant felicities obtain. It is indeed true that there is a strong resemblance, but I have deliberately avoided using the idea of a felicity because this concept tends to imply that there can be an exhaustive enumeration of all speech situations or felicities (or motifs) appropriate to them. This is something that I want to avoid. The attempt to enumerate all possible speech situations and their salient features seems to be a relapse into a kind of language realism, although a partial enumeration of speech situations or a discussion of some of their appropriate felicities may be useful for clarifying certain issues. What I want to do with the concept of a motif which I have begun to develop is to examine how motifs of necessity would function in narrative practices relevant to politics. For this purpose it is important to be aware that since it depends upon the context, what is an appropriate or faithful speech act can change historically. This is true not only in the sense that contexts change, but in the sense that, as we saw in our discussion of Polanyi, all contexts have a dynamic element to them that points beyond themselves; thus, what we had once thought was an appropriate speech act for a given context may eventually be discovered to be inappropriate, and this change will in no way cause us to lapse into relativism.

Attempting exhaustively to enumerate speech situations, however, can cause us to forget this important insight.

The above discussion leads to an important possible objection to what has been developed so far, which is that the concept of necessity, or of a motif, as developed here, may harbor a subtle mind-body dualism. Specifically, if, at the phenomenological level of the "generic" speech act, the necessity that governs the speech act—the necessity that a speech act must be intelligible at some level, or that we must acritically rely upon the context of the speech act—is absolute, since we cannot at this level withdraw from the context, while at other levels, for example in ethical or political contexts, we can be said to be unfaithful, or to abstract ourselves from the context (which is to say, in these contexts, that the relevant felicities do not obtain absolutely), it would seem to follow that there is something qualitatively different about the different levels, i.e., that the "generic" speech act represents some kind of noumenal level while the political speech act represents some kind of phenomenal level, or something of the sort. This problem only arises, however, when one has understood necessity to mean determination, as opposed to the idea we have developed whereby it means something more like setting limits. If we understand necessity to mean the limits relevant to a given situation, our explication of the generic speech act as subject to absolute necessity simply means that at the phenomenological level the limits on our actions are narrower than at the ethical or political level, just as the limits on a mechanical system are narrower than those on a biological system. The two levels are in this sense (as in many others) different, but they are not somehow fundamentally or qualitatively different.

The third point to consider is that the idea of faithfulness I have developed will undoubtedly sound something like the existentialist notion of authenticity. Both ideas have at their core the idea of being true to one's words or being responsible. But the idea of faithfulness developed here is different in that it depends crucially on the context. The key problem for the existentialist notion of authenticity is that it is completely indeterminate. It is never clear what could count as an authentic (i.e., responsible or truthful) act. But the idea of faithfulness, as we have developed it, is limited precisely by the context. Only certain acts in a given context would actually be faithful acts. Hannah Pitkin has observed that Wittgenstein's understanding of language leads to a set of limits imposed by the relevant context:

Wittgenstein reminds us that notions like responsibility, action, consequences, are made to be used in actual cases where we converse with one another about particular actions in our lives. In assigning responsibility for action, we speak always against the background of particular circumstances, as particular individuals. There, our concepts of responsibility and consequences are at home; there they make sense. But they are also finite. They do not fully make sense applied to our entire lives in the abstract and in general.[25]

We can see in this statement an implicit version of Poteat's formulation: it is precisely because of the particularly of the circumstances and individuals that the acts involved are absolutely contingent or unique, but also because of this particularity that they are subject to necessity or finitude.

As a corollary to the above, we should consider the objection that although the idea of faithfulness is not completely indeterminate in the way existentialist authenticity is, it still appears to be politically indeterminate, or perhaps is determinate in the wrong way. In the context of a tyrannical political system, it might be asked, would not faithfulness to the context mean obedience to tyranny? The answer, briefly, is "no," but it will require further elaboration of how the concept of faithfulness applies in the context of a narrative practice to understand how this is so. As we shall see, the idea of faithfulness developed here implies that, if one finds oneself in a tyrannical system, faithfulness to one's context means fighting the tyranny. Faithfulness is not the same thing as obedience, although in certain contexts, a provisional obedience may be part of faithfulness.[26]

A fourth important consideration at this point is that the concept of necessity we have developed here fits our model of what a non-objectivist conception of necessity would have to be like. I earlier characterized the concepts of objectivism as impersonal, abstract, dualistic, static, unaware of the relevant communal context, and based on an untenable universal skepticism. Thus, a non-objectivist conception of necessity should be personal, concrete, nondualistic, dynamic, communally oriented, and based upon faith rather than skepticism. Our model meets these requirements. It is personal in that it is based on personal speech acts and on the irreducible personal aspect of knowing. It eschews abstraction; the crucial indication of unfaithfulness is precisely abstraction from the relevant context. The faithful speech act remains tied to the concrete context appropriate to it. It is nondualistic in that it relies on Polanyi's triadic model of the generation of an object of perception or knowledge from the context rather than on a subject-object dichotomy. Another way to put this is that it is based on a model of words as actions rather than as referents. This in turn points to the fact that it is dynamic, using sound rather than a static, visual model as its starting point. It is, further, communally oriented in that the model of the speech act we have developed here articulates certain aspects of one person speaking to another. And it is, of course, based centrally upon faith rather than skepticism.

Finally, we can now see why it was necessary to discuss at some length matters that were not explicitly political. Without the detailed discussion of the characteristic features of objectivism and the subtle ways that a literate visual orientation promotes objectivist thinking, it would have been extremely difficult to construct the conception of necessity as we have done in this chapter. The discussion of necessity and contingency has depended centrally upon an understanding of the nature of objectivism and its experiential sources. Hence, the crucial feature of our initial formulation—that the speaker not abstract himself or herself from his or her context—is the obverse of both the basic failing of objectivism and the most fundamental aspect of literate consciousness, i.e., abstraction from context. Our discussion of objectivism revealed that its primary characteristic, upon which its other typical features are substantially dependent, is the tendency to understand objects of knowledge in abstraction from their necessary context. Similarly, our examination of the experiential basis of objectivism in literate visualism showed that the most basic feature of this orientation is the decontextualization, or abstraction, of language and the phenomena it articulates. Thus, our antidote to the disease of objectivism is a conception of knowledge and action that makes faithfulness to, or nonabstraction from, the relevant context its basic criterion of validity.

To reiterate, then, the result of our investigation, we can say that as a rudimentary formulation, every speech act is subject to necessity from its context in that at the most basic phenomenological level the speaker must acritically rely upon that context, or that in an ethical or political context, only certain things a speaker can say will be appropriate for or faithful to that context. Necessity means that the speaker cannot withdraw from, or abstract himself or herself from, the context of his or her speech act.

At this point, having developed a conception of necessity based upon the speech act, we can say that we now have a concrete standard for judging actions that we can apply to ethics and politics, i.e., whether or not a given speaker in a given context was faithful to his or her words. Of course, this must be stated in a more concrete fashion, and of course there will be disputes as to whether a given speaker or listener was, in a given case, faithful or not, but the standard is there. How this formulation would be made more concrete and how these disputes would be settled requires us to examine more carefully the context of political speech acts. Let us therefore now see how we could apply this formulation to MacIntyre's concept of a narrative practice.

5

SPEECH, PLACE, AND NARRATIVE PRACTICE

I have already briefly argued that the speech act, or rather, particular speech acts in particular contexts, can provide places that allow individuals to orient themselves and can thus set limits to the activities and relations within narrative practices. As I have also explained, by places I do not mean geographical locations or situations within social hierarchies, but rather places of faithfulness to a particular speaker. To explicate this conception of place in detail and thus extend Alasdair MacIntyre's approach to moral reasoning and action, I will begin by examining again the structure of and possible difficulties with his own extension of Aristotle.

For MacIntyre, a virtue is a quality the possession and exercise of which enables us to achieve certain goods, the goods internal to practices. A practice, in turn, involves centrally the pursuit of goals that define and are defined by the practice. Practices are located in the larger context of narratives, which give coherence to the lives of individuals by ordering the events and actions in each individual's life into a story. Narratives in turn are grounded in and form the groundwork for a tradition, which establishes goals for the future based upon the past. The overall structure expands the conception of a virtue beyond the relatively narrow goals embodied in practices to the broader human goods implied in the structure of narratives and traditions.

As we have already mentioned, the questions that immediately arise for this scheme are, how do we attain critical distance from the narrative practice of which we find ourselves a part, and how do we adjudicate among apparently incommensurable narrative practices? Or more concretely, we might ask, how do we know whether the practice we are currently engaged in is indeed a good or legitimate practice? From the structure of MacIntyre's scheme, it would appear that we must refer to the narratives of the individuals involved in the practice. At this point, however, the question that would immediately arise is, how can we judge the validity of the relevant narratives? This question would presumably refer us to the tradition of which we are part. Again, however, the question comes up, how can we evaluate the history and goals of the tradition? It seems that we can make this evaluation only if we can know the ultimate goal of the tradition, which would seem to require that we have some conception of an overall goal for humanity. As I have already mentioned, J. Budzisewski has argued that MacIntyre can only solve this problem with some kind of "metaphysical history." And indeed, MacIntyre's final formulation of his approach to moral reasoning does seem to have a circular or infinitely regressive quality to it, as he is able to say only that "the good life for man consists in seeking the good life for man."

To find our way out of this difficulty, we must examine a little more closely the mode of reasoning we have employed in analyzing MacIntyre's schema. It seems that we have employed what amounts to a deductive model to explicate the relationship between the various components of the schema. To answer the question of the validity of a particular practice, we have looked at the narratives of the individuals involved, as if something in these narratives would contain the key regulative principle for practices in general or at least certain kinds of practices, from which we could deduce what is correct for this particular practice. Similarly, we have attempted to discover the correct structure of individual narratives by looking for some principle in the tradition encompassing them from which we could deductively construct proper narratives. And finally, we have looked for a definitive telos which would allow us to deduce standards of appropriateness for the history of a tradition.

If asked why we have proceeded this way, we presumably would reply that we think that, given MacIntyre's construction of the schema, each higher, or more general, element of the schema should in some way set limits to what can occur in the lower or less general elements. That is, narratives should be able to set limits to what goes on in practices, and the overall tradition should eliminate, or make inappropriate, certain possibilities for the narratives that draw upon it. Recalling our discussion in the previous chapter, we notice that we have given here two of the formulations of necessity there developed. Necessary conditions set limits to what can happen in certain situations or they make certain things appropriate, others inappropriate. Our attempt to deduce limiting conditions for practices from narratives, in turn from traditions, and finally from the contexts of traditions seems to be an application of this concept of necessity. But, as we have just seen, MacIntyre's scheme does not seem to allow us to apply the concept in a fruitful way.

We may find a way out of this dilemma, however, by examining more closely other possible implications of our concept of necessity. As we have seen, the root etymological meaning of necessary is not to move away from, not to withdraw, not to retire. Our speech acts are limited by necessity in that they cannot move away from their contexts. Another way to state this could be that necessary conditions connect things (or events). We can illustrate this by recalling the example of the machine discussed in the previous chapter. The operational principles of the machine cannot be reduced to, but are limited by, its physico-chemical characteristics. The operational principles of the machine, that is, cannot withdraw from its physico-chemical conditions. But this is to say that its operational principles must in some way be connected to its physico-chemical characteristics. Hence, the idea of a connection may be a helpful way to understand motifs of necessity. If we want something in a narrative that can set limits to practices within it, we might want to examine how the narrative and the practices are connected, rather than looking for some principle within the narrative from which we can deduce rules for the various practices. We may be able to get around the apparent infinite regress implied in a deductive model by thinking in terms of connections or linkages. Indeed, what I will argue is that a motif is a place, in the sense described above, i.e., a location of faithfulness to another speaker, that links the elements of a narrative practice and thus sets limits by connecting. This will in turn allow us to explicate more concretely what we mean by a place.

The Polis as a Place

We can begin to understand this meaning of place by examining a somewhat different problem that could arise from MacIntyre's schema. We might ask, what do the various practices enclosed within my narrative have to do with each other? Or, how are the various narratives within our tradition related? Do we really have a tradition or just many mutually unconnected narratives? The problem here is essentially that of incommensurability. It could be extended to traditions with the question, how is our tradition related to other, rival traditions? Again the question is about the connections between the elements of MacIntyre's schema.

We can approach this problem by reexamining the concept of necessity we derived in the previous chapter in light of the questions just raised. We have said that, in an ethical or political context, necessity consists in motifs—events, situation, themes—that set limits to what

may appropriately be said in a particular speech act, that is, motifs that
determine what constitutes a faithful or unfaithful speech act. These
motifs would determine what constitutes speakers abstracting
themselves from context. Our discussion above has shown that the
context of a practice will in fact be the narratives of the various people
engaged in the practice, and that for the practice to be limited, it must in
some way be demonstrably connected to those narratives. It would
appear then that the motifs that would provide elements of necessity for
a practice, or for the speech acts that make up the practice, would be
events or themes of some kind which connect the practices and the
narratives of those who engage in the practice, or rather that connect the
speech acts that form the practice and the speech acts that make up the
narratives. If we have determined the kinds of events or themes that
would connect a practice to the narratives of its practitioners, or the
narratives of the members of a tradition to the tradition, or a tradition to
the world in which it is embedded, or to other traditions, we can then
determine what speech acts would be faithful or unfaithful in these
various contexts.

In order to do this, we must become much clearer about what is
meant by a motif. At the moment, this concept is still extremely vague.
We earlier observed that a motif was a type of incident, a particular
situation, a character, event, situation, or theme. More fundamentally, it
is an obsolete form of motive, etymologically derived from move and
thus related to movement. Let us begin to clarify and sort out these
possibilities with a central example from MacIntyre that may fit the
characteristics of what I have termed a motif. This is the Greek polis. In
his discussion of Aristotle's understanding of practical rationality,
MacIntyre says:

> It is thus only within those systematic forms of activity within
> which goods are unambiguously ordered and within which
> individuals occupy and move between well-defined roles that the
> standards of rational action directed toward the good and the best
> can be embodied. To be a rational individual is to participate in
> such a form of social life and to conform, as far as is possible, to
> those standards. It is because and insofar as the *polis* is an arena of
> systematic activity of just this kind that the *polis* is the locus of
> rationality. And it was because Aristotle judged that no form of
> state but the *polis* could integrate the different systematic activities
> into an overall form of activity in which the judgement of each
> kind of good was given its due that he also judged that *only a polis*

could provide that locus. No practical rationality outside the *polis* is the Aristotelian counterpart to *extra ecclesiam nulla salus*.[1]

MacIntyre clearly understands the polis as something that set limits, or indicates what should or should not be done. He gives an example of an analogous situation:

It may be constructive to consider those contemporary social contexts in which we do still find application for something very like Aristotelian conceptions of practical rationality. A hockey player in the closing seconds of a crucial game has an opportunity to pass to another member of his or her team better placed to score a needed goal. Necessarily, we may say, if he or she has perceived and judged the situation accurately, he or she must immediately pass. What is the force of this "necessarily" and this "must"? It exhibits the connection between the good of that person *qua* hockey player and member of that particular team and the action of passing, a connection such that were such a player not to pass, he or she must *either* have falsely denied that passing was for their good *qua* hockey player *or* have been guilty of inconsistency *or* have acted as one not caring for his or her good *qua* hockey player and member of that particular team. That is to say, we recognize the necessity and immediacy of rational action by someone inhabiting a structured role in which the goods of some systematic form of practice are unambiguously ordered. And in so doing we apply to one part of our social life a conception which Aristotle applies to rational social life as such.[2]

What MacIntyre is saying here is that for Aristotle, all of social life is like a practice in that there are more-or-less definitive, or exemplary, right and wrong ways to act in a given situation. The polis is analogous to the game of hockey, and at first sight, it might appear that the polis plays essentially the role of a tradition in MacIntyre's formulation of moral reasoning. By this I mean that the polis in some way provides a framework for the individual narratives of those who live in it, and thus for the practices they engage in. From the purpose of the polis in the overall scheme of things, therefore, we can deduce the relevant goals for rational human beings (or, in MacIntyre's terms, the narratives of particular individuals), from which in turn we deduce the relevant goods for or limits upon specific practices in which humans may engage.

If we examine MacIntyre's discussion more closely, we can see that he has actually adumbrated one of the essential features of the concept of necessity that we developed in the previous chapter. Specifically, we can see from MacIntyre's example how a person acting in a way contrary to his or her good would be abstracted from his or her context, since the context only allows certain actions, or at least requires certain actions if the person in question is to act intelligibly. (We could say that in a very real sense this person doesn't know where he or she is.) This is true both in the case of playing hockey—one must have somehow denied one's status as a hockey player in order to act contrary to what is good in this situation—and in the case of the polis, where failure to act rationally demonstrates that one does not belong in the polis. In this sense, the practice of hockey and the polis appear to fit the criterion of what we termed a motif, i.e., they set limits by determining what would be a valid or invalid (abstracted) action. But if we draw this conclusion, it is not clear how what we have called a motif of necessity is different from a practice, narrative, or tradition. Furthermore, it is clear that this understanding of a motif is not quite what we want, since it still leaves us with the problem we discussed earlier, i.e., how can we be sure about the role of the polis in the overall scheme of things? That is, even if we could say that membership in the polis (or on a hockey team) implies that certain actions are appropriate and others inappropriate (abstracted), we would still have to answer the question of whether or not it is appropriate to be a member of the polis (or a hockey team) in the first place. It would seem that although there may be important analogies between the polis and the practice of hockey, there are also important disanalogies. Again, we seem to be at an impasse.

We might, however, returning to our earlier discussion, consider that the polis *connects* individual narratives to a tradition of some sort, rather than providing a general principle from which specific rules may be deduced, that is, rather than being itself a tradition. In other words, the polis may correspond to neither a narrative or a tradition in MacIntyre's framework, but rather to something else that links these two. This is what Hannah Arendt may be getting at in her discussion of the polis. For Arendt, the polis is the place of action. It has two functions: first, it is the place that enables "men to do permanently, albeit under certain restrictions, what otherwise had been possible only as an extraordinary and infrequent enterprise," that is, "to multiply the occasions to win 'immortal fame'"; and, second, it is a place that offers "a remedy for the futility of action and speech," that is, where one's great deeds can be retold so that they will not be forgotten.[3]

Here we have a situation where the polis connects individual narratives with some kind of tradition. Specifically, the polis is the place of connection because it is the place where the relevant speech acts occur. We can see this from the two functions of the polis discussed by Arendt. By providing a place where individual narratives can be incorporated into a tradition, the polis allows for the possibility of more individual narratives of the kind it is supposed to foster, since the presence of the tradition can inform and inspire individual action, and the tradition itself can be formed from what otherwise would be fragments, individual narratives unconnected to anything else that might give them a larger coherence.

In the terminology developed earlier, we can also see that the polis is indeed a motif of necessity, in that when it connects narrative to tradition it sets limits to both. Any narrative legitimately developed from the context of the polis must conform to certain limits imposed by the tradition, and the tradition itself is limited by the narratives that make it up. A narrative that approved of cowardly actions, for example, would not be a legitimate possibility.

We now have the beginnings of a clearer idea of what we mean when we talk about motifs of necessity to provide limits for narrative practices. It appears that we mean something that limits by connecting, that is, by providing a place where practices and narratives or narratives and traditions can mutually generate each other. In other words, we seem to have isolated a human activity that, while clearly relevant to ethical practice in the sense MacIntyre understands it, does not fit any of the concepts he has developed to describe ethical practice. Our next step would be to elaborate this concept further. We have used the term "place" here, and we can begin by observing that the polis, as we have described it, is in fact an example of a place, in the sense we used earlier when discussing the differences between oral and visual conceptualizations of experience. As we have seen, William H. Poteat understands place as acritical reliance upon context, manifested most fundamentally in our primordial bodily orientation in the world. The polis also fits this model. It is a place of acritical reliance upon a context of mutually generating narratives and tradition. This is a clear implication of Arendt's discussion. She says that "it is as though the men who returned from the Trojan War had wished to make permanent the space of action which had arisen from their deeds and sufferings, to prevent its perishing with their dispersal and return to their isolated homesteads."[4] The reason that, without the polis, action is so futile and glorious deeds are so rare is that there exists no established context that can be acritically relied upon to engage in action. The polis, at least on Arendt's account, fulfills the same function for action as does reliance upon established scientific opinion in Michael Polanyi's account of scientific discovery—providing just such a context for expanding the body of scientific opinion. Indeed, the parallel is quite close. Just as established scientific opinion consists of accumulated findings from scientific practice woven into a body of theory with regulative force for scientific practice, the polis generates the collection of stories and narratives that imply a certain organization of common life. Says Arendt: "The *polis*, properly speaking, is not the city-state in its physical location; it is the organization of the people as it arises out of acting and speaking together, and its true space lies between people living together for this purpose, no matter where they happen to be."[5] The citizen of the polis relies upon the public space that it provides to engage in action just as the scientist relies upon the established body of scientific knowledge and practices to gain new knowledge, and in both cases the action made possible by the context will in turn become part of the context. Hence, the polis—our initial example of a motif—seems to be a place of acritical reliance that links elements of MacIntyre's framework in such a manner that it limits them.

The polis as we have described it here also displays another important aspect of the speech act, which, it will be recalled, is our basic model. Poteat points out that "my act of owning my words [i.e., of being faithful, the basic motif of the speech act] presupposes these [the various contexts of the speech act] but is not reducible to nor derivable from them."[6] The polis, similarly, depends on the context of narrative and tradition but is not reducible to the relevant narratives and traditions. That is, the "space of action" which Arendt says had "arisen from their deeds and sufferings" could not be independent of those deeds but also could not be reduced to them, just as the action of the scientist cannot be independent of established scientific opinion but also cannot be reduced to it.[7]

We should also note one other way that the polis fits the concept of a motif developed for the speech situation in the last chapter. Specifically, it is not like the motif of the eight-tone scale, which eternally determines all of the possibilities for a piece of music. Rather, the possibilities inherent in the polis, while limited or bounded (by the tradition and narratives that form it and which it allows to form), are still infinite. Arendt stresses the unpredictability, that is the contingency, of action, and thus of the life of the polis, established to create possibilities for action. Thus, we can say that the polis, at least as understood by Arendt, and in this context by MacIntyre, is not equivalent to a tradition or a narrative but is a place that links or connects and thus limits both, and in providing limits is an example of a motif of the type we discussed in the previous chapter. More generally, we might suspect that the motifs which we want to provide necessity for practices, narratives, and traditions must be places similar to the polis.

In another sense, however, this conclusion—that the polis is a place, and that motifs of necessity are places like the polis—might seem to be at odds with our earlier discussion of motif, which indicated that we want something along the lines of an event, or perhaps something pertaining to movement. This does not seem to apply very well to the polis, or to the idea of a place generally, which we tend to understand as something static. But we can certainly see that the earlier discussed conception of a place, as an acritical reliance upon context for orientation, could be described as an event or a movement. Recall that Poteat argues that "space is primordially a pre-reflective vectorial orientation, and this precisely is my body in its pre-reflective integration into a world. . . . It is within an oriented *whence* that primordial spatiality lies and it is from within this *whence* that all orientation derives."[8] The movement, or event, in Poteat's conception of place is precisely the acritical reliance upon the context.

We can make this clearer by examining Polanyi again. In his formulation, we attend from the context to a comprehension of the whole. This is what happens when a scientist relies upon the context of scientific practice to generate new knowledge. It is also what happens in the more basic cases of perception and tool-using. We attend from what we are subsidiarily aware of (the context) to what we are focally aware of (the object of perception). The acritical reliance upon context to generate a whole from its constituent parts—what Polanyi calls tacit knowledge—is itself an event or movement, or as Polanyi would say, a process. It is this from-to movement that constitutes place as Poteat is using the term. Thus, it does make sense to talk of a place that is an event, and this seems to be another example of how recapturing an oral/aural orientation can recover aspects of our experience that atrophy if we think exclusively in visual terms, which tend to make us think of a place as something static.

Now if we return to the polis, we can understand more clearly what we mean by speaking of the polis as a place that is also an event. Let us examine Arendt's formulation again. The polis is "the organization of the people as it arises out of acting and speaking together . . . ." This is to say, the acritical reliance upon a context of narrative and tradition, here manifested in action and speech, generates a further context of narrative and tradition which is regulative for further action and speech. The polis is an event or movement in the same way that the scientist's acritical reliance upon received scientific opinion or the perceiver's acritical reliance upon perceptual context are dynamic events or movements.

Another way to understand this is to observe that when Arendt talks about the polis as a space, she seems to be using space in the sense that Walter Ong talks about oral/aural inhabited space. "The space of appearance comes into being whenever men are together in the manner of speech and action," says Arendt. "Its peculiarity is that, unlike the spaces which are the work of our hands, it does not survive the actuality of the movement which brought it into being, but disappears not only with the dispersal of men . . . but with the disappearance or arrest of the activities themselves."[9] When Arendt says that the space created by speech and action disappears with the stoppage of speech and action, she seems to have in mind the kind of space that is inhabited by speakers (or at least beings that make sounds and thus manifest themselves in person-like ways) and that disappears when its inhabitants become silent and thus no longer manifest themselves. When she contrasts this to the spaces that are the work of our hands, she seems to have in mind for the latter the visual (or visual-tactile) space that has the quality of enduring presence, i.e., in which, as we discussed in the previous chapter, one can imagine an eternally enduring configuration, something one cannot do with dynamic oral-aural phenomena. The polis is therefore an event in the sense that it is a dynamic, inhabited oral-aural space generated by the speech acts of its citizens.

One final possible source of confusion should be cleared up at this point. This is the association I have made between the polis and necessity. For Arendt, the polis, or the public realm, is the place of freedom, while the private realm, the household, is the realm of necessity. It might seem strange, therefore, that I want to say that the polis provides for necessity. This confusion can be cleared up by recognizing that I am using the term differently than Arendt. In the way I am using the terms, both the polis and the household are characterized by necessity and contingency. To say that the polis is the realm of freedom while the household is the realm of necessity is to use the term necessity to mean something more like determination, or at least something that sets such severe limits as to extinguish freedom. Similarly, to say that the polis is the realm of freedom does not mean that it is a realm of pure contingency. To say that the polis provides necessity for human action, then, is not to contradict Arendt's understanding but rather to discuss a different use of the word.

Let us summarize how the polis is an example of a motif of necessity such as we discussed in the previous chapter. We initially said that if we examine the concepts of necessity and contingency from an oral/aural as opposed to a visual starting point, we can argue that the two concepts are not mutually exclusive and that the speech act can be said to be absolutely contingent but still subject to necessity from its context. In the context of a generic speech act, this necessity is absolute in that the speaker must be fundamentally faithful to or intelligible to those to whom he or she is speaking. In other contexts, the necessity consists of motifs that will set limits to what may be faithfully, i.e., appropriately, said. In the specific political context of MacIntyre's discussion of narrative practice, we concluded that the relevant motifs for this context must in some way connect the various aspects of MacIntyre's scheme and in so doing set limits by determining what would count as valid, appropriate, non-abstracted, or faithful speech acts. The polis is an example of such a motif: it connects narrative and tradition by being the place of speech acts that generate narratives and traditions and in the process of generating narrative and tradition allows them mutually to limit each other. As a place, it is an event or movement (or process) in the sense that it is the acritical reliance upon a context (the developed narratives and traditions of the polis) for the generation of a whole (the more fully developed narratives and traditions of the polis), just as the scientist acritically relies upon established scientific opinion to further scientific knowledge, or the perceiver acritically relies upon the context of the act of perception to generate the object perceived. As we noted before, the polis cannot be reduced to the narratives and traditions that it generates, but at the same time cannot be independent of the context they provide.

Hence, we conclude that the polis, a motif that provides necessity for tradition and narrative by connecting and thus limiting them, is an event that constitutes a dynamic place. Necessity for the common life of humans comes, not from the closed cosmos of Aristotle, but from their acritical reliance upon a mutually generating context of narrative and tradition to further develop this context. This act or event of acritical reliance is the polis, or the speech acts that make up the polis. What we need to do now is develop the idea of a place in a more general way.

Place as a General Concept

We can begin to generalize the concept of place with the Abraham story. This story will illustrate more clearly than the polis the salient features of the concept. Although Arendt does observe that the polis should not be understood as a specific geographical place, or even a particular institutional form, it could be rather easily misunderstood as such. More importantly, the polis explicitly excludes much of the population, those subject to necessity in the sense of labor, from the place it provides. And most importantly, the example of the polis has not yet given us clear criteria for what constitute legitimate or illegitimate speech acts. The Abraham story overcomes these limitations. Specifically, the Abraham story illustrates a place that cannot be understood as any particular geographical location or institutional form, and it shows how a place can include all persons, and indeed why we would think that a place *should* include all persons. Further, the Abraham story also allows us to discern from its structure some ideas about what criteria we may apply to determine what is indeed a proper place, that is, what constitute legitimate or illegitimate speech acts. We shall see that a place that constitutes a motif of necessity will meet two criteria: first, it must be such that it allows one to recognize that one's acritical reliance upon the relevant context was justified; and second, it must be such as to allow one to recognize the universal in the particular. I shall elaborate these criteria as we examine the Abraham story.

As Eric Auerbach has pointed out, the details of the story of Abraham's sacrifice of Isaac are terse in the extreme. When God calls Abraham, the actual geographical location of the two speakers is not stated. When Abraham says "Here I am," the Hebrew word means something like "behold me," and indicates a moral position with respect to God. "Where he is actually," observes Auerbach, "whether in Beersheba or elsewhere, whether indoors or in the open air, is not stated . . . and what Abraham was doing when God called to him is left in the same obscurity."[10] Similarly, the journey itself "unrolls with no episodes in a few independent sentences whose syntactical connection is of the most rudimentary sort."[11] It is "like a silent progress through the indeterminate and the contingent, a holding of the breath, a process which has no present, which is inserted, like a blank duration, between what has passed and what lies ahead. . . ."[12] The destination of the journey is stated, but it is "significant not so much as the goal of an earthly journey, in its geographical relation to other places, as through its special election, through its relation to God, who designated it as the scene of the act. . . ."[13] We could say that in this story, Abraham's moral place—that of being faithful to another personal speaker—is described in the most primordial terms, stripped of all obscuring details. In the stories of the polis, by contrast, the fundamental aspect of faithfulness to another speaker is never presented so clearly, presumably because it is not so well understood by the relevant authors. Says Auerbach:

> The human beings in the Biblical stories have greater depths of time, fate, and consciousness than do the human beings in Homer; although they are nearly always caught up in an event engaging all their faculties, they are not so entirely immersed in its present that they do not remain continually conscious of what has happened to them earlier and elsewhere; their thoughts and feelings have more layers, are more entangled. Abraham's actions are explained not only by what is happening to him at the moment, nor yet by his character (as Achilles' actions by his courage and pride, and Odysseus' by his versatility and foresightedness), but by his previous history; he remembers, he is constantly conscious of, what God has promised him and what God has already accomplished for him—his soul is torn between desperate rebellion and hopeful expectation; his silent obedience is multilayered, has background. Such a problematic psychological situation as this is impossible for any of the Homeric heroes, whose destiny is clearly defined and who wake every morning as if it were the first day of their lives: their emotions, though strong, are simple and find expression instantly.[14]

The greater psychological depth of the biblical characters derives from their (or their authors') greater recognition of the fundamental aspect of faithfulness. The clearest manifestation of the difference between the Bible and Homer in this regard can be seen in the biblical portrayal of God as the paradigmatic personal speaker, whose words are always ultimately faithful, whereas Zeus and the other Homeric gods are human in their unfaithfulness.

Because it goes right to the heart of the problem, the Abraham story also indicates very clearly the first important criterion for judging the appropriateness or faithfulness of speech acts. This is the transformative aspect of a speech-based motif of necessity, that is of faithfulness to a personal speaker. We can see this by asking what would have happened if Abraham had not acted faithfully. The answer is clear: if Abraham had not attempted to sacrifice Isaac, he would never have received God's revelation. John W. Dixon, Jr., observes:

> With Abraham the order of things was first transformed. Living in an order that required blood offerings to God, Abraham submitted,

against all hope, in obedience to the vengeful will. Against all hope, the beloved son was given back to him, and only symbolic blood required.[15]

For Dixon, the Abraham story contains a striking paradox in that freedom was established through obedience: "What Abraham's obedience did was enable us to see ourselves apart from the order of things. To see ourselves as selves apart from fixity into the fatality of sacred order."[16] What Dixon means is that if Abraham had failed to be faithful to the paradigmatic personal speaker, who promises always to be faithful, he would never have received the revelation that humans are free from the cosmological order of sacrifice. Hence, Abraham's place of faithfulness allowed obedience to be transformed into freedom. What is essential to this transformation is that Abraham's faithfulness, or acritical reliance upon God, was shown to be justified. If God had not stopped him from sacrificing Isaac, nothing new would have been learned. But God's revelation, showing Abraham that human sacrifice was not desired, and therefore that humans are (at least partly) free from natural fate, allowed Abraham to see that his earlier faithfulness was justified by this new knowledge. This transformation runs parallel to the kind of transformation discussed by Polanyi in the contexts of perception or scientific knowledge. Our acritical reliance allows us to perceive or discover something we could not otherwise have known; this new knowledge allows us to see that the earlier faithfulness was justified. Hence we now have a very fundamental criterion for determining what kinds of speech acts are valid and thus what kinds of structures, or rather, events, provide the places where these speech acts can occur.

A further consideration of the Abraham story, this time with regard to how the revelation was achieved, illustrates the second important criterion of faithfulness provided by speech-based motifs of necessity. This is the way in which such places reveal the universal through the particular. Says Dixon:

As sacrifice, Isaac, the beloved, was not a person. He was an old man's hope, an old woman's desire. . . . But, given back to Abraham, Isaac was free, a free gift of the grace of God and not the will of man. The shattered old man, irrevocably torn by three days in the knowledge of Hell, could only look with wonder. For Isaac is now something other than himself. Isaac has become a person.[17]

After God's revelation, Isaac has an identity that transcends the particulars of his situation as Abraham's son. He is a gift from God. But this identity could never have been revealed without the particulars of Abraham's situation. If Abraham had had many sons, or if he and Sarah were young enough to anticipate having more, or again if Abraham had not been faithful, the revelation of Isaac's personhood could not have come about. That is, Abraham's place of faithfulness allowed the particularities of his situation to reveal a universal aspect of human existence—that all humans, as unique creatures in God's image, have an identity and a dignity that transcends the particulars of their location in any social system or hierarchy.

Again, this feature of the Abraham story, or of Abraham's place of faithfulness, is captured in Polanyi's epistemology. Polanyi observes that we generate universal concepts through tacit reliance upon particular experiences and examples: "In speaking of man in general we are not attending to any kind of man, but relying on our subsidiary awareness of individual men, for attending to their joint meaning. This meaning is a comprehensive entity, and its knowledge is wiped out by attending to its particulars in themselves."[18] The universal term "man" is generated by the subsidiary awareness we have of all men we have ever seen, and could not be generated without these particulars.

We might note two additional points about the Abraham story. First, the story illustrates an essential aspect of place or motif that we earlier discussed, i.e., that Abraham's place of faithfulness is not possible apart from its context but also is not reducible to it. We have observed that the generic speech act, our basic model for motif or place, displayed this characteristic, and that this was true of the polis; we can see it again in this more complex situation. Second, we should also note that the Abraham story certainly establishes the possibility of the modern contextless self. Since it strips the place of faithfulness to its bare essentials, to the context of faithfulness to God, it makes it conceivable that one could imagine the self free of all context. We have briefly mentioned that the implications of the biblical picture of reality are that if faithfulness in God becomes problematic, the world will become a placeless chaos. Analogously, or rather as a particular manifestation of this situation, if the self's place, or context, is recognized as ultimately nothing but faithfulness to God, it is quite possible that this minimal context will be lost, leaving the self utterly abandoned.

The Abraham story thus indicates more clearly what it is about motif or place that allows us to distinguish faithful from unfaithful acts. Let us reiterate the two criteria: first, the place that makes up the motif of necessity must be such that it allows one to recognize that one's acritical reliance was justified, just as Abraham's discovery of human freedom allowed him to realize that his obedience to God was justified; second, the place that makes up the motif of necessity must be such that it allows one to recognize the universal through the particular, just as Isaac's identity as a person independent of any particular social status was revealed through the particulars of his situation. I shall elaborate these criteria more fully shortly when I discuss concrete examples of places of faithfulness.

Now let us look again at MacIntyre's discussion of narrative practice. Drawing upon our discussion to this point, we can locate within MacIntyre's discussion the reason why he may have difficulty addressing the charges of relativism that could be brought against his conception. Specifically, I believe we can now say that MacIntyre's conceptual scheme does not seem to be grounded because it is missing an essential element—the concept of place which we have just developed. MacIntyre begins his development of the concept of a virtue thus:

> There are no less than three stages in the logical development of the concept which have to be identified in order, if the core conception of a virtue is to be understood, and each of these stages has its own conceptual background. The first stage requires a background of what I shall call a practice, the second an account of what I have already characterized as the narrative order of a single human life and the third an account a good deal fuller than I have given now of what constitutes a moral tradition. Each later stage presupposes the earlier, but not *vice-versa*. Each earlier stage is both modified by and reinterpreted in the light of, but also provides an essential constituent of each later stage.[19]

The essential phrase in this passage is where MacIntyre says that "each later stage in the development of the concept presupposes the earlier, but not *vice-versa*." The earlier stages become essential features of the later stages (practices become essential features of narratives), but, as MacIntyre appears to understand it, or at least as he states it here, one can have a concept of a practice without necessarily having a concept of a narrative or a tradition. For MacIntyre, the concept of a narrative is necessary only to complete (or to begin to complete) the concept of a practice. This is because the concept of a practice cannot provide a complete account of the virtues, since there would be conflicts between different goals and practices, and no coherent ordering of which goals and practices were more important, without a narrative.[20] But if we examine MacIntyre's definition of a practice, it seems that the concept of a practice must also presuppose the concepts of narrative and tradition: "any coherent and complex form of socially established cooperative human activity through which goods internal to that form of activity are realized in the course of trying to achieve those standards of excellence which are appropriate to, and partially definitive of, that form of activity, with the result that human powers to achieve excellence, and human conceptions of the ends and goods involved, are systematically extended."[21] This definition seems to assume, not as something that only completes a practice but rather as something it also presupposes, a very definite social context of some complexity, that is, a context of narrative and tradition. We can see a more concrete manifestation of this if we consider the following passage: "It belongs to the concept of a practice as I have outlined it . . . that its goods can only be achieved by subordinating ourselves within the practice in our relationship to other practitioners."[22] The decision to enter a practice and subordinate ourselves initially to its practitioners is, it would seem, something that can only occur within the context of a narrative. Note specifically that the difficulty with attempting to understand the concept of a practice without the concept of a narrative is not just, as MacIntyre points out, that the practice, or choice of practice, would or could seem to be arbitrary, so that the concept of a practice must be supplemented and extended by the concept of a narrative. Rather, it seems that the concept of a practice must presuppose the concept of a narrative because otherwise the person involved could not understand what it means to enter into the practice and subordinate himself or herself to the practioners.

So, MacIntyre's problem is not just that the concept of a virtue would be incomplete in the context of a practice and nothing else, it is that the concept of a practice seems to presuppose something like a narrative. If the relationship is one of mutual presupposition, or mutual dependence, the question that then arises is, what provides the linkage or connection between the two concepts? It would seem to be something like the idea of a place that I have developed. That is, what would hold together a particular practice in which I am engaged with the particular narrative from which I render intelligible my various activities and aspirations, is the concrete place provided by my faithful speech acts which relate my various activities to each other and to their settings. From the way I have developed the concept of a place, it would seem that the relation between practice and narrative is not so much the hierarchy that MacIntyre proposes, but rather something more like mutual presupposition, which as we have seen, seems to be required by the rest of his analysis. Therefore we can conclude that what is needed to ground, or better, to hold together or connect, MacIntyre's conceptual scheme is the concept of place of necessity, which we have developed from our analysis of the speech act.

We can clarify the above point by examining MacIntyre's schema a bit more closely. We earlier said that a fundamental characteristic of a speech act (or more generally of any acritical reliance upon context) and thus of a place, is that although it is dependent in many ways upon its context, it cannot be reduced to its context. We might say that MacIntyre's key failing is that he has reduced what I have called place—acritical reliance upon context—to the context, that is, practice and narrative, itself. MacIntyre's scheme has no room for place because the acritical reliance upon context that constitutes place has been collapsed into the context. My faithful speech acts which link, and thus allow universal meaning to emerge from and therefore limit, my particular activities and aspirations, have been reduced to those particular activities and aspirations, leaving them radically contingent and without limit precisely because of their unconnected particularity. Or, at least, they become so without some definitive telos, such as would have to be provided by a metaphysical biology or metaphysical history.

We can also gain a clearer understanding of the problem if we examine briefly Habermas's discussion of the speech act and of what he calls the ideal speech situation. Habermas's more recent work has modified many of his early formulations, but his essential idea of ultimately grounding political practice in rational consensus has remained constant, and his early conception of the ideal speech situation turns out to be particularly illuminating when compared with my concept of place. Here we may see the opposite problem to MacIntyre's, i.e., that Habermas abstracts excessively from context. Habermas begins with the assumption that regulative force for human action and practice must come from the structure of the speech act. He wants to elucidate the necessary conditions for a rational consensus in institutionally unbound situations. This is what can provide a normative guide for political life. The key test is whether or not agreement was reached solely on the force of the argument made, not upon contingent factors such as ideological or psychological delusion. The only permissible motive would be the cooperative search for truth. This would have to mean that no elements of the argument were systematically exempted from critical analysis. This in turn would mean that all participants would have a symmetrical or equal distribution of chances to speak. It is this situation that Habermas would refer to as the ideal speech situation. Habermas wants to argue that all of our speech acts necessarily (tacitly) assume such a situation as normative, or else the very notion of discourse as a search for truth becomes meaningless. From the structure of the ideal speech situation we can deduce concrete applications to political life.[23]

The ideal speech situation has been subject to considerable misunderstanding. It is not meant as a description of any possible empirical situation, nor as a utopian social goal to be achieved. Rather, it could be understood as functioning somewhat like Plato's vision of the Good in that it attempts to articulate symbolically certain fundamental dimensions of human experience. Specifically, just as the vision of the Good articulates the fundamental unchanging structure of the cosmos which (Plato thinks) we tacitly know as the condition of all knowledge, however distorted our explicit perception of reality, the ideal speech situation articulates the fundamental structure of human communication which we tacitly assume as the condition of all speech, however distorted actual communication might be. Or to put it another way, the ideal speech situation can be seen as a symbolic articulation of Polanyi's concept of tacit knowledge in the context of speech. The critical difference between Plato and Habermas, of course, is that while the vision of the Good articulates a cosmic order independent of human agency, the ideal speech situation symbolizes a world ultimately structured by human speech.

On the other hand, if we compare the ideal speech situation to the Abraham story, we notice one very striking difference. As we have seen, the fundamental aspects of my concept of place, of the speech act's acritical reliance upon context, are here illustrated most starkly. The institutional constraints, if we may use this term, relevant to Abraham's response to God are completely ignored. But nevertheless Abraham is still thoroughly embedded in a specific, unique context, one indeed brought about by his earlier faithfulness to God's call, and his place of faithfulness to God cannot be made intelligible without this specific context. The ideal speech situation, by contrast, attempts to explicate the conditions and consequences of faithful human speech acts that can provide limits or necessity for human actions *independent* of context. That is, the ideal speech situation seems to be a speech situation involving two (or more) paradigmatic personal speakers, always faithful to their words. This is what Habermas seems to be tacitly assuming when he specifies conditions such as the motives of the speakers or, derivatively, the arrangement of speech opportunities. Whereas the biblical stories articulate the dimensions of conversations in various contexts between concrete, often unfaithful human beings and an ever-faithful speaker, the ideal speech situation describes the dimensions of a conversation between two or more ever-faithful speakers. From the biblical standpoint, no human can be always faithful, which is to say that no human can fully transcend the contingencies of his or her situation. Habermas's problem, from this perspective, is in attempting to specify what cannot be specified, i.e., necessary conditions that would hold in every conceivable context. Habermas seems to be falling into just the opposite trap that MacIntyre does, i.e., he seems to be attempting to completely abstract place—acritical reliance on context—from context. That is, my faithful speech acts, which link and thus limit my particular activities and aspirations, although they cannot be reduced to those particularities, also cannot be specified or explicated apart from those particularities; Habermas attempts to specify what faithful speech acts would unite and thus limit particular activities without actually speci-fying any particular activities. If MacIntyre tends to lose the universal in the particular, it could be said that Habermas tends to lose the particular in the universal. My formulation recognizes that the universal can only be revealed through the particular but that only those particulars that can reveal the universal are valid.

Richard J. Mouw's response to one aspect of MacIntyre's work can also help to illustrate this issue.[24] Mouw observes that when MacIntyre opposes premodern conceptions of the self to modern conceptions, he places that of the Protestant reformers in the modern category. According to MacIntyre, the agent "now stands alone before God, stripped of all social characteristics."[25] Mouw wants to argue that although the position of the reformers could have *led* to such a context-less agent (as we have noted when discussing the Abraham story), this was not what they themselves had in mind. He points out that Luther "can be interpreted as believing that he had a role in the heavenly community. And it just so happened that there came a time when he no longer thought that his role in the earthly church harmonized with his role in the heavenly community—although he was very quick to establish a new churchly community in which role-harmonization could be achieved."[26] More generally, MacIntyre argues that God's commands became arbitrary, that is, without rational justification, when the teleology of medieval thought was lost. But Mouw points out that the reformers' position was more nuanced than this. Calvin thought that God's commands were rational to God, but that humans, limited in their capacities, might not always fully understand this rationale and therefore must trust in God's commands. What MacIntyre interprets as a destruction of context could conversely be understood as a more subtle appreciation of context.[27] Indeed, as Mouw points out, we might see in medieval scholasticism, with its idea of natural truths available without revelation, a precursor of the modern notion of autonomous reason, abstracted from any context of trust.[28] The point here is that when MacIntyre says that the agent "now stands alone before God, stripped of all social characteristics," and thus without a context, he has forgotten that standing before God is itself a context (that is, a place), and in fact the only context that can order all the other contextual characteristics peculiar to the agent. Without the place given by the individual's attempts to be faithful to other speakers and thus to the paradigmatic speaker, all other elements of the person's social context become disconnected and arbitrary.

We can summarize our discussion of what is lacking in MacIntyre's conception, as well as that of Habermas, by saying that MacIntyre, in reacting against the modern self as it has developed, has thrown out the Abrahamic revelation of humankind as ultimately a responsible speaker (as opposed to a natural being) along with the modern notion of the autonomous self to which it could lead. Habermas, conversely, has attempted to recover the reality of the responsible speaker but has forgotten the context that is the condition of this speaker's appearance. Only by thinking in terms of both a responsible speaker and the context of that speaker's speech acts can we avoid the problems inherent in these two formulations.

I have now taken the concept of place illustrated by the polis and developed it in a more general form. We can now see that what can provide elements of necessity—what will set limits—for practice, narrative, and tradition are what we have called motifs, that is, events of movement that provide the places for speech acts and in so doing provide criteria for which are valid or invalid, faithful or unfaithful speech acts. This concept can address some of the crucial problems that arise for MacIntyre and also for Habermas. The concept, however, is still quite abstract. By discussing some examples of places, I will make it more concrete, and will also elaborate more fully the criteria of what constitutes a legitimate place. This will be the final stage in clarifying the concept.

Paradigmatic Places for Narrative Political Practice

Before I begin to elaborate specific places appropriate to political practice, one extremely important point must be made. The following list of places is certainly not intended to be exhaustive, and it is a fundamental implication of the concept of place that no list of places ever could be exhaustive. That is, the concept of place as we have developed it rests precisely on the understanding that reality does not have an unchanging constitution but rather changes in an intelligible manner. Places are intended not to provide a static standard from which may be deduced eternal ethical and political principles but rather are intended to make coherent the dynamic changes involved in narrative practices. It is quite conceivable that the development of a particular tradition may substantially alter the tradition's earlier understanding of a particular place, develop new places, or even eventually recognize that what was once thought to be a legitimate place actually is not. Hence, the following discussion should be approached with the understanding that it merely sketches a few basic elements of a complex, dynamic phenomenon.

Our discussion must begin with the paradigmatic place—my (or your) integral mindbody. As we have already seen, Poteat regards the human mindbody as the primordial place of orientation for all of our activities:

> The ground of all my discriminations and articulations of space, both reflected and as yet unreflected—visual, olfactory, tactile, audial, kinaesthetic, proprioceptive—is the radical *whence* of my lived, as yet unreflected mindbody in its worldly circumambience. It is in other words a *place*: *the archaic place* from "within" which all my *acts of placing*—both gestural and spoken—proceed. Spatiality as *place* is a *whereon-to-stand* from which you and I and all others jointly make our mindbodily appearance with one another in our mutual world.[29]

Our conceptions of space, knowledge, truth, and even good and evil are generated out of the place of our mindbodies. The world we experience articulately is one that we have mindbodily spoken into existence. All places of necessity that we might discuss in the context of political society are derivative from this primordial place. That is to say, our mindbodies are the fundamental context of speech. In fact, our mindbodies are the sources of the three basic features of a place that we have so far explicated: they are an acritical reliance upon context, they allow us to see that this reliance was justified, and they reveal the universal in the particular.

We have already observed, when developing the concept of place, that our mindbodies are an acritical reliance upon context: "Space is primordially a pre-reflective vectorial orientation, and this precisely is my body in its pre-reflective integration into a world. . . . It is within an oriented *whence* that primordial spatiality lies and it is from within this *whence* that all orientation derives."[30] Furthermore, this acritical reliance upon context is shown to be justified by the fact that the categories and perceptions of intelligibility that we mindbodily generate are more fundamental than the categories and perceptions of unintelligibility that we create. Our later, articulate analysis of our fundamental orientation and the linguistic structures it generates shows that our primordial, inarticulate trust in reality was justified. Finally, we have also seen that our acritical reliance upon context enables us to generate universal concepts or terms from particular cases. Our most elementary perceptual and linguistic experience is the ground for the far more complex social places upon which we must rely.

Two very fundamental political considerations derive from the mindbody as the primordial and paradigmatic human place.

First, to say that the fundamental human place is the mindbody, with its capacity to generate a world of infinite possibilities through its linguistic and even sublinguistic discriminations and orientations, and more specifically with its capacity to generate all the other places with which we orient ourselves, implies that each human mindbody should be treated with dignity and respect because each human can potentially, in some way, contribute to creating the place of each other human. If the places with which we orient ourselves as human beings are not fixed in a hierarchical natural order but rather are created from the infinite possibilities of the speech act, every single human act of speech, and indeed every single human act, has world-transforming and indeed world-creating possibilities, and therefore attention must be given to each human speaker. Whereas to regard the fundamental human capacity as that of abstract rational thought or aesthetic creativity implies hierarchy, since humans clearly differ in these capacities, to say that the specifically human capacity is that of being a faithful speaker implies a fundamental equality, since in any given unique context, any human may speak faithfully.

On the other hand, recognizing the mindbody as the fundamental human place, and recognizing its implications of equality, dignity, and respect for each person, still is to recognize the reality of human finitude and the legitimacy of authority, education, discipline, and even punishment for a political community. To say that *any* practice of habituation or restraint is necessarily a transgression of the body, as post-Nietzschean theorists such as Michel Foucault have assumed, is really tacitly to conceive of the human body as something unbounded. Although many disciplinary practices will, or may be, coercive, the finitude of the mindbody implies that at least some practices that order and limit it can be noncoercive, since at least some ordering practices will conform to its limits. Alienation from all authority structures or extreme civil libertarianism are not characteristics of a politics grounded in the place of the mindbody.

Moving beyond this fundamental paradigm into derivative cases, an excellent example of a place can be found in the activity of apprenticeship, which has been extensively discussed by Polanyi, among others. The particular orientation assumed by the individuals in an apprenticeship relation is an example of how acritical reliance upon context can set definite limits to human activity. We have already examined this briefly. For our purposes here, the essential feature of apprenticeship is that the specific type of acritical reliance upon context involved links narrative and practice and thus limits both.

For the apprentice, it is essential that within the context of a practice he or she submit to the authority of those who know more. As Polanyi describes it,

> This assimilation of great systems of articulate lore by novices of various grades is made possible only by a *previous act of affiliation*, by which the novice accepts apprenticeship to a community which cultivates this lore, appreciates its values and strives to act by its standards. This affiliation begins with the fact that a child submits to education within a community, and it is confirmed throughout life to the extent to which the adult continues to place exceptional confidence in the intellectual leaders of the same community. Just as children learn to speak by assuming that the words used in their presence mean something, so throughout the whole range of cultural apprenticeship in the intellectual junior's craving to understand the doings and sayings of his intellectual superiors assumes that what they are doing and saying has a hidden meaning which, when discovered will be found satisfying to some extent. . . . Such granting of one's personal allegiance is—like an act of heuristic conjecture—a passionate pouring of oneself into untried forms of existence. The continued transmission of articulate systems, which lends public and enduring quality to our intellectual gratifications, depends throughout on these acts of submission.[31]

As we have already seen in our discussion of MacIntyre, this submission to authority requires certain decisions and predispositions within the apprentice's own narrative. Hence, apprentices cannot simply do as they please; they must recognize their own ignorance and strive to emulate those who have greater knowledge. Similarly, the position within the practice of those in authority will constitute at least some part, possibly a substantial part, of their narrative self-understandings. They cannot do anything they please, either; their position in the relation charges them with definite obligations as to the knowledge and skills they must impart to the apprentice, and definite criteria of failure if they abuse their superior position.

It is also important to be clear that the place of apprenticeship is not reducible to the other elements in MacIntyre's conceptual scheme, i.e., virtue, practice, narrative, or tradition. We would not say that apprenticeship is a virtue; it seems to be rather something that both requires and develops certain virtues, or better that its structure defines the kinds of virtues necessary in various practices. We would not say that it is a practice, although we might say that it could be something essential for any proper practice, since a proper practice must be in some way linked to the narratives of the individuals involved. Similarly, it might be essential to a particular narrative or a particular tradition, but we would not identify it with these on a one-to-one basis. It is better to recognize apprenticeship as something conceptually distinct, as a place that connects particular practices with particular narratives.

If we recall our two criteria for evaluating places, we can see that the place of apprenticeship meets these criteria. If apprenticeship is to be truly a place, the apprentice must be able (at least in principle, since of course failures may occur) eventually to regard his or her acritical reliance as having being justified. This would occur if the apprentice eventually became the equal or colleague of the teacher, which is indeed the goal of apprenticeship. Hence, if an apprenticeship reaches its goal, the apprentice does indeed recognize that his or her earlier submission to authority was justified. If the relationship between teacher and apprentice degenerates into a patron-client relation, the teacher has failed, since the apprentice will never be in a position to judge his or her earlier submission. Indoctrination could never be a place in our sense because it would never allow the person being indoctrinated to see that his or her acritical reliance was justified.

Similarly, a true place must reveal the universal through the particular. Polanyi would argue that the structure of articulate systems based on apprenticeship does this. In any but the simplest of practices, no one expert will understand all of the details of the practice. But he or she can confidently rely upon the expertise of others because all have undergone the same process of apprenticeship. Experts' own particular experiences of apprenticeship, allowing them to achieve their particular expertise, allows them to have confidence in other experts since they will (or should) have undergone a similar process. Hence, from the particular experience and situation of a number of individuals arises a universal bond and (within its specific context) a universal articulate structure.

From the above discussion, we can see that, in ethical or political terms, what is essential about the place of apprenticeship is that its structure, or rather its movement, provides definite criteria for which the more powerful member of the relationship can be called to account. The structure of apprenticeship, in addition to placing obvious limitations on the apprentice, also places very definite limitations on the action of the expert or teacher. As we mentioned before, teachers who do not at least attempt to make their apprentices into their equals or colleagues have failed. Of course the concrete, specific institutional structures which will allow for an accounting will depend on particular circumstances, but the basic structure or process stands available for us—it links specific practices to specific narratives in a way that sets limits upon individual goals and actions and especially upon the power of those in positions of authority.

It might be thought that apprenticeship, with its stress upon the apprentice's submission to authority, would have conservative implications for political and social order. To some extent this is true, and in this sense the place of apprenticeship serves as a reminder of human finitude—of the impossibility of full autonomy. On the other hand, however, it seems to me that it also has implications that are quite radical. Very little present-day work, for example, is modelled upon the apprenticeship relation; current work routines tend to be characterized by rigid hierarchies where those in authority use (supposedly) esoteric knowledge to control those below them. Any political society dedicated to making apprenticeship a fundamental ordering place for its citizens would therefore be required to eliminate mindless, dead-end jobs and to require that experts make themselves in some way intelligible to non-experts. Indeed, our discussion so far implies that the very concept of an "expert," as currently understood, would require fundamental revision. In our discussion of Polanyi, we observed that his argument about autonomy for cultural authorities seemed to imply an epistemological privilege inconsistent with other aspects of his theory. Our discussion of apprenticeship can perhaps clarify this point: we could say that experts should remain autonomous in that non-experts should not decide or influence issues purely internal to the relevant practice (scientific or otherwise), but experts must explain what they are doing to non-experts when their expert activity will have an effect on those outside the practice. Education into the demands of public accountability would itself become an important part of the apprenticeship process.

Apprenticeship is a place that connects, and thus limits, practice and narrative. An example of a place that links narrative and tradition is ritual. It should be relatively obvious that rituals will (or should) link the narratives of particular individuals to the traditions of which those individuals are a part. What is particularly illuminating is the way in which rituals do this. Ritual is one of several activities that establish mediation, or as Poteat calls it, "room." According to Poteat, room is what allows us to make sense of the world:

> In an important sense *room* is required no less for our making the world intelligible to ourselves—and here room means both time and distance and all the variations upon these in their literal and derived meanings and the points at which these literal and derived meanings intersect. Time, room, distance, are necessary if we are to comprehend, to order, to hierarchize, and to integrate the immediacies of our fugitive affective lives and of our no less fleeting perceptions. . . . We cannot be persons when we have no room within which to comprehend our experience. Indeed, we cannot, lacking time and distance, properly have experience. We are condemned rather to the mere suffering of whatever happens to us. Existence becomes one undifferentiated happening.[32]

Ritual creates mediation because it takes time and distance. For Russian Orthodox theologian Alexandr Schmemann, ritual, or at least the Orthodox liturgy, takes time and distance because it constitutes a journey to a destination. In the case of the Eucharist, the journey begins when Christians leave their homes and separate worlds to come together in one place, thus creating distance between the assembly of believers and the world, that is, mediating the world. It continues with the entrance, where the participants ascend to a holy place. With the offering of the gifts, the participants are transformed as they offer themselves to Christ. The kiss of peace refers to the love of Christ, "the eternal wonder of which consists precisely in the fact that it transforms the *stranger* (and each stranger, in his depths, is an *enemy*) into a *brother*. . . ."[33] Finally, when receiving communion the participants have reached the goal of the journey. Elizabeth Newman, in discussing Schmemann's liturgical theology, points out that ritual necessarily takes time because it is rhythmic: "The liturgy or ritual as rhythmic movement takes time: time to breathe, time to sit at the table, to partake of the bread and wine, to offer the kiss of peace, to recite the Lord's prayer. . . ."[34] The rhythmic journey of the liturgy—our words, breath, gestures—mediates God, the world, others, and even ourselves to us, and in so creating room enables us to orient ourselves in the world.

If we again refer to our criteria of a legitimate place, we can see that the liturgy as Schmemann describes it is an acritical reliance which transforms the participants and reveals the universal in the particular. The liturgy is clearly an acritical reliance upon context in that we acritically submit to its formalized repetition. And we have already stressed its transformative powers in our discussion: the journey of the Eucharistic liturgy generates distance that transforms the participants and their orientation in the world in such a way that their earlier acritical reliance is justified. The Eucharist also reveals the universal in the particular in that all of its particular components display the fundamental, universal human place before God. The room generated by the space and time of the journey allows us to recognize our place before God in a way that pure immediacy would not.

Putting this in a more clearly political context, we now have some definite reasons for why public rituals are important for political order, and some definite criteria about how we may distinguish a valid communal ritual from forms of indoctrination and demagoguery. Specifically, public rituals are needed to provide mediation (or room), and only those public rituals that do provide mediation are acceptable. It is a fairly common observation that in any political community, various intermediary institutions and associations are required to protect the individual from centralized power. Tyrannical governments always attempt to break down such intervening structures. A healthy political order will have, among other mediating structures, public ceremonies that allow citizens to orient themselves in the same way the Orthodox liturgy does for Schmemann. By contrast, in a sick political order public rituals degenerate into "mere" rituals, or become calculated attempts at manipulation, breaking down the mediation that ritual can provide and thus reducing citizens' capacities to make sense of their common life.

Another example of a place that links narrative to tradition can be found in the biblical phenomenon of prophecy. Walter Brueggemann has argued that prophecy is fundamentally not mere social criticism, but a response to a profound crisis of a tradition. It arises when a tradition is corrupted and flounders, and attempts, not merely to revive or reform a tradition that has become corrupt, but to transform the tradition into something new. Brueggemann points out that the governing metaphor for the prophetic literature, or at least that of Jeremiah, Ezekiel, and Second Isaiah, is that of exile. Exile, of course, implies some kind of displacement. The displacement addressed by the prophets is that which arises when the narrative tradition, or the linkage between narrative and tradition, has broken down to the point where it no longer provides a reliable place of acritical reliance from which to orient ourselves. The prophet is one who recognizes this and is able to draw upon the tradition in such a way that it can be transformed. According to Brueggemann, the prophet "appeals to the old memories and affirmations in an astonishing way to jar the perceptual field of Israel and to cause a wholly new discernment of reality."[35]

In the example of prophecy we again see a place of acritical reliance that transforms. Prophets do not doubt that the context of tradition ultimately makes sense—indeed, there is an important sense in which they *cannot* doubt this, since their entire orientation toward the world is derived from their tradition—but they do recognize that the tradition has become or is becoming incoherent and is in need of transformation. They recognize its incoherence from their perception that the world the tradition articulates is nearing an end. "The overriding historical, theological reality in Jeremiah's perception," says Brueggeman, "is that God's people are to be given over into the hands of the Babylonian empire."[36]

The process by which the prophet recognizes that his or her tradition has become incoherent has been illuminated by MacIntyre himself in his discussion of what he calls epistemological crises. For MacIntyre, people are experiencing an epistemological crisis when "what they took to be evidence pointing unambiguously in some one direction now turns out to have been equally susceptible to rival interpretations."[37] The epistemological crisis is resolved by a dramatic narrative:

> When an epistemological crisis is resolved, it is by the construction of a new narrative which enables the agent to understand *both* how he or she could intelligibly have held his or her original beliefs *and* how he or she could have been so drastically misled by them. The narrative in terms of which he or she at first understood and ordered experiences is itself made into the subject of an enlarged narrative. The agent has come to understand how the criteria of truth and understanding must be reformulated.[38]

MacIntyre also points out that the reformulation of the tradition depends upon an acritical reliance upon the tradition. Discussing Descartes' skepticism he observes that "someone who really believed that he knew nothing would not even know how to begin on a course of radical doubt; for he would have no conception of what his task might be, of what it would be to settle his doubts and to acquire well-founded beliefs. Conversely, anyone who knows enough to know *that* does indeed possess a set of extensive epistemological beliefs which he is not putting in doubt at all."[39]

Prophecy provides the place from which the narratives of a given tradition can be reformulated to account for why the tradition appeared to be breaking down. MacIntyre himself points in this direction when discussing scientific discovery:

> The criterion of a successful theory is that it enable us to understand its predecessors in a newly intelligible way. It, at one and the same time, enables us to understand precisely why its predecessors have to be rejected or modified and also why, without and before its illumination, past theory could have remained credible. It introduces new standards for evaluating the past. It recasts the narrative which constitutes the continuous reconstruction of the scientific tradition.
>
> This connection between narrative and tradition has hitherto gone almost unnoticed, perhaps because tradition has usually been taken seriously only by conservative social theorists. Yet those features of tradition which emerge as important when the connection between tradition and narrative is understood are ones which conservative theorists are unlikely to attend to. For what constitutes a tradition is a conflict of interpretations of that tradition, a conflict which itself has a history of rival interpretations. . . .
>
> A tradition then not only embodies the narrative of an argument, but is only to be recovered by an argumentative retelling of that narrative which will itself be in conflict with other argumentative retellings. Every tradition therefore is always in danger of lapsing into incoherence and when a tradition does so lapse it sometimes can only be recovered by a revolutionary reconstitution. Precisely such a reconstitution of a tradition which had lapsed into incoherence was the work of Galileo.[40]

When MacIntyre discusses the connection between narrative and tradition, he appears to mean a place of public discussion. Indeed, the continuous argument, or ongoing discussion, he describes sounds very much like the polis. It appears that any tradition, if it is vital, will have a place of public debate about the tradition, even if not as explicitly institutionalized as the polis. The prophet comes into play when this ongoing discussion has become confused. His or her acritical reliance upon narrative and tradition can generate renewed narrative and tradition and thus renew the public space of discussion. The polis needs prophecy to survive.

If we consider our two criteria of legitimate place, we can see that, in the context of the prophet's call, they provide a means of distinguishing between true and false prophets and between legitimate and illegitimate traditions. The true prophet must be able to present a vision that transforms the tradition while allowing it to remain recognizable as the same tradition. Hence, prophets who claim a completely new vision cannot be true to their own epistemological situation or their own tradition. Also, the prophet's vision must reveal the universal in the particularities of the tradition. That is, true prophets must be able to show how the tradition has the resources to extend itself by transcending its current crisis and how it can make itself intelligible to other traditions.

This feature of legitimate prophecy also indicates how the problem of commensurability of traditions can be dealt with. Frequently, although not always, an epistemological crisis within a tradition will be caused by contact with another, alien, tradition. The test of which tradition is more legitimate or truthful rests with which tradition contains the resources successfully to resolve the epistemological crises created by the rival tradition, since this would reveal a more universal understanding through the tradition's own particularities. That is, a tradition is truly legitimate if, or to the extent that, it is capable of generating prophetic voices that can explain how the tradition's current interpretation of reality has become incoherent or inadequate and how it could be corrected. A tradition that cannot produce prophets will, and should, die.

We can perhaps illustrate what we have just argued by examining MacIntyre's discussion of patriotism. MacIntyre wants to say that it is fundamentally important to distinguish between patriotism as love of or loyalty to one's country because it is one's country, that is precisely because of its particularity, and liberal pseudo-patriotism which attempts to confine love of one's country within the limits of a broader, universalistic morality. True patriotism and universalistic morality are simply incompatible, argues MacIntyre, because morality is ultimately always generated out of a concrete, particular tradition:

It is not just that I first apprehend the rules of morality in some socially specific and particularised form. It is also and correlatively that the goods by reference to which and for the sake of which any set of rules must be justified are also going to be goods that are socially specific and particular. For central to those goods is the enjoyment of one particular kind of social life, lived out through a particular set of social relationships and thus what I enjoy is the good of *this* particular social life inhabited by me and I enjoy *it* as what it is. . . . Goods are never encountered except as thus particularised. Hence the abstract general claim, that rules of a certain kind are justified by being productive and constitutive of goods of a certain kind, is true only if these and these and these particular sets of rules incarnated in the practices of these and these and these particular communities are productive of or constitutive of these and these and these particular goods enjoyed at certain times and places by certain specifiable individuals.

It follows that *I* find *my* justification for allegiance to these rules of morality in *my* particular community; deprived of the life of that community, *I* would have no reason to be moral.[41]

MacIntyre goes on from here to argue that patriotism is thus a virtue because loyalty to a particular community is thus necessary to sustain morality, that is, all other virtues. It is true, therefore, that patriotism places certain aspects of the relevant tradition beyond question and thus is not fully rational, at least in the sense modernity has understood rationality. This is why liberalism views patriotism with suspicion. Of course—and this is a point that MacIntyre perhaps does not make as well as he should—the "fully rational" morality of liberal modernity is itself simply an illusion, since it establishes as universal a particular set of goods and rules from a particular tradition, but there is a sense in which the liberal critique does point out again the difficulty with MacIntyre's approach to moral reasoning, i.e., that he so thoroughly particularizes morality as to be unable to avoid the charge of relativism.

Our discussion of prophecy as a place can show the way out of this dilemma. Any tradition will, as MacIntyre points out, contain many unexamined assumptions. Under certain conditions some of these unquestioned assumptions will come into question because events have brought the tradition's self-understanding into question. Since any valid tradition will contain the resources to (partly) transcend its particularity, a valid tradition would be able to examine and rearticulate, modify, or even discard those assumptions that have been called into question, while still remaining recognizable as the same tradition. A tradition unable to do this would be untruthful. Hence, the dichotomy MacIntyre establishes, i.e., of particular vs. universal morality, is really a false one; the proper distinction is between traditions capable of revealing the universal in their particularities and thus being capable of reforming and transcending themselves, and traditions that cannot do so and that will thus eventually become incoherent and die.

The concrete political implications of the above analysis are considerable. The criterion elucidated immediately places under considerable suspicion the modern nation-state, since in fact the traditions that constitute modern nation-states do not seem to have the resources to transcend their particularity. Similarily, modern liberalism becomes suspect because its "universal" morality can easily be shown to be extremely parochial, and parochial in such a way that it cannot transcend itself.

A further implication of the above analysis is that a person should owe his or her allegiance only to a tradition that can generate prophetic voices and reform itself, and when one discovers that one has been part of a tradition that cannot do this, one must undergo the painful but necessary process of abandoning the inadequate and dying tradition for a more truthful one. Conversion would be a central place of necessity in any adequate political theory.

Our analysis of prophecy also indicates a very important instance where one of Macintyre's formulations should be modified. MacIntyre represents the narrative of an individual life as a search for an only partially understood goal: "The virtues therefore are to be understood as those dispositions which will not only sustain practices and enable us to achieve the goods internal to practices, but which will also sustain us in the relevant kind of [narrative] quest for the good, by enabling us to overcome the harms, dangers, temptations and distractions which we encounter, and which will furnish us with increasing self-knowledge and knowledge of the good."[42] But the biblical prophets are depicted not as *searching* but rather as *responding to a call*. The idea of a search or quest seems to be more appropriate to the Platonic idea of the Good than to the speech-based places we have discussed so far. The central feature of such places is that they establish necessary conditions of responsibility for human speakers in terms of other human speakers, rather than in terms of an abstractly defined goal. Whereas the critical question in a search is whether or not the searcher is getting closer to the goal, something only that individual (or group of individuals) can answer, the critical question in my conception of a place is whether or not a speaker has become abstracted from the context of responsibility to other speakers—*something the other speakers can probably answer better*. The concept of place articulates more clearly, it seems to me, the absolutely critical dimension of attentiveness to the voice of the other.

Of course, MacIntyre does ultimately say that the good for humanity does consist centrally of a responsible life within a community,[43] but there is nevertheless an important shift in emphasis from "searching for the good" to "responding to a call." Since, as we have just seen, the latter formulation contains more clearly the sense of another concrete personal speaker, it should be less likely to degenerate into a potentially destructive abstraction, such as a rigid doctrine. One does not have to be a deconstructionist to recognize how tyrannical a vision of the good community could become if it turned into an abstract doctrine intelligible only to a part of that community. Or, to put it in terms of our basic question of limits, the requirement of non-abstraction from context and thus faithfulness to other speakers seems to present a more reliable limit on human actions than a goal that, even though it may primarily consist of responsible action in a community and, when properly symbolized, articulates the inexhaustible mystery of human existence, could be misunderstood as something to be grasped and possessed. MacIntyre's description of the good life should thus be changed from "the good life for man is the life spent in seeking the good life for man," to "the good life for a person is an orientation of attunement to the ever-changing ambiguities and nuances of that person's speech-location, as they appear in the persons of other speakers."

Finally, our examination of these three paradigmatic places can now allow us to address an important issue raised in the preceding chapter, i.e., that the idea of faithfulness is politically indeterminate or even destructive in the sense that faithfulness to context could mean obedience to whatever power structure happens to exist, even a tyrannical one. As we have seen in this chapter, faithfulness to context would require that one attempt to construct, uphold, and reform paradigmatic places of orientation such as apprenticeship, ritual, and prophecy. If existing institutional structures do not provide such places, that is, if apprenticeship has been replaced by indoctrination, ritual has degenerated into manipulation, or a tradition produces false prophets, then individuals and communities acting faithfully must attempt to reconstruct those places and thus resist an order that has become tyrannical. Indeed, faithfulness not only demands resistance to tyranny, it is necessary to recognize a tyrannical situation—one that has destroyed fundamental places—to begin with.

I will conclude by reiterating the salient features of the concept of a place, and in so doing, showing how it fulfills my original goal of establishing the rudiments of a speech-based political vocabulary. As we have seen, necessity for MacIntyre's concept of narrative practice comes from places of faithfulness which connect practice with narrative or narrative with tradition. These places are themselves events or movements in the sense that any acritical reliance upon context is an event or movement. The structure of the process involved reveals the two features of place that serve as guidelines for evaluating the faithfulness of the speaker. First, a true place must transform those who inhabit it in such a way that they can recognize that their acritical reliance upon their context of practice, narrative, and tradition was justified. Second, a true place will reveal the universal through the particular.

There are three ways in which the concept of place as I have developed it fulfills my original goal of articulating some basic elements of a speech-based political vocabulary. First, the concept is derived directly from our phenomenological consideration of the speech act. The model of a place appropriate for political practice parallels the place inherent in the structure of the speech act. Just as the context of the speech act provides necessity in a situation of absolute contingency, the structure of a place sets limits in a situation of infinite possibilities.

Second, my development of the concept of place has attempted, as much as possible, to recapture a sense of the oral/aural. I have attempted to use terms and examples that avoid the impersonal, abstract, dualistic, static, skeptical, and individualistic connotations of a visually-oriented vocabulary, and that imply the personal, contextual, holistic, dynamic, non-skeptical, and communal features of oral/aural experience. In one sense, the ultimate goal of the discussion has been to change the reader's conceptual orientation to the point where speaking of place as a speech event, or space as an inhabited aural phenomenon, or the world as something spoken into existence does not seem awkward, but rather sounds more sensible than the vocabulary of objectivism. To the extent that my discussion has accomplished this, it will have recaptured dimensions of experience largely lost by the visual objectivist paradigm of modernity. This of course is another reason why the non-political chapters were essential to the argument; a speech-based political vocabulary would only make sense if it was preceded by a discussion of more general oral/aural phenomena.

Finally, and in practical terms, most importantly, a political practice based upon the concepts discussed here would, to put it most simply, involve more speaking. That is, a narrative political tradition limited by places such as the ones described above would be one in which speech and hearing could rival visual phenomena in their influence on individuals' perceptual and conceptual frameworks, since all of these places are fundamentally oriented toward speech—whether through debate, rhythmic ritual, or the verbal example implied by apprenticeship. Such a political tradition would not represent a return to an oral culture, something we would not find desirable anyway, but could redress somewhat the present imbalance between vision and hearing in our sensory orientation. If my argument is correct that a literate/visual orientation tends to promote an objectivist mindset, with its correlative destruction of limits and loss of any sense of finitude, and that the postliterate visual orientation produced by the electronic media pushes this tendency to its logical conclusion in relativism, this reorientation in itself, more than any specific institutional arrangement, would allow us to recapture a sense of finitude and escape our current relativistic dilemma.

CONCLUSION:
SPEECH, PLACE, AND THE
POSTMODERN PUBLIC REALM

Our investigation has finally come full circle. After having developed the concept of a speech-based place and examined specific places appropriate to political practice, I want to conclude by putting the concept of place in a larger political context, and by so doing addressing the issue raised at the very beginning of this study: what implications this conception of place has for a postmodern political order—that is for a political order that can recapture a sense of human finitude but that also grants modernity credit for its egalitarian achievements and its recognition of human creative capacities.

First of all, it should be clear that the concept of place developed here does not provide a blueprint for a good society. Indeed, I explicitly argued in the previous chapter that the specific, concrete places discussed are not tied to any particular institutional framework. Rather, these places will set limits on political practice by eliminating as unacceptable certain institutional frameworks. It is of fundamental importance that they do not set any particular institutional framework in stone and in fact encourage institutional change as those in authority are called to account.

What *is* basic to the concept of a place is that it establishes the potential for the development of a political vocabulary that can revive a public realm of debate and discussion about, and action to establish, the common good. I mentioned earlier that the most important thing that any political theory does is not so much to establish a comprehensive vision of political order, but rather to provide, or contribute to, a political vocabulary. This conclusion is congruent with the general thrust of post–World War II political theory. The concept as it has been developed here would develop a public realm in a very particular manner, however. It clearly implies a situation where all areas of life would be, or at least could be, politicized. This is clear, for example, in our discussion of apprenticeship. Although apprenticeship is indeed a place of acritical reliance where the apprentice submits to the superior knowledge of the master, a true apprenticeship situation should bring about the eventual equality of apprentice and master. Thus, institutional mechanisms must exist to call those in power to account if they do not fulfill their duty. But this is to say that masters are subject to political review, that is, subject to question and debate over whether they actually have fulfilled their duty to the common good of the community as it relates to the particular practice in question. Hence, education, far from being apolitical or somehow above politics, is a thoroughly political undertaking. The same, or a similar, analysis could apply to work, family relations, and other aspects of life.

Three important points need to be made about this matter. To begin with, in potentially politicizing all areas of life, the concept of a place simply recognizes another major insight of twentieth-century political theory, i.e., that nothing can be exempted from politics. This insight is, of course, at odds not only with modern liberalism, but also with classical Greek thought, which typically attempts to exempt certain areas of reality (the natural order of the cosmos, the private realm of the household) from politics. It is, however, strikingly congruent with the biblical understanding of reality, where even God is political. The possibility of politicizing all areas of life is, of course, one that is profoundly dismaying to liberal sensibilities. But this is because liberalism perceives politics as essentially or even exclusively a matter of coercion, and perceives this coercion to be potentially limitless. This leads to our next two points: First, the concept of place recognizes that politics is not only, indeed most emphatically not even primarily, a matter of coercion. Indeed, politics is not necessarily even a matter of debate and discussion. As our discussion of ritual demonstrated, public ceremonies are an important part of the political realm, as they contribute to establishing the common good, but they do not normally involve debate and discussion. Second, as we have established while developing the concept, speech-based places would limit politics not by exempting certain areas from politics but by providing a set of built-in limitations to politics.

Stated in its most general form, then, one implication of my argument would be to elaborate specific places of responsibility and then to explicate changes in human thought and action that would allow such places to develop. Out of such a project would develop the local practices and communities, and simultaneously the narratives and traditions, that theorists such as Alasdair MacIntyre and Stanley Hauerwas see as essential to sustaining and restoring morality and civility. At the same time the traditions that would develop would be limited by the places that inform them. This would develop a politics devoted to finding and establishing the common good, which would recognize that all aspects of life are potentially political but which at the same time sets limits to political action.

We can make this general statement more concrete by placing the modern understanding of politics within the framework just developed. Modern liberalism attempts to make a fairly sharp distinction between the state, or the public realm, on the one hand, and civil society, or the private realm, on the other. Civil society is seen as the realm of voluntary cooperation, based upon free contract, of more or less autonomous individuals, and is conceived to be characterized by something approximating natural harmony. The state is seen as primarily or exclusively an instrument of coercion, which uses law to settle the occasional disagreements or coercive actions that arise in civil society. State power must be limited to preserve individual freedom and will be limited because civil society is characterized on the whole by individuals peacefully pursuing their own private goals.

The fatal flaw in this conception is of course the assumption that civil society is a realm of "natural harmony." If disagreement or coercion turns out to be endemic to civil society, then there may be no limits to the role of state coercion in its attempt to adjudicate the conflicts of civil society. This is why it was so important, for example, for classical liberals such as Adam Smith to assume that humans have a "natural propensity" to engage in market activity; without this assumption the market could be a realm of considerable coercion and thus could be subject to extensive regulation. But, as Hobbes perceived, if civil society consists of nothing but dissociated individuals, then as a matter of sheer logic, the private realm *will* be a place of continual conflict requiring potentially unlimited state coercion simply to maintain peace. And, empirically, it has been readily demonstrated that many of the social institutions of liberal society are indeed perceived as coercive by those subject to them. Hence, the paradoxical tendency of liberal societies is toward a continual growth of centralized state power in the name of individual freedom.

More recent versions of liberalism, recognizing this growth as inevitable, attempt to mitigate the coercive essence of the state by democratizing it. The attempt to democratize the state, however, ultimately amounts to an attempt to transfer the earlier model of civil society, with its assumption of equal opportunity to pursue one's goals, to the political realm, with the result that the political process is now subject to the same coercive distortions as civil society, especially when it takes the form of representation. Indeed, the attempt to democratize the state may actually strip it of any autonomy based on law and turn it into a tool of the most powerful social interests. Politically, liberalism is parasitical upon premodern conceptions of nature in the same way that, as we have already seen, it is ontologically parastical upon such understandings. When these remnants of the earlier natural order are lost, liberal theory disintegrates into a welter of absurdities and contradictions, just as liberal society degenerates into a mass of isolated, easily manipulated individuals and liberal politics degenerates into a spectacle played out in the mass media. The more radical modern ideologies simply recognize more clearly than liberalism the implications of the loss of a natural order.

If we use the terminology we have developed in our discussion, we can pinpoint the crucial point of confusion in liberalism. This is that early liberalism still tacitly retained, albeit frequently in somewhat altered form, many premodern, "natural" places of orientation in its understanding of civil society, particularly, of course, in its under-standing of such institutions as the family. As these places were eventually broken down by the universalization of the subjectivistic individualism upon which civil society was supposedly built, civil society tended to degenerate into the realm of perpetual conflict envisioned by Hobbes, with its correlative expansion of state power. The appearance of natural harmony among subjective wills could only be maintained by the partial survival of older forms of authority and subordination, which would collapse once the idea of the autonomous individual was taken with full seriousness. Premodern, status-based, natural authorities and hierarchies embedded in the structure of a supposedly contractual civil society were what actually provided places with which liberal society could order itself.

What is needed to break out of the dilemma of late modern societies, then, is a reconstruction of authoritative places of orientation— not, however, by attempting to revive a conception of natural, fixed, hierarchical order, but rather by constructing places of faithful speech acts which will allow institutional structures to be open to criticism and modification. What this in turn implies is that the sharp distinction made by liberalism between public and private is false and destructive. If places of orientation based upon faithful speech acts must be established in all realms of human activity, then all human activities have an irreducible public dimension to them.

From the above considerations we can begin to derive a new understanding of participation in the public realm. The model of the polis assumes that the public realm is a place of debate and action distinct from the private realm of the household, which requires that all citizens be able to come together and meet in a face-to-face manner. This model is obviously inapplicable to any large-scale political organization and thus tends to be replaced with various forms of representation, which of course dilute the possibilities for citizenship. If, however, we understand the public realm not as a discrete area but rather as an irreducible element of all human activities, we can see that all human activities contain possibilities for citizenship. What in liberal societies are understood as private associations are in an important sense political and thus can be places of citizenship. To understand citizenship this way is to allow for the reconstruction of a public realm that is not monolithic or inaccessible to local participation. A political society constructed upon this understanding of the public realm would replace the monolithic sovereignty of the state with a variety of overlapping authorities. This kind of pluralistic associational life is precisely what Tocqueville admired most about the America of his time and what many other modern commentators admire most about the medieval order. What it would require in order both to become fully democratic and to remain coherent and not disintegrate into a welter of mutually conflicting subcultures and interest groups, however, would be precisely the kinds of ordering places, and institutional structures to sustain those places, that we have discussed. Hence, my conception of place holds out the possibility of developing local traditions of self-government and citizenship without attempting to return to the tribalistic politics of the polis.

We can make the above point more concrete by examining Jürgen Habermas's discussion of Thomas Aquinas. As Habermas understands it, Aquinas becomes the unwitting precursor of the modern liberal understanding of politics and society when he transforms Aristotle's political science into a science of society. Whereas Aristotle understands the polis as a political association, and exempts the household, or the private realm of labor, from the political realm, Aquinas includes labor, dignified by Christianity, as a legitimate aspect of the community, but in so doing depoliticizes the community: "The opposition of *polis* and *oikos* has been reduced to the common denominator of *societas*; and this is interpreted by analogy to the patriarchically organized domestic and family life, thus actually apolitically by Aristotle's criteria. The order of the *polis* was actualized in the participation of the citizens in administration, legislation, justice, and consultation; the *ordo* retained by Thomas sacrifices the political substance of the citizen's politically oriented will and consciousness as formed in public discussion. . . ."[1] From the argument I have developed so far, we could say that Thomas's mistake was not so much in replacing the political with the social as in failing to recognize that every aspect of the social has a political dimension to it. Participation, and thus formation of political will and consciousness through public discussion and public ritual, would come through the attempt to bring about accountability and responsibility in everyday life by developing and maintaining places of faithfulness such as apprenticeship structures in work, educational, familial, etc. contexts. As earlier mentioned, what impressed Tocqueville about Jacksonian America was not so much its formal political institutions but rather the manifestations of its relatively egalitarian culture found in its associational life. Similarly, the basic tension that Habermas sees in modernity—that is, between communicative rationality and subject-centered reason—has its practical embodiment in the conflict between, on the one hand, the promise of breaking down older ascriptive hierarchies and thus creating capacities for self-government for larger numbers of people and, on the other hand, the creation of new, more subtle, and ultimately more relentlessly dominating hierarchies based upon modern technology. The development of places of faithfulness would allow for the critique of both types of hierarchies, while simultaneously realizing the necessity of the kinds of provisional hierarchies implied in such places as apprenticeship.

We can also understand this issue by considering Hannah Arendt's discussion of the active life for humans.[2] As Arendt sees it, or rather as she presents the prephilosophical Greeks as understanding it, the active life has three components: labor, work, and action. Labor consists of those human activities most closely involved in maintaining the life-cycle, and thus is the aspect of human existence closest to nature or least specifically human. Work partly transcends nature by building an objective world of enduring artifacts which allows humans to orient themselves and escape the subjectivity of the labor process. Action, finally, is the activity in which humans most completely transcend nature and establish themselves as unique individuals in a political community through speech and deeds. For the ancients, action was the highest activity within the active life and was reserved for citizens; labor was relegated to the private realm of women and slaves. The sharp separation between public and private realms was necessary to keep the less fully human, indeed even subhuman, laboring activity from corrupting the fully human activity of action. Modernity, as Arendt sees it, has inverted the proper hierarchy within the active life and thus threatens to reduce all people to a slavelike existence.

Although Arendt's discussion of the active life and its components articulates vital dimensions of human experience, it nevertheless has serious limitations as a political theory applicable to postmodernity because of the hierarchy or exclusion apparently implied in the sharp distinction Arendt wants to make between public and private, itself implied by the hierarchy of activities. If full humanity can only be achieved in a life of action unconcerned with mere labor or even work, it seems that the bulk of humanity must be consigned to a subordinate or even marginal position. Or, conversely, if the capacity for action can be democratized, it seems that action can be sustained only for short durations, as with revolutionary movements, before it is eclipsed by the mundane necessities of work and labor.

We can see a way out of this dilemma by considering one of the implications of our discussion of the speech act. If action, or speech, does not allow us to transcend a given natural order (the earth to which Arendt sees us as irrevocably tied), but rather actually *creates* the natural order as an articulate conceptual entity, then the sharp distinction made among the elements of the active life no longer holds. Work and even labor can themselves contain dimensions of action and as such can be sources of fully human activity. Or, we could say that just as what modern liberalism takes to be private, apolitical voluntary organizations actually have a political dimension, so what Arendt takes to be private, subpolitical activities also have a public, political dimension to them. The laboring process may provide opportunities for citizenship just as associational life does. It is possible that the life of action may be available to all people and in all dimensions of human existence.

We can now make the implications of my argument more explicit: we must articulate those places that can allow individuals to achieve citizenship within the bounds of overlapping local associations and practices while still binding those associations and practices into a coherent whole. This effort in turn would constitute the beginnings of a narrative tradition about the recovery of a sense of place from the void of late modernity.

A specific example of this can be given by an examination of Peter Berger's discussion of the concepts of honor and dignity.[3] Honor is an essentially premodern concept; in this understanding, one's identity is essentially found in one's social roles, and one's honor has been damaged when one fails to fulfill one's role or roles. Dignity, by contrast, is a typically modern concept wherein one's essential identity is found apart from all social roles. (Actually, as discussed in the previous chapter, we can see the beginnings of the concept of dignity—of an identity that transcends the particulars of one's situation—in the Abraham story.) Berger does not intend to critique the concept of dignity, and he recognizes the many benefits of understanding individuals as having an identity apart from any specific social role. He points out that "the conviction that even the weakest members of society have an inherent right to protection and dignity; the proscription of slavery in all its forms, of racial and ethnic oppression; the staggering discovery of the dignity and rights of the child; the new sensitivity to cruelty . . . the new recognition of individual responsibility for all actions . . . all these and others are moral achievements that would be unthinkable without the peculiar constellations of the modern world."[4] But Berger does think that with the loss of the concept of honor and its grounding of identity in concrete social roles, modern societies have suffered a loss of reliable identity. He recommends recovering the concept of honor without losing the idea of dignity: "The ethical test of any future institutions, and of the codes of honour they will entail, will be whether they succeed in embodying and in stabilizing the discoveries of human dignity that are the principal achievements of modern man."[5]

It would seem that something along these lines would be implied by our understanding of a postmodern public realm. We said that we wanted to develop local traditions of self-government and citizenship within a context of overlapping authorities by recognizing the public or political dimension of all human activities, which would require the development of the kinds of places we have discussed. According to our earlier discussion, legitimate places will transform us in such a way that they allow us to see that our earlier faithfulness, or acritical reliance upon authority, was justified, and they will reveal the universal in the particular. We can see that the concept of honor could be a place in the sense we have developed, if it is linked to the concept of dignity. That is, if honor allows one to understand one's social roles as transforming one into a citizen, and if it is able to reveal the universal characteristics of citizenship in one's particular social roles, therefore indicating an identity beyond one's particular social roles, or in other words, establishing dignity, then it would be a legitimate place. One concrete application, then, of our discussion would be to elaborate conceptions of honor in such a way that honor would be a true place in our sense, and thus could coexist with a conception of dignity lying beyond any specific social role.

We can elaborate an even more specific application of the concept of place by considering the contemporary political economy, which we surveyed briefly in the first chapter. We have already mentioned the new global capitalist economy, with its potential for unprecedented social dislocation, as perhaps the most thoroughgoing manifestation of what I called the radical contingency of late modernity. Jeremy Rifkin, among others, has in fact argued that the new high-tech economy will have revolutionary consequences for the social structures of both industrialized and industrializing societies. Specifically, in *The End of Work*, Rifkin argues that computer and related technologies will permit most economic production to be done by a relatively small percentage of the population. These new technologies thus hold out the serious possibility of what for most of human history has been only a wildly utopian dream: material plenty with very little labor. This possibility, however, has a frightening downside to it. Unless the transition embodied in this "third industrial revolution" is handled properly, that is, unless economic and social institutions are reformed accordingly, the result of the information revolution, with its elimination of many existing types of work, could be massive un- and underemployment, homelessness, crime, and terrorism, accompanied by fascistic responses from the privileged minority which benefits spectacularly from the new technologies, possibly culminating in a worldwide economic collapse as an increasingly unequal distribution of income and the creation of a vast surplus population ultimately destroy the mass purchasing power necessary to sustain a high-consumption economy.

Rifkin has two main proposals to prevent this scenario from occurring. First, the work week must be shortened (possibly to twenty hours a week within a generation) to provide employment opportunities for more people (and also to give people more time for civic and family activities); and second, many more people should be provided with positions in the non-profit sector, performing various types of community services. Obviously, this would require major political action, since it entails a significant, albeit indirect, redistribution of income.[6]

The concept of place I have developed here is relevant to Rifkin's argument in three ways. First, and most obviously, it can, in ways we have already discussed, contribute to the revival of the public realm that would be required by both of his proposals for avoiding the potentially destructive effects of the information revolution. Only a highly motivated and well-organized political movement could bring about the far-reaching institutional reforms he recommends, and at the same time, only a thoroughgoing public debate could ensure the justice of those institutional changes.

Second, and ultimately more importantly, Rifkin's proposals imply something much more fundamental than just political action to restructure economic institutions. What is ultimately implied is a fundamental cultural or ethical transformation away from the modern Protestant work ethic, with its idea of serving the common good through economically productive labor—the increasing irrelevance of which is apparent in its degeneration into an ethos of purely individual success—and toward a different understanding of achievement or fulfillment.

This new understanding of human fulfillment would in certain ways resemble premodern conceptions of the human good in that it would encompass community service that is not necessarily productive in a narrowly economic sense, civic activities directed toward finding and achieving the common good, and ultimately perhaps the spiritual dimension of human existence. If this is indeed the case, it can be seen that the conception of place we have developed could be fundamental to such a reorientation, partly because it would provide a different model of human identity and activity but also because it could do so in a relatively egalitarian way. This would be perhaps the most concrete implication of the idea of a speech-based place.

Finally, and most crucially, if the future holds an increased reliance on the new electronic media, with their tendency to create a post-objectivist or relativist orientation, then it becomes fundamentally important to develop experiential alternatives. If the sources of modern objectivism and late modern relativism lie at least partly in an excessively visual orientation, then the only way these patterns of thought can be overcome is through a recovery of an orientation toward speech and hearing. Hence, it would be essential to counter the use of computers and television with activities that recover and heighten our sense of the oral/aural. The face-to-face oral demonstration implied in the place of apprenticeship, the acoustic space created by the time and rhythm of ritual, and the debate implied in the place of prophecy, to take just three examples, could achieve this. Indeed, such a reorientation could recapture realms of human experience, such as the religious, that have become utterly opaque to our visual culture, and thus contribute to the ethical transformation just discussed. Developing places of faithfulness to recover morality and community and reorienting our sensorium would be mutually reinforcing goals.

We can summarize these implications of our concept of speech-based place by saying that, most concretely, by providing both a sense of finitude and a new ethical model, the concept of place could contribute to preventing our current technological revolution from fulfilling Nietzsche's prophecy of an utterly nihilistic world, and more positively, could help allow us to regain dimensions of human experience that we have largely lost in modernity without, however, sacrificing the scientific and democratic achievements of modernity. Oral/aural places of faithfulness hold out the possibility, not of a utopian future, but of a world more livable than the one our current objectivist/relativist dilemma threatens to produce.

I would like to close by summarizing the broader implications of the concept of place that I have developed. I have mentioned that it is possible to discern the beginnings of a new approach to our comprehension of reality in recent philosophy, theology, and political theory. One central feature of these undertakings is the abandonment of notions of strict linear causality and their replacement with an attempt to recognize and understand configurations that make certain events more or less probable. The most basic aspect, I believe, of this emerging orientation toward the world is that it recognizes both the inescapability and the enabling capacity of context. In the course of my argument, I have examined in some detail some of the reasons why modernity has tended to ignore context, and of course context has been fundamental to the concept of place. My discussion then, beyond being an attempt to articulate some of the rudiments of a speech-based political vocabulary, can be understood as a contribution to the developing articulation of this orientation in the world.

This new orientation toward, or rather within, reality offers as elements of necessity, not a set of fixed absolutes in either the Platonic sense or the sense of modern forms of methodism nor a knowable historical goal as with much nineteenth-century thought, but rather hints and clues about experience, knowledge, and even redemption yet to be attained. These hints and clues may themselves change, but they change in an intelligible manner. Our necessary acritical reliance upon context in everything we do indicates this, since it means that what is intelligible is more fundamental than what is unintelligible. The picture that emerges from recent epistemological-ontological investigations is one that is teleological, but with a teleology that could be described as hidden or dynamic, where we proceed with a confidence that is based on the clues we have already received but also with a sense of our limitations. We attempt to remain faithful in our articulate activities just as we unavoidably remain faithful in our primordial, inarticulate orientation in the world, realizing that we will often fail but that out of our failures can come greater understanding. Such a position, or rather such a place, is one that could be described as a rational faith.

NOTES

Introduction

1. Broad overviews of the development and later demise of modern liberal rationalism can be found in Thomas A. Spragens, Jr., *The Irony of Liberal Reason* (Chicago: University of Chicago Press, 1981); Roberto Mangabeira Unger, *Knowledge and Politics* (New York: The Free Press, 1975); William M. Sullivan, *Reconstructing Public Philosophy* (Berkeley: University of California Press, 1986); and John H. Hallowell, *The Decline of Liberalism as an Ideology* (Berkeley: University of California Press, 1943). For more general discussions of the breakdown of modern scientific rationalism, see Richard Bernstein, *Beyond Objectivism and Relativism: Science, Hermeneutics and Practice* (Philadelphia: University of Pennsylvania Press, 1988), and Alfred North Whitehead, *Science and the Modern World* (New York: Macmillan, 1925). In addition to the classic discussions of Tocqueville and Weber, influential sociological studies of modern individualism include Robert Nisbet, *The Quest for Community: A Study in the Ethics of Order and Freedom* (Oxford: Oxford University Press, 1953); David Riesman, *The Lonely Crowd: A Study of the Changing American Character* (New Haven: Yale University Press, 1961); Richard Sennett, *The Fall of Public Man: On the Social Psychology of Capitalism* (New York: Random House, 1974); Christopher Lasch, *The Culture of Narcissism: American Life in an Age of Diminishing Expectations* (New York: W. W. Norton, 1978); and Robert N. Bellah *et al.*, *Habits of the Heart: Individualism and Commitment in American Life* (New York: Harper & Row, 1985).

2. Early statements of postmodern themes can be found in Martin Heidegger, *Nietzsche*, vol. 4: *Nihilism*, trans. Frank A. Capuzzi, ed. David Farrell Krell (San Francisco: Harper & Row, 1982), and especially in "The Question Concerning Technology," in *Basic Writings*, ed. David Farrell Krell (New York; Harper & Row, 1977), pp. 283–318. Definitive works by Derrida include *Speech and Phenomena: And Other Essays On Husserl's Theory of Signs*, trans. David B. Allison (Evanston: Northwestern University Press, 1973), and *Of Grammatology*, trans. Gayatri Chakravorty Spivak (Baltimore: Johns Hopkins University Press, 1976). Foucault's position is most fully developed in *Discipline and Punish: The Birth of the Prison*, trans. Allan Sheridan (New York: Vintage Books, 1979); *The History of Sexuality*, vol. I: *An Introduction*, trans. Robert Hurley (New York: Random House, 1979); and *Power/Kowledge*, ed. Colin Gordon (New York: Pantheon Books, 1980). See also Jean-Francois Lyotard, *The Postmodern Condition: A Report on Knowledge*, trans. Geoff Bennington and Brian Massumi (Minneapolis: University of Minnesota Press, 1984).

3. See Allan Bloom, *The Closing of the American Mind* (New York: Simon & Schuster, 1987), p. 154.

4. See Leo Strauss, *Natural Right and History* (Chicago: University of Chicago Press, 1950).

5. Strauss argues that the fundamental question for political theory is whether nature is functional or mechanistic (see *Natural Right and History*, pp. 7–8), but this misses the point. The real question is whether it is meaningful to talk about a "nature" independent of human agency in the first place.

6. A more detailed discussion can be found in Jürgen Habermas, *Knowledge and Human Interests*, trans. Jeremy J. Shapiro (Boston: Beacon Press, 1971), pp. 301–317.

7. See Eric Voegelin, *The New Science of Politics: An Introduction* (Chicago: University of Chicago Press, 1952); Hannah Arendt, *The Human Condition* (Chicago: University of Chicago Press, 1958); Habermas, *Knowledge and Human Interests* and *Theory and Practice*, trans. John Viertel (Boston: Beacon Press, 1973); Alasdair MacIntyre, *After Virtue: A Study in Moral Theory*, 2nd ed. (Notre Dame: University of Notre Dame Press, 1984); and Charles Taylor, *Sources of the Self: The Making of the Modern Identity* (Cambridge, Mass.: Harvard University Press, 1989).

8. See Bernstein, *Beyond Objectivism and Relativism*.

9. See MacIntyre, *After Virtue*, and Stanley Hauerwas, *A Community of Character: Toward a Constructive Christian Social Ethic* (Notre Dame: University of Notre Dame Press, 1981), and *The Peaceable Kingdom: A Primer in Christian Ethics* (Notre Dame: University of Notre Dame Press, 1983).

10. Throughout the discussion, I will use the term "postmodern" to mean simply "after what is modern," while reserving the terms "postmodernism" or "postmodernist" to refer to the ideas of theorists such as Foucault, Derrida, etc.

1. The Concept of a Narrative Practice
as an Alternative to Objectivism

1. See Habermas, *Knowledge and Human Interests*, pp. 301–317, and Bernstein, *Beyond Objectivism and Relativism: Science, Hermeneutics, and Practice*.

2. In the historical sketch that follows, I will employ terms such as "man," "he," "his," and "him" rather than such expressions as "humanity," "he or she," etc., because the theorists in question have indeed been concerned mainly with men.

3. The doctrine of creation *ex nihilo* is not stated clearly in Genesis but is worked out later in the Bible and in Christian theology. See Thorlief Boman,

Hebrew Thought Compared with Greek, trans. Jules S. Moreau (Philadelphia: Westminister Press, 1961), p. 63. Explicit doctrines aside, even the oldest strata of biblical stories contain a strong sense of the world's contingency and also imply human creative capacities. The most obvious example is the Abraham story, which I shall discuss in chapter 5. See also Reinhold Niebuhr, *The Nature and Destiny of Man: A Christian Interpretation*, vol. I: *Human Nature* (New York: Charles Scribner's Sons, 1941), and William H. Poteat, *Polanyian Meditations: In Search of a Post-Critical Logic* (Durham: Duke University Press, 1985), pp. 104–132.

4. The discussion here is quite simplified. Nietzsche recognized that modern science depended upon Christianity, and the potential disenchantment of the world inherent in biblical religion is an important theme in Weber. The first systematic explication of this idea was by Alfred North Whitehead in *Science and the Modern World*. For an early detailed treatment of this question, see M. B. Foster, "The Christian Doctrine of Creation and the Rise of Modern Science," *Mind* 43 (1934): 447–468; "Christian Theology and Modern Science of Nature—I," *Mind* 44 (1935): 439–466; and "Christian Theology and Modern Science of Nature—II," *Mind* 45 (1936): 1–27. Some of the themes discussed by Foster are developed further in Poteat, *Polanyian Meditations*.

5. See William H. Poteat, "Persons and Places," in *Art and Religion as Communication*, ed. James Waddell and F. W. Dilliston (Atlanta: John Knox Press, 1974), pp. 175–195.

6. The discussion here is again quite simplified. The debate about how much Greek philosophy could be compatible with the biblical worldview has extended over the entire history of Christianity. The nominalist movement does, however, represent the decisive rejection of Aristotle.

7. The classic discussion of this phenomenon is by Robert N. Bellah, "Civil Religion in America," in *American Civil Religion*, ed. Russell E. Richey and Donald G. Jones (New York: Harper & Row, 1974), pp. 21–44.

8. In this regard, see, for example, Voegelin, *The New Science of Politics: An Introduction* , pp. 187–189.

9. This has been one of Michel Foucault's main themes. See also Sheldon Wolin's discussion in *Politics and Vision: Continuity and Innovation in Western Political Thought* (Boston: Little, Brown and Company, 1960), pp. 309–325, 343–351.

10. Rawls's *A Theory of Justice* (Cambridge, Mass.: The Belknap Press of Harvard University Press, 1971) remains the classic statement of postwar reform liberalism.

11. *A Theory of Justice*, pp. 65–90.

12. Undoubtedly the most famous version of this thesis is Francis Fukuyama's "The End of History?" *The National Interest* (Summer 1989): 3–18.

13. For examinations of the recent changes in the world economy, see Robert Reich, *The Work of Nations: Preparing Ourselves for Twenty-first Century Capitalism* (New York: Alfred A. Knopf, 1991), and Jeremy Rifkin, *The End of Work: The Decline of the Global Labor Force and the Post-Market Era* (New York: G. P. Putnam's Sons, 1995). Rifkin focuses especially upon the dislocative effects of the new computer and computer-related technologies. See also the analysis in Scott Lash and John Urry, *The End of Organized Capitalism* (Madison: University of Wisconsin Press, 1987), especially pp. 285–300, with regard to cultural tendencies in recent capitalism. Kevin Phillips argues that much of the new elite is relatively unproductive, even parasitical, in *The Politics of Rich and Poor: Wealth and the American Electorate in the Reagan Aftermath* (New York: Random House, 1990).

14. See Rifkin, *End of Work*, pp. 165–217, especially pp. 208–217. For similar views, see the replies to Fukuyama following "The End of History?" pp. 19–35.

15. See Habermas's discussion in *Knowledge and Human Interests*, pp. 274–300, as well as MacIntyre's discussion in *After Virtue: A Study in Moral Theory*, pp. 109–120, 256–263. See also Habermas's critique of post-Nietzschean thought in *The Philosophical Discourse of Modernity: Twelve Lectures*, trans. Frederick Lawrence (Cambridge: MIT Press, 1987).

16. For a more complete argument, see Niebuhr, *The Nature and Destiny of Man*, and also Poteat, *Polanyian Meditations*.

17. See Berlin's discussion in "Two Concepts of Liberty," in *Four Essays on Liberty* (Oxford: Oxford University Press, 1969), pp. 118–172; the quotation is on p. 168.

18. See Michael Walzer, *Spheres of Justice* (New York: Basic Books, 1983), and Daniel Bell, *Communitarianism and Its Critics* (Oxford: Clarendon Press, 1993). This Daniel Bell is not the same person as the sociologist Daniel Bell, author of *The Cultural Contradictions of Capitalism* (New York: Basic Books, 1976).

19. See Eric Voegelin, "Necessary Moral Bases for Communication in a Democracy," in *Problems of Communication in a Pluralistic Society*, Papers delivered at a conference on Communication, the fourth in a series of Anniversary Celebrations, March 20, 21, 22, and 23, 1956 (Milwaukee: The Marquette University Press, 1956), pp. 53–68; the quotation is on p. 62.

20. See Bell, *Communitarianism and Its Critics*, pp. 70–73; the quotation is on p. 72. It is quite possible, incidentally, that Bell is being subtly ironic here, as his dialogue is very well constructed and does not flinch from acknowledging weaknesses in communitarian positions.

21. See Bell, *Communitarianism and Its Critics*, pp. 76–77.

22. See Stanley Hauerwas and David Burrell, "From System to Story: An Alternative Pattern for Rationality in Ethics," in Stanley Hauerwas *et al.*,

Truthfulness and Tragedy: Further Investigations in Christian Ethics (Notre Dame: University of Notre Dame Press, 1977), pp. 15–39; the quotation is on pp. 37–38. In a more recent book devoted specifically to medical ethics, Hauerwas frequently puts the word "nature" in quotation marks to indicate that the concept may be problematic, but nevertheless states that "the rise of 'medical ethics' is due more to the confused moral world we inhabit than to our technological revolution." But, as I have argued, the confused moral world we inhabit is itself the result, not of technology per se, but of the breakdown of the classical natural cosmos which has made the modern technological revolution possible. See *Suffering Presence: Theological Reflections on Medicine, the Mentally Handicapped, and the Church* (Notre Dame: University of Notre Dame Press, 1986); the quotation is on p. 1.

23. MacIntyre, *After Virtue*, p. 191.

24. Ibid., p. 187.

25. Ibid., pp. 187–194; the quotations are on pp. 193–194.

26. Ibid., pp. 204–225.

27. See J. Budziszewski, *The Resurrection of Nature: Political Theory and the Human Character* (Ithaca: Cornall University Press, 1986), pp. 62–64.

28. See *Whose Justice? Which Rationality?* (Notre Dame: University of Notre Dame Press, 1988), and *Three Rival Versions of Moral Enquiry: Encyclopaedia, Genealogy, and Tradition* (Notre Dame: University of Notre Dame Press, 1990).

2. Scientific Practice and
Its Implicit Critique of Objectivism

1. See Michael Polanyi, *Personal Knowledge: Towards a Post-Critical Pholosophy* (Chicago: University of Chicago Press, 1958), pp. 33–34.

2. *Ibid.*, pp. 18–27, 49–63.

3. *Ibid.*, pp. 69–131, 327–346.

4. *Ibid.*, p. 73.

5. *Ibid.*, p. 101.

6. *Ibid.*, pp. 124–131.

7. *Ibid.*, pp. 195–202, 367–368.

8. *Ibid.*, p. 99.

9. *Ibid.*, pp. 134–149.

10. *Ibid.*, pp. 4–5.

11. *Ibid.*,„ pp. 195–202, 367–368.

12. *Ibid.*, pp. 249–324.

13. Much of the following discussion is drawn from Polanyi's later work. In *The Tacit Dimension* (Garden City, N.Y.: Doubleday, 1966) and *Knowing and Being: Essays by Michael Polanyi*, ed. Marjorie Grene (Chicago: University of Chicago Press, 1969), Polanyi extends the analysis of tacit knowing originally set out in *Personal Knowledge*, and recognizes that this solidifies the structure of faith and commitment earlier explicated.

14. Polanyi, *Knowing and Being*, p. 139.

15. *Ibid.*, pp. 139–140.

16. Polanyi, *Personal Knowledge*, pp. 55–56.

17. Ludwig Wittgenstein, *Philosophical Investigations*, 3rd ed., trans. G. E. M. Anscombe (New York: Macmillan, 1958), p. 179e.

18. See Wittgenstein, *Philosophical Investigations*, para. 626, and Polanyi, *Personal Knowledge*, pp. 55–56.

19. See Polanyi, *Personal Knowledge*, pp. 49–50.

20. Polanyi, *Knowing and Being*, p. 119.

21. *Ibid.*, p. 117.

22. See Polanyi, Knowing and Being, pp. 9–15.

23. Polanyi, *Knowing and Being*, p. 119.

24. *Ibid.*, pp. 119–120.

25. It is instructive to observe that Kuhn's attempt to save himself from charges of relativism relies heavily on Polanyi's idea of tacit knowledge. See Thomas S. Kuhn, *The Structure of Scientific Revolutions*, 2nd ed. (Chicago: University of Chicago Press, 1970), pp. 174–210, especially pp. 187–198.

26. See chapter 5.

27. Wittgenstein, *Philosophical Investigations*, para. 104.

28. This is a fairly common theme in the revisionist literature. In addition to Kuhn, see Stephen Toulmin, *The Philosophy of Science: An Introduction* (London: Hutchinson University Library, 1953). See also Poteat, *Polanyian Meditations: In Search of a Post-Critical Logic*.

29. See Norwood Hanson, *Patterns of Discovery: An Inquiry Into the Conceptual Foundations of Science* (Cambridge: Cambridge University Press, 1958).

30. Wittgenstein would argue that there are many things that we are certain of, i.e., that we cannot seriously doubt, such as the fact that the world has existed for a long time before we were born, even though they cannot be exhaustively specified. See *On Certainty*, ed. G. E. M. Anscombe and G. H. von Wright, trans. Denis Paul and G. E. M. Anscombe (New York: Harper & Row, 1969), especially pp. 12e–16e.

31. See chapter 4.

32. See Polanyi, *Personal Knowledge*, pp. 269–298.

33. See, for example, Polanyi, *Personal Knowledge*, pp. 347–380.

34. *Ibid.*, p. 169.

35. Polanyi, *Knowing and Being*, p. 149; see also pp. 181–207.

36. Wittgenstein, *Philosophical Investigations*, para. 437.

37. See chapter 4.

38. Polanyi, *Personal Knowledge*, p. 329.

39. *Ibid.*, pp. 328–332.

40. Polanyi, *Knowing and Being*, p. 169.

41. Polanyi, *Personal Knowledge*, p. 203.

42. See Polanyi, *Knowing and Being*, pp. 49–58.

43. *Ibid.*, pp. 87–96.

44. See chapter 5.

45. See Polanyi, *Personal Knowledge*, pp. 203–224

3. The Written Word as an Experiential Source of Objectivism

1. For the most part, only a few scattered references exist in journals devoted to political theory, philosophy, and theology. An excellent treatment of Walter Ong, probably the best-known writer in the field, can be found in Clarence Walhout, "Christianity, History, and Literary Criticism: Walter Ong's Global Vision," *Journal of the American Academy of Religion* LXII (1994): 435–460, although this discussion focuses on broader issues than just oral-literate differences. Other recent works that apply this literature include Paul J. Achtmeier, "*Omne Verbum Sonat:* The New Testament and the Oral Environment of Late Western Antiquity," *Journal of Biblical Literature* 109 (1990): 3–27; Robert J.

Conners, "Greek Rhetoric and the Transition from Orality," *Philosophy and Rhetoric* 19 (1986): 38–65; Timothy W. Crusius, "Orality in Kenneth Burke's Dialectic," *Philosophy and Rhetoric* 21 (1988): 116–130; Hwa Yol Jung, "Vico's Rhetoric: A Note on Verene's *Vico's Science of the Imagination*," *Philosophy and Rhetoric* 15 (1982): 187–202; Werner H. Kelber, "In the Beginning Were the Words: Apotheosis and Narrative Displacement of the Logos," *Journal of the American Academy of Religion* LVIII (1990): 69–98; William S. Kurz, "Narrative Approaches to Luke Acts," *Biblica* 68 (1987): 195–220; Tony M. Lentz, "Spoken versus Written Inartistic Proof in Athenian Courts," *Philosophy and Rhetoric* 16 (1983): 242–261; Joanne B. Waugh, "Heraclitus: The Postmodern Presocratic?" *Monist* 74 (1991): 605–623; and D. Wiebe, "The Prelogical Mentality Revisited," *Religion* 17 (1987): 29–61. See also my "Sight, Sound, and Epistemology: The Experiential Sources of Ethical Concepts," *Journal of the American Academy of Religion* LXIV (1996): 1–25.

2. For a basic discussion of this work, see Walter J. Ong, S.J., *Orality and Literacy: The Technologizing of the Word* (London: Methuen, 1982), pp. 16–27; the quotation is on p. 20. It is cited from Adam Parry's introduction to Milman Parry, *The Making of Homeric Verse: The Collected Papers of Milman Parry, ed. Adam Parry* (Oxford: Clarendon Press, 1971), p. xix. This work discusses the issues raised here in more detail. See especially Adam Parry's introduction.

3. See Eric A. Havelock, *Preface to Plato* (Cambridge, Mass.: The Belknap Press of Harvard University Press, 1963). Subsequent works by Havelock have continued to develop these ideas. See *Origins of Western Literacy* (Toronto: Ontario Institute for Studies in Education, 1976); *The Greek Concept of Justice: From Its Shadow in Homer to Its Substance in Plato* (Cambridge, Mass.: Harvard University Press, 1978); *The Literate Revolution in Greece and Its Cultural Consequences* (Princeton, N.J.: Princeton University Press, 1982); and *The Muse Learns to Write: Reflections on Orality and Literacy from Antiquity to the Present* (New Haven: Yale University Press, 1986). See also Eric A. Havelock and Jackson P. Herschell, eds., *Communication Arts in the Ancient World* (New York: Hastings House, 1978).

4. Walter J. Ong, S.J., *Ramus, Method, and the Decay of Dialogue* (Cambridge, Mass.: Harvard University Press, 1958). Other important works by Ong include *The Presence of the Word: Some Prolegomena for Cultural and Religious History* (New Haven: Yale University Press, 1967; reprint ed., Minneapolis: University of Minnesota Press, 19??); *Rhetoric, Romance, and Technology: Studies in the Interaction of Expression and Culture* (Ithaca: Cornell University Press, 1971); *Interfaces of the Word: Studies in the Evolution of Consciousness and Culture* (Ithaca: Cornell University Press, 1977); and *Orality and Literacy*.

5. J.C. Carothers, "Culture, Psychiatry, and the Written Word," *Psychiatry* 22 (1959): 307–320.

6. Jack Goody and Ian Watt, "The Consequences of Literacy," *Comparative Studies in Society and History* 5 (1963): 304–345. This article appeared later in

Jack Goody, ed., *Literacy in Traditional Societies*, (Cambridge: Cambridge University Press, 1968), pp. 27–84. Other studies by Goody include *The Domestication of the Savage Mind* (Cambridge: Cambridge University Press, 1977); *The Logic of Writing and the Organization of Society* (Cambridge: Cambridge University Press, 1986); and *The Interface Between the Written and the Oral* (Cambridge: Cambridge University Press, 1987).

7. Albert B. Lord, *The Singer of Tales*, Harvard Studies in Comparative Literature, 24 (Cambridge, Mass.: Harvard University Press, 1960).

8. Boman, *Hebrew Thought Compared with Greek*. The problem of the relative sensory orientations of Hebrew and Greek thought is a complicated one. William M. Ivins, Jr., in *Art and Geometry: A Study in Space Intuitions* (Cambridge, Mass.: Harvard University Press, 1946), argues that the ancient Greeks showed relatively little visual orientation compared to modern Western people, being instead more tactilely oriented. Goody also discusses important effects of literacy and visual orientation in Hebrew thinking; see *The Logic of Writing*, pp. 39–41. Of course, none of these findings are mutually contradictory. It would be quite possible to say that the Greeks were less visually oriented than modern people but more so than the Hebrews, who in turn, although heavily oriented to sound, had been affected more by literacy than, say, tribal societies with no writing at all. On the differences between the Semitic and Greek alphabets and what these differences imply for visual orientation, see below.

9. Claude Levi-Strauss, *The Savage Mind* (Chicago: University of Chicago Press, 1966).

10. Marshall McLuhan, *The Gutenberg Galaxy: The Making of Typographic Man* (Toronto: University of Toronto Press, 1962).

11. See Harvey J. Graff, *The Literacy Myth: Literacy and Social Structure in the Nineteenth-Century City* (New York: Academic Press, 1979); *The Legacies of Literacy: Continuities and Contradictions in Western Culture and Society* (Bloomington: Indiana University Press, 1987); and *The Labyrinths of Literacy: Reflections on Literacy Past and Present* (London: the Falmer Press, 1987). Also see Michael Cole and Sylvia Scribner, *Culture and Thought: A Psychological Introduction* (New York: John Wiley & Sons, 1974), and Sylvia Scribner and Michael Cole, *The Psychology of Literacy* (Cambridge, Mass.: Harvard University Press, 1981). Other works that attempt to develop more complex models of oral-literate differences and interactions include Rosalind Thomas, *Literacy and Orality in Ancient Greece* (Cambridge: Cambridge University Press, 1992); Ruth Finnegan, *Literacy and Orality: Studies in the Technology of Communication* (Oxford: Basil Blackwell, 1988); and Brian V. Street, *Literacy in Theory and Practice* (Cambridge: Cambridge University Press, 1984).

12. Havelock, *The Muse Learns to Write*, pp. 30–33.

13. See Ong, *Presence of the Word*, pp. 49–50.

14. See Ong, *Orality and Literacy*, pp. 31–33, 71–74, and *Presence of the Word*, pp. 111–175. I shall discuss the matter of how sight and sound may be conceptualized in more detail in chapter 4.

15. See Ong, *Orality and Literacy*, pp. 68–69, and Carothers, "Culture, Psychiatry, and the Written Word," pp. 311–312, 314–316.

16. Ong, *Orality and Literacy*, p. 12.

17. See Ong, *Orality and Literacy*, pp. 33–36, and *Presence of the Word*, pp. 22–35.

18. See Ong, *Orality and Literacy*, pp. 57–68.

19. Cole and Scribner, *Culture and Thought*, pp. 126–134.

20. See Ong, *Orality and Literacy*, pp. 57–68, and Havelock's discussion of oral (i.e., poetic) memory in *Preface to Plato*, pp. 36–193.

21. Ong, *Orality and Literacy*, pp. 37–38; the quotations are on p. 37.

22. *Ibid.*, pp. 38–39; the quotation is on p. 38.

23. *Ibid.*, pp. 39–41.

24. *Ibid.*, pp. 41–42.

25. Goody, ed., *Literacy in Traditional Societies*, pp. 30–34.

26. Ong, *Orality and Literacy*, pp. 46–49.

27. *Ibid.*, pp. 42–43.

28. *Ibid.*, pp. 43–45. See also *Presence of the Word*, pp. 195–222. ·

29. Ong, *Orality and Literacy*, pp. 45–46; the quotation is on p. 45. See also Havelock, *Preface to Plato*, pp. 145–160.

30. Ong, *Orality and Literacy*, pp. 49–57. Cole and Scribner argue that the ability to answer intelligence test questions "correctly" is the result of modern methods of schooling, not literacy. See Scribner and Cole, *Psychology of Literacy*, pp. 235–260. This may be true in a sense (we might imagine Plato doing miserably on a modern intelligence test), but modern schools are themselves a product of literacy; therefore literacy remains a fundamental factor.

31. See Ong, *Orality and Literacy*, pp. 38–39. See also Havelock, *Preface to Plato*, pp. 234–253.

32. See Ong, *Orality and Literacy*, pp. 83–93; the quotation is on p. 84. See also Havelock, *Origins of Western Literacy*, especially pp. 9–43.

33. See Ong, *Orality and Literacy*, pp. 88–93, 101–103. See also Havelock, *Origins of Western Literacy*, pp. 22–50; Ong, *Presence of the Word*, pp. 35–47; and Goody, ed., *Literacy in Traditional Societies*, pp. 38–44.

34. Ong, *Orality and Literacy*, p. 91.

35. See Ong, *Orality and Literacy*, 93–101, 103–116, and *Presence of the Word*, pp. 53–63, 76–87.

36. See Ong, *Orality and Literacy*, pp. 117–135, and *Presence of the Word*, pp. 47–53, 63–76. See also the discussions in Elizabeth L. Eisenstein, *The Printing Press as an Agent of Change: Communications and Cultural Transformation in Early Modern Europe*, 2 vols. (Cambridge: Cambridge University Press, 1979).

37. See Ong, *Orality and Literacy*, pp. 135–138, and *Presence of the Word*, pp. 87–92, 256–260, 290–291, 301–303. The effect of television and other electronic media on emotional orientations seems to be rather complicated. Although the tendency toward neutralizing emotions that Ong mentions can be seen in certain contexts, television on the whole seems to be a very emotionally charged medium. Ong argues that new media of communication can have the paradoxical effect of actually intensifying certain aspects of older communicative orientations, even while transforming others. For example, the rhetorical tradition, which intensified the kind of formal argumentation found in oral cultures, arose during the early stages of literacy, since writing allowed people to analyze the process of argumentation, something that could not be done to any great degree in an entirely oral situation, and thus expand the possibilities inherent in oral debate. Similarly, although writing and printing ultimately have tended to tone down the agonistic element of debate (by abstracting knowledge from the frequently contentious lifeworld), the earliest stages of print literacy saw the level of vitriolic argument reach a historical maximum. What Ong initially took to be the tendency of the electronic media to neutralize the lifeworld may be another example of this.

38. A good overview of the subject matter can be found in a conversation between Camille Paglia and Neil Postman, "She Wants Her TV! He Wants His Book!" *Harper's*, March 1991, pp. 44–55. Postman has written extensively about television in a variety of contexts. See *Amusing Ourselves to Death: Public Discourse in the Age of Show Business* (New York: Viking, 1985); *Conscientious Objections: Stirring Up Trouble About Language, Technology, and Education* (New York: Alfred A. Knopf, 1988); and *Teaching as a Conserving Activity* (New York: Delacorte Press, 1979).

39. See Ong, *Presence of the Word*, pp. 166–169.

40. See Ong, *Orality and Literacy*, pp. 33–36, 57–62, 69–71.

41. See Goody, *The Domestication of the Savage Mind*, especially pp. 52–73.

42. See Ong, *Orality and Literacy*, pp. 117–123, and *Presence of the Word*, pp. 169–175.

43. See Ong, *Orality and Literacy*, pp. 103–105. Elsewhere, Ong notes that the majority of our analytical vocabulary is etymologically related to vision; see *Interfaces of the Word*, pp. 132–137. John Verhaar observes that we inevitably use visual/spatial categories when we attempt to think analytically; see *Some Relations Between Perception, Speech, and Thought: A Contribution Towards the Phenomenology of Speech* (Assen, Netherlands: Van Gorcum, 1963), pp. 36–43.

44. See Ong, *Presence of the Word*, pp. 222–231; *Orality and Literacy*, pp. 131–132; *Presence of the Word*, pp. 71–74; and McLuhan, *Gutenberg Galaxy*, pp. 22–23.

45. Ong, *Orality and Literacy*, pp. 132–135; the quotation is on pp. 132–33.

46. *Ibid.*, pp. 134–135.

47. See Goody, ed., *Literacy in Traditional Societies*, pp. 45–49.

48. *Ibid.*, pp. 61–63.

49. Ong, *Orality and Literacy*, pp. 54–55. See also Goody, ed., *Literacy in Traditional Societies*, pp. 61–63.

50. Ong, *Orality and Literacy*, pp. 151–155, 69–71.

51. This is an observation by George Steiner, cited in Ong, *Orality and Literacy*, pp. 130–131.

52. Ong, *Orality and Literacy*, p. 131.

53. See the essays by Postman cited above, especially *Amusing Ourselves to Death*, pp. 64–80. The thesis that a loss of analytical capacities occurs in a culture dominated by television is supported by recent physiological findings. According to David Gress, "Psychologists have pointed out that a culture based on reading demands the exercise—and hence refinement—of more complex, higher-order brain functions than are needed to absorb the messages of purely visual images or of sound." See "Diagnosis of a 'Kulturkampf'," *The New Criterion*, May 1987, p. 28.

54. See Joshua Meyrowitz, *No Sense of Place: The Impact of Electronic Media on Social Behavior* (New York: Oxford University Press, 1985), especially pp. 226–263.

55. See Postman, *Teaching as a Conserving Activity*, pp. 47–70 for a discussion of the emotional effects of television.

56. Paglia agrees in large part with Postman's characterization of post-literate consciousness, but thinks the irrationalism brought about by television is

acceptable because the world is, indeed, irrational. Paglia actually argues that the emerging culture is in certain ways a return to earlier preliterate culture, which she claims is based upon images, not words. Clearly she has in mind here *written* words, not spoken words. Although preliterate cultures make some use of images, their fundamental orientation, as we have seen, is to sound as exemplified by the spoken word. Hence it would be incorrect to argue (on this basis at least) that a postliterate visual culture would be very similar to a preliterate culture.

57. See Havelock, *Preface to Plato*, pp. 234–253.

58. *Ibid.*, pp. 254–275; the quotation is on p. 270.

59. Ong, *Presence of the Word*, p. 73.

60. *Ibid.*, p. 118.

61. See chapter 5.

62. Ong, *Orality and Literacy*, p. 167.

63. *Ibid.*, pp. 101–103.

64. *Ibid.*, pp. 168–169. Actually, our discussion of the electronic media would tend to indicate that deconstruction is experientially linked to television, not writing.

65. See Poteat, *Polanyian Meditations: In Search of a Post-Critical Logic*, especially pp. 27–103.

66. Rush Rees, ed., *Recollections of Wittgenstein* (Oxford: Oxford University Press, 1984), p. 161.

4. Beyond Objectivism: The Logic of the Speech Act

1. Poteat has coined the term "mindbody" to emphasize the unity of "mind" and "body" in *Polanyian Meditations: In Search of a Post-Critical Logic.*

2. Poteat, *Polanyian Meditations*, p. 57.

3. See Hans Jonas, *The Phenomenon of Life: Toward a Philosophical Biology* (New York: Harper & Row, 1966; rpt. ed., Chicago: Phoenix Books, University of Chicago Press, 1982), pp. 135–151.

4. Poteat, Polanyian Meditations, pp. 65–66.

5. See the discussion of Havelock's interpretation of Plato in chapter 3.

6. Poteat, *Polanyian Meditations*, p. 62.

7. *Ibid.*, p. 63.

8. *Ibid.*, pp. 70–80; the quotation is on p. 80.

9. *Ibid.*, pp. 80–86.

10. *Ibid.*, pp. 86–92.

11. *Ibid.*, p. 91.

12. *Ibid.*, p. 91.

13. *Ibid.*, pp. 59–60.

14. *Ibid.*, p. 95.

15. Wittgenstein, *On Certainty*, para. 231.

16. See Ong, *The Presence of the Word: Some Prolegomena for Cultural and Religious History* pp. 162–167; the quotations are on p. 163 and p. 164.

17. Jonas, *Phenomenon of Life*, p. 138.

18. See Poteat, "Persons and Places: Paradigms in Communication," in *Art and Religion as Communication*, pp. 175–195; the first three quotations are from p. 182, the last from p. 185.

19. Peter Strawson argues that a purely auditory concept of space is impossible, but this does not really affect the arguments of Ong and Poteat, since they are not talking about a "purely auditory" concept of space but rather an inhabited space, dependent on kinaesthetic experience as well, which is ultimately best understood through sound. See Peter Strawson, *Individuals: An Essay in Descriptive Metaphysics* (London: Methuen, 1959), pp. 59–86.

20. See Fred Dallmyr, *Language and Politics: Why Does Language Matter to Political Philosophy?* (Notre Dame: University of Notre Dame Press, 1984), pp. 106–109; the quotation is on p. 109.

21. Wittgenstein, *Philosophical Investigations*, p. 59e.

22. See Eric Partridge, *Origins: A Short Etymological Dictionary of Modern English* (New York: Macmillan, 1958), pp. 417–418.

23. See Poteat, *Polanyian Meditations*, pp. 94–97, 127–128.

24. See Niebuhr's discussion in *The Nature and Destiny of Man*, vol. I: Human Nature, pp. 150–264; the quotation is on p. 241.

25. Hannah Pitkin, *Wittgenstein and Justice: On the Significance of Ludwig Wittgenstein for Social and Political Thought* (Berkeley: University of California Press, 1972), p. 334.

26. See chapter 5.

5. Speech, Place, and Narrative Practice

1. MacIntyre, *Whose Justice? Which Rationality?*, p. 141.

2. *Ibid.*, pp. 140–141.

3. Arendt, *The Human Condition*, pp. 196–197.

4. *Ibid.*, p. 198.

5. *Ibid.*, p. 198.

6. Poteat, *Polanyian Meditations: In Search of a Post-Critical Logic*, p. 127.

7. Note that objectivist accounts of scientific knowledge will typically make one of these mistakes.

8. Poteat, "Persons and Places," in *Art and Religion as Communication*, p. 182.

9. Arendt, *Human Condition*, p. 199.

10. Eric Auerbach, *Mimesis: The Representation of Reality in Western Literature*, trans. Willard R. Trask (Princeton: Princeton University Press, 1953), p. 8.

11. *Ibid.*, p. 9.

12. *Ibid.*, p. 10.

13. *Ibid.*, p. 10.

14. *Ibid.*, p. 12.

15. John W. Dixon, Jr., *The Physiology of Faith: A Theory of Theological Relativity* (New York: Harper & Row, 1979), p. 260.

16. *Ibid.*, p. 261.

17. *Ibid.*, p. 261.

18. Polanyi, *Knowing and Being: Essays by Michael Polanyi*, p. 149.

19. MacIntyre, pp. 186–187.

20. *Ibid.*, pp. 210–203.

21. *Ibid.*, p. 187.

22. *Ibid.*, p. 191.

23. Habermas's main discussion is in "What is Universal Pragmatics?" in *Communication and the Evolution of Society*, trans. Thomas McCarthy (Boston: Beacon Press, 1979), pp. 1–68. See also McCarthy's discussion in *The Critical*

Theory of Jurgen Habermas (Cambridge: MIT Press, 1978), pp. 272–333, especially pp. 291–310. For more recent elaborations of these basic themes, see *The Theory of Communicative Action*, vol. 1: *Reason and the Rationalization of Society*, trans. Thomas McCarthy (Boston: Beacon Press, 1984); *The Theory of Communicative Action*, vol. 2: *Lifeworld and System: A Critique of Functionalist Reason*, trans. Thomas McCarthy (Boston: Beacon Press, 1987); *Moral Consciousness and Communicative Action*, trans. Christian Lenhardt and Shierry Weber Nicholson, intro. Thomas McCarthy (Cambridge: MIT Press, 1990), especially pp. 43–115; and *Justification and Application: Remarks on Discourse Ethics*, trans. Ciaran Cronin (Cambridge: MIT Press, 1993).

24. Richard J. Mouw, "Alasdair MacIntyre on Reformation Ethics," *Journal of Religious Ethics* 13 (Fall 1985): 243–257.

25. *Ibid.*, pp. 246–247.

26. *Ibid.*, p. 250.

27. *Ibid.*, pp. 249–250.

28. *Ibid.*, pp. 250–256.

29. Poteat, *Polanyian Meditations*, p. 271.

30. Poteat, "Persons and Places," p. 182.

31. Polanyi, *Personal Knowlege: Towards a Post-Critical Philosophy*, pp. 207–208.

32. See "Persons and Places," pp. 187–188.

33. Alexander Schmemann, *The Eucharist* (Crestwood, N.Y.: St. Vladimir's Seminary Press, 1977), p. 139. Quoted in Elizabeth Newman, "A Hermeneutics of Worship" (Ph.D. dissertation, Duke University, 1990), p. 187.

34. Newman, "Hermeneutics of Worship," pp. 258–259.

35. Walter Brueggeman, *Hopeful Imagination: Prophetic Voices in Exile* (Philadelphia: Fortress Press, 1986), p. 96.

36. *Ibid.*, p. 16.

37. Alasdair MacIntyre, "Epistemological Crises, Dramatic Narrative and the Philosophy of Science," *Monist* 60:4 (October 1977): 453–472; the quotation is on p. 453.

38. *Ibid.*, p. 455.

39. *Ibid.*, p. 458.

40. *Ibid.*, pp. 460-461.

41. Alasdair MacIntyre, "Is Patriotism a Virtue?" The Lindley Lecture, University of Kansas, March 26, 1984 (Lawrence: Department of Philosophy, University of Kansas, 1984), pp. 9–10.

42. See MacIntyre, *After Virtue*, pp. 215–220; the quotation is on p. 219.

43. *Ibid.*, pp. 219–225.

Conclusion

1. See Habermas, *Theory and Practice*, pp. 47–49; the quotation is on p. 48.

2. See Arendt, *The Human Condition*, especially pp. 22–78.

3. See Peter Berger, "On the Obsolescence of the Concept of Honour," in *Liberalism and Its Critics*, ed. Michael Sandel (New York: New York University Press, 1984), pp. 149–158.

4. *Ibid.*, pp. 157–158.

5. *Ibid.*, p.158.

6. Rifkin, *The End of Work: The Decline of the Global Labor Force and the Dawn of the Post-Market Era.*

BIBLIOGRAPHY

Achtemeier, Paul J. *"Omne Verbum Sonat:* The New Testament and the Oral Environment of Late Western Antiquity." *Journal of Biblical Literature* 109 (1990): 3–27.

Angus, Ian, and Lenore Langsdorf, eds. *The Critical Turn: Rhetoric and Philosophy in Postmodern Discourse.* Carbondale, Ill.: Southern Illinois University Press, 1993.

Arendt, Hannah. *The Human Condition.* Chicago: University of Chicago Press, 1958.

Auerbach, Eric. *Mimesis: The Representation of Reality in Western Literature.* Translated by Willard R. Trask. Princeton: Princeton University Press, 1953.

Austin, J. L. *How To Do Things With Words,* 2nd ed. Edited by J. O. Urmson and Marina Sbisa. Cambridge, Mass.: Harvard University Press, 1962.

Ayer, A. J., ed. *Logical Positivism.* New York: The Free Press, 1959.

Ball, Terence, ed. *Idioms of Inquiry: Critique and Renewal in Political Science.* Albany: SUNY Press, 1987.

———. *Transforming Political Discourse: Political Theory and Critical Conceptual History.* London: Basil Blackwell, 1988.

Barber, Benjamin R. *Strong Democracy: Participatory Politics for a New Age.* Berkeley: University of California Press, 1984.

Baynes, Kenneth, James Bohman, and Thomas McCarthy, eds. *After Philosophy: End or Transformation?* Cambridge, Mass.: MIT Press, 1987.

Beiner, Ronald. *Political Judgement.* Chicago: University of Chicago Press, 1983.

———, ed. *Theorizing Citizenship.* Albany: SUNY Press, 1995.

Bell, Daniel. *Communitarianism and Its Critics.* Oxford: Clarendon Press, 1993.

Bell, Daniel. *The Cultural Contradictions of Capitalism.* New York: Basic Books, 1976.

Bellah, Robert N. "Civil Religion in America." In *American Civil Religion,* pp. 21–44. Edited by Russell E. Richey and Donald G. Jones. New York: Harper & Row, 1974.

———, et al. *Habits of the Heart: Individualism and Commitment in American Life.* New York: Harper & Row, 1985.

Berlin, Isaiah. *Four Essays On Liberty.* Oxford: Oxford University Press, 1969.

Bernstein, Richard J. *Beyond Objectivism and Relativism: Science, Hermeneutics, and Praxis.* Philadelphia: University of Pennsylvania Press, 1988.

———, ed. and intro. *Habermas and Modernity.* Cambridge, Mass.: MIT Press, 1985.

Bloom, Allan. *The Closing of the American Mind.* New York: Simon & Schuster, 1987.

Boman, Thorlief. *Hebrew Thought Compared with Greek.* Translated by Jules C. Moreau. New York: W. W. Norton, 1960.

Bowers, C. A. *Elements of a Post-Liberal Theory of Education.* New York: Teacher's College Press, 1987.

Brueggemann, Walter. *Hopeful Imagination: Prophetic Voices in Exile.* Philadelphia: Fortress Press, 1986.

Budziszewski, J. *The Resurrection of Nature: Political Theory and The Human Character.* Ithaca: Cornell University Press, 1986.

Burtt, Edwin Arthur. *The Metaphysical Foundations of Modern Physical Science: A Historical and Cultural Essay.* London: Routledge and Kegan Paul, 1924.

Carothers, J. C. "Culture, Psychiatry, and the Written Word." *Psychiatry* 22 (1959): 307–320.

Cavell, Stanley. *Must We Mean What We Say? A Book of Essays.* Cambridge: Cambridge University Press, 1969.

Cole, Michael, and Sylvia Scribner. *Culture and Thought: A Psychological Introduction.* New York: John Wiley & Sons, 1974.

Conners, Robert J. "Greek Rhetoric and the Transition From Orality." *Philosophy and Rhetoric* 19 (1986): 38–65.

Crusius, Timothy W. "Orality in Kenneth Burke's Dialectic." *Philosophy and Rhetoric* 21 (1988): 116–130.

Dallmyr, Fred. *Language and Politics: Why Does Language Matter to Political Philosophy?* Notre Dame: University of Notre Dame Press, 1984.

Daly, Markate, ed. *Communitarianism: A New Public Ethics.* Belmont, Cal.: Wadsworth Publishing Co., 1994.

Derrida, Jacques. *Of Grammatology.* Translated by Gayatri Chakravorty Spivak. Baltimore: Johns Hopkins University Press, 1976.

————. *Speech and Phenomena: And Other Essays on Husserl's Theory of Signs.* Translated by David B. Allison. Evanston: Northwestern University Press, 1973

Dixon, John W., Jr. *The Physiology of Faith: A Theory of Theological Relativity.* New York: Harper & Row, 1979.

Duhem, Pierre. *The Aim and Structure of Physical Theory.* Foreward by Prince Louis de Broglie. Translated by Philip D. Wiener. Princeton: Princeton University Press, 1954.

Eisenstein, Elizabeth L. *The Printing Press as an Agent of Change: Communications and Cultural Transformations in Early Modern Europe,* 2 vols. Cambridge: Cambridge University Press, 1979.

Finnegan, Ruth. *Literacy and Orality: Studies in the Technology of Communication.* Oxford: Basil Blackwell, 1988.

Finnis, John. *Natural Law and Natural Rights.* Oxford: Clarendon Press, 1980.

Fleischacker, Samuel. *The Ethics of Culture.* Ithaca: Cornell University Press, 1994.

Foster, M. B. "The Christian Doctrine of Creation and the Rise of Modern Science." *Mind* 43 (1934): 447–468.

————. "Christian Theology and Modern Science of Nature—I." *Mind* 44 (1935): 439–466.

————. "Christian Theology and Modern Science of Nature—II." *Mind* 45 (1936): 1–27.

Foucault, Michel. *Discipline and Punish: The Birth of the Prison.* Translated by Allan Sheridan. New York: Vintage Books, 1979.

————. *The History of Sexuality.* Vol. I: *An Introduction.* Translated by Robert Hurley. New York: Random House, 1979.

————. *Power/Knowledge.* Edited by Colin Gordon. New York: Pantheon Books, 1980.

Fukuyama, Francis. "The End of History?" *The National Interest* (Summer 1989): 3–35.

Gibbons, Michael. T., ed. *Interpreting Politics.* New York: New York University Press, 1987.

Gillespie, Michael Allen. *Hegel, Heidegger, and the Ground of History.* Chicago: University of Chicago Press, 1984.

Glendon, Mary Ann, and David Blankenhorn, eds. *Seedbeds of Virtue: Sources of Competence, Character, and Citizenship in American Society.* Lanham, Md.: Madison Books, 1995.

Goody, Jack. *The Domestication of the Savage Mind*. Cambridge: Cambridge University Press, 1977.

———. *The Interface Between the Written and the Oral*. Cambridge: Cambridge University Press, 1987.

———, ed. *Literacy in Traditional Societies*. Cambridge: Cambridge University Press, 1968.

———. *The Logic of Writing and the Organization of Society*. Cambridge: Cambridge University Press, 1986.

———, and Ian Watt. "The Consequences of Literacy." *Comparative Studies in Society and History* 5 (1963): 304–345.

Gould, Carol C. *Rethinking Democracy: Freedom and Social Cooperation in Politics, Economy, and Society*. Cambridge: Cambridge University Press, 1988.

Graff, Harvey J. *The Labyrinths of Literacy: Reflections on Literacy Past and Present*. London: The Falmer Press, 1987.

———. *The Legacies of Literacy: Continuities and Contradictions in Western Culture and Society*. Bloomington: Indiana University Press, 1987.

———. *The Literacy Myth: Literacy and Social Structure in the Nineteenth-Century City*. New York: Academic Press, 1979.

Gress, David. "Diagnosis of a 'Kulturkampf.'" *The New Criterion* (May 1987): 28.

Gutmann, Amy. "Communitarian Critics of Liberalism." *Philosophy and Public Affairs* 14 (1985): 308–322.

Haan, Norma, *et al.*, ed. *Social Science as Moral Inquiry*. New York: Columbia University Press, 1983.

Habermas, Jürgen. *Communication and the Evolution of Society*. Translated by Thomas McCarthy. Boston: Beacon Press, 1979.

———. *Justification and Application: Remarks on Discourse Ethics*. Translated by Ciaran Cronin. Cambridge, Mass.: MIT Press, 1993

———. *Knowledge and Human Interests*. Translated by Jeremy J. Shapiro. Boston: Beacon Press, 1971.

———. *Legitimation Crisis*. Translated by Thomas McCarthy. Boston: Beacon Press, 1975.

———. *Moral Consciousness and Communicative Action*. Translated by Christian Lenhardt and Shierry Weber Nicholsen. Introduction by Thomas McCarthy. Cambridge, Mass.: MIT Press, 1990.

———. *The Philosophical of Discourse of Modernity: Twelve Lectures.* Translated by Frederick Lawrence. Cambridge, Mass.: MIT Press, 1987.

———. *Postmetaphysical Thinking: Philosophical Essays.* Translated by William Mark Hohengarten. Cambridge, Mass.: MIT Press, 1992.

———. *Theory and Practice.* Translated by John Viertel. Boston: Beacon Press, 1973.

———. *The Theory of Communicative Action,* 2 vols. Translated by Thomas McCarthy. Boston: Beacon Press, 1984–87.

Hallowell, John H. *The Decline of Liberalism as an Ideology.* Berkeley: University of California Press, 1943.

Hanson, Norwood Russell. *Patterns of Discovery: An Inquiry Into the Conceptual Foundations of Science.* Cambridge: Cambridge University Press, 1958.

Hauerwas, Stanley. *A Community of Character: Toward a Constructive Christian Social Ethic.* Notre Dame: University of Notre Dame Press, 1981.

———. *The Peaceable Kingdom: A Primer in Christian Ethics.* Notre Dame: University of Notre Dame Press, 1983.

———. *Suffering Presence: Theological Reflections on Medicine, the Mentally Handicapped, and the Church.* Notre Dame: University of Notre Dame Press, 1986.

———, and L. Gregory Jones, eds. *Why Narrative? Readings In Narrative Theology.* Grand Rapids: William B. Eerdmans, 1989.

———, et al. *Truthfulness and Tragedy: Further Investigations in Christian Ethics.* Notre Dame: University of Notre Dame Press, 1977.

Havelock, Eric A. *The Greek Conception of Justice: From Its Shadow in Homer to Its Substance in Plato.* Cambridge, Mass.: Harvard University Press, 1978.

———. *The Literate Revolution in Greece and Its Cultural Consequences.* Princeton: Princeton University Press, 1982.

———. *The Muse Learns to Write: Reflections on Orality and Literacy From Antiquity to the Present.* New Haven: Yale University Press, 1986.

———. *Origins of Western Literacy.* Toronto: The Ontario Institute for Studies in Education, 1976.

———. *Preface to Plato.* Cambridge, Mass.: The Belknap Press of Harvard University Press, 1963.

———, and Jackson B. Hershbell, eds. *Communication Arts in the Ancient World.* New York: Hastings House, 1978.

Heidegger, Martin. *Basic Writings*. Edited by David Ferrel Krell. New York: Harper & Row, 1977.

———. *Nietzsche*. Vol. 4: *Nihilism*. Translated by Frank A. Capuzzi. Edited by David Farrell Krell. San Francisco: Harper & Row, 1982.

Hiley, David R., James F. Bohman, and Richard Shusterman, eds. The *Interpretive Turn: Philosophy, Science, and Culture*. Ithaca: Cornell University Press, 1991.

Innis, Harold A. *Art and Geometry: A Study in Space Intuitions*. Cambridge, Mass.: Harvard University Press, 1946.

———. *The Bias of Communication*. Toronto: University of Toronto Press, 1951.

Ivins, William M., Jr. *Prints and Visual Communication*. New York: Da Capo Press, 1969.

Jonas, Hans. *The Phenomenon of Life: Toward a Philosophical Biology*. New York: Harper & Row, 1966; reprint ed., Chicago: Phoenix Books, University of Chicago Press, 1982.

Jung, Hwa Yol. "Vico's Rhetoric: A Note on Verene's *Vico's Science of the Imagination*." *Philosophy and Rhetoric* 15 (1982): 187–202.

Kelber, Werner H. "In the Beginning Were the Words: The Apotheosis and Narrative Displacement of the Logos." *Journal of the American Academy of Religion* LVIII (1990): 69–98.

Kuhn, Thomas S. *The Structure of Scientific Revolutions*, 2nd ed. Chicago: University of Chicago Press, 1970.

Kurz, William S. "Narrative Approaches to Luke-Acts." *Biblica* 68 (1987): 195–220.

Lakatos, Imre, and Alan Musgrave, eds. *Criticism and the Growth of Knowledge*. Proceedings of the International Colloquium in the Philosophy of Science, London, 1965, vol. 4. Cambridge: Cambridge University Press, 1970.

Langford, Thomas A., and William H. Poteat, eds. *Intellect and Hope: Essays in the Thought of Michael Polanyi*. Durham: Duke University Press, 1968.

Langsdorf, Lenore, and Andrew R. Smith, eds. *Recovering Pragmatism's Voice: The Classical Tradition, Rorty, and the Philosophy of Communication*. Albany: SUNY Press, 1995.

Lasch, Christopher. *The Culture of Narcissism: American Life in an Age of Diminishing Expectations*. New York: W. W. Norton, 1978.

Lash, Scott, and John Urry. *The End of Organized Capitalism*. Madison: University of Wisconsin Press, 1987.

Lentz, Tony M. "Spoken versus Written Inartistic Proof in Athenian Courts." *Philosophy and Rhetoric* 16 (1983): 242–261.

Levi-Strauss, Claude. *The Savage Mind.* Chicago: University of Chicago Press, 1966.

Lindblom, Charles E. "The Market as Prison." *Journal of Politics* 44 (1982): 324–336.

Lord, Albert B. *The Singer of Tales.* Harvard Studies in Comparative Literature, 24. Cambridge, Mass.: Harvard University Press, 1960.

Lowi, Theodore J. *The End of Liberalism: The Second Republic of the United States,* 2nd ed. New York: W. W. Norton, 1979.

Lyotard, Jean-Francois. *The Postmodern Condition: A Report on Knowledge.* Translated by Geoff Bennington and Brian Massumi. Minneapolis: University of Minnesota Press, 1984.

MacIntyre, Alasdair. *After Virtue: A Study in Moral Theory,* 2nd ed. Notre Dame: University of Notre Dame Press, 1984.

———. *Against the Self-Images of the Age: Essays on Ideology and Philosophy.* Notre Dame: University of Notre Dame Press, 1978.

———. "Epistemological Crises, Dramatic Narrative and the Philosophy of Science." *Monist* 60 (1977): 453–472.

———. *Is Patriotism A Virtue?* The Lindley Lecture, University of Kansas, March 26, 1984. Lawrence: Department of Philosophy, University of Kansas, 1984.

———. *A Short History of Ethics.* New York: Collier Books, Macmillan, 1966.

———. *Three Rival Versions of Moral Enquiry: Encyclopaedia, Genealogy, and Tradition.* Notre Dame: University of Notre Dame Press, 1990.

———. *Whose Justice? Which Rationality?* Notre Dame: University of Notre Dame Press, 1988.

Marsh, James L. *Critique, Action, and Liberation.* Albany: SUNY Press, 1995.

McCarthy, Thomas. *The Critical Theory of Jurgen Habermas.* Cambridge, Mass.: MIT Press, 1978.

McLuhan, Marshall. *The Gutenberg Galaxy: The Making of Typographic Man.* Toronto: University of Toronto Press, 1962.

Melzer, Arthur M., Jerry Weinberger, and M. Richard Zinman, eds. *History and the Idea of Progress.* Ithaca: Cornell University Press, 1995.

Meyrowitz, Joshua. *No Sense of Place: The Impact of Electronic Media on Social Behavior.* Oxford: Oxford University Press, 1985.

Midgley, Mary. *Can't We Make Moral Judgements?* New York: St. Martins Press, 1991.

Mouw, Richard J. "Alasdair MacIntyre on Reformation Ethics." *Journal of Religious Ethics* 13 (1985): 243–257.

Mulhall, Stephen, and Adam Swift. *Liberals and Communitarians*. Oxford: Blackwell, 1992.

Nathanson, Stephen. "In Defense of 'Moderate Patriotism.'" *Ethics* 99 (1989): 535–552.

Newman, Elizabeth. "A Hermeneutics of Worship." Ph.D. dissertation, Duke University, 1990.

Niebuhr, Reinhold. *The Nature and Destiny of Man: A Christian Interpretation.* Vol. I: *Human Nature*. New York: Charles Scribner's Sons, 1941.

Nisbet, Robert. *The Quest for Community: A Study in the Ethics of Order and Freedom.* Oxford: Oxford University Press, 1953.

Ong, Walter J., S. J. *Interfaces of the Word: Studies in the Evolution of Consciousness and Culture*. Ithaca: Cornell University Press, 1977.

————. *Orality and Literacy: The Technologizing of the Word.* London: Methuen, 1982.

————. *The Presence of the Word: Some Prolegomena for Cultural and Religious History.* New Haven: Yale University Press, 1967. Reprint ed., Minneapolis: University of Minnesota Press, 1981.

————. *Ramus, Method, and the Decay of Dialogue: From the Art of Discourse to the Art of Reason.* Cambridge, Mass.: Harvard University Press, 1958.

————. *Rhetoric, Romance, and Technology: Studies in the Interaction of Expression and Culture.* Ithaca: Cornell University Press, 1971.

Parry, Milman. *The Making of Homeric Verse: The Collected Papers of Milman Parry.* Edited by Adam Parry. Oxford: Clarendon Press, 1971.

Partridge, Eric. *Origins: A Short Etymological Dictionary of Modern English.* New York: Macmillan, 1958.

Phillips, Derek L. *Looking Backward: A Critical Appraisal of Communitarian Thought.* Princeton: Princeton University Press, 1993

Phillips, Kevin. *The Politics of Rich and Poor: Wealth and the American Electorate in the Reagan Aftermath.* New York: Random House, 1990.

Pitkin, Hanna Fenichel. *Wittgenstein and Justice: On the Significance of Ludwig Wittgenstein for Social and Political Thought.* Berkeley: University of California Press, 1972.

Polanyi, Michael. *Knowing and Being: Essays by Michael Polanyi.* Edited by Marjorie Grene. Chicago: University of Chicago Press, 1969.

———. *The Logic of Liberty: Reflections and Rejoinders.* London: Routledge and Kegan Paul, 1951.

———. *Personal Knowledge: Towards a Post-Critical Philosophy.* Chicago: University of Chicago Press, 1958.

———. *Science, Faith and Society.* Chicago: University of Chicago Press, 1946.

———. *The Study of Man.* Chicago: University of Chicago Press, 1959.

———. *The Tacit Dimension.* Garden City, N.Y.: Doubleday, 1966.

Popper, Karl. *The Logic of Scientific Discovery.* New York: Harper and Row, 1959.

Postman, Neil. *Amusing Ourselves to Death: Public Discourse in the Age of Show Business.* New York: Viking, 1985.

———. *Conscientious Objections: Stirring Up Trouble About Language, Technology, and Education.* New York: Alfred A Knopf, 1988.

———. *Teaching as a Conserving Activity.* New York: Delacorte Press, 1979.

Poteat, William H. "Persons and Places." In *Art and Religion as Communication,* pp. 175–195. Edited by James Waddell and F. W. Dilliston. Atlanta: John Knox Press, 1974.

———. *Polanyian Meditations: In Search of a Post-Critical Logic.* Durham: Duke University Press, 1985.

Rawls, John. *A Theory of Justice.* Cambridge, Mass.: The Belknap Press of Harvard University Press, 1971.

Rees, Rush, ed. *Recollections of Wittgenstein.* Oxford: Oxford University Press, 1984.

Reich, Robert. *The Work of Nations: Preparing Ourselves for Twenty-First Century Capitalism.* New York: Alfred A. Knopf, 1991.

Riesman, David. *The Lonely Crowd: A Study of the Changing American Character.* New Haven: Yale University Press, 1961.

Rifkin, Jeremy. *The End of Work: The Decline of the Global Labor Force and the Dawn of the Post-Market Era.* New York: G. P. Putnam's Sons, 1995.

Rorty, Richard. "The Priority of Democracy to Philosophy." In *The Virginia Statute for Religious Freedom,* pp. 257–282. Edited by Merrill Peterson and Robert Vaughan. Cambridge: Cambridge University Press, 1987.

Sandel, Michael, ed. *Liberalism and Its Critics.* New York: New York University Press, 1984.

————. *Liberalism and the Limits of Justice*. Cambridge: Cambridge University Press, 1982.

Scribner, Sylvia, and Michael Cole. *The Psychology of Literacy*. Cambridge, Mass.: Harvard University Press, 1981.

Sennett, Richard. *The Fall of Public Man: On the Social Psychology of Capitalism*. New York: Random House, 1974.

Shapiro, Michael J. *Language and Politics*. New York: New York University Press, 1984.

"She Wants Her TV! He Wants His Book!" *Harper's* (March 1991): 44–55.

Spragens, Thomas A., Jr. *The Irony of Liberal Reason*. Chicago: University of Chicago Press, 1981.

————. *The Politics of Motion: The World of Thomas Hobbes*. Foreward by Antony Flew. Lexington: The University Press of Kentucky, 1973.

————. *Reason and Democracy*. Durham: Duke University Press, 1990.

Strauss, Leo. *Natural Right and History*. Chicago: University of Chicago Press, 1950.

Strawson, Peter. *Individuals: An Essay in Descriptive Metaphysics*. London: Methuen, 1959.

Street, Brian V. *Literacy in Theory and Practice*. Cambridge: Cambridge University Press, 1984.

Sullivan, William M. *Reconstructing Public Philosophy*. Berkeley: University of California Press, 1986.

Tannen, Deborah, ed. *Spoken and Written Language: Exploring Orality and Literacy*. Norwood, N.J.: Ablex Publishing, 1982.

Taylor, Charles. *Philosophical Papers*, 2 vols. Cambridge: Cambridge University Press, 1985.

————. *Sources of the Self: The Making of the Modern Identity*. Cambridge, Mass.: Harvard University Press, 1989.

Thomas, Rosalind. *Literacy and Orality in Ancient Greece*. Cambridge: Cambridge University Press, 1992.

Thompson, John B., and David Held, eds. *Habermas: Critical Debates*. Cambridge, Mass.: MIT Press, 1982.

Toulmin, Stephen. *The Philosophy of Science: An Introduction*. London: Hutchinson University Library, 1953.

Tully, James. "Wittgenstein and Political Philosophy: Understanding Practices of Critical Reflection." *Political Theory* 17 (1989): 172–204.

Unger, Roberto Mangabeira. *Knowledge and Politics.* New York: The Free Press, 1975.

Verhaar, John W. M., S. J. *Some Relations Between Perception, Speech and Thought: A Contribution Towards the Phenomenology of Speech.* Assen, Netherlands: Van Gorcum, 1963.

Voegelin, Eric. "Necessary Moral Bases for Communication in a Democracy." In *Problems of Communication in a Pluralistic Society,* Papers delivered at a conference on Communication, the fourth in a series of Anniversary Celebrations, March 20, 21, 22, and 23, 1956, pp. 53–68. Milwaukee: The Marquette University Press, 1956.

———. *The New Science of Politics: An Introduction.* Chicago: University of Chicago Press, 1952.

———. *Order and History,* 5 vols. Baton Rouge: LSU Press, 1957–87.

Wadell, Paul J., C. P. *Friendship and the Moral Life.* Notre Dame: University of Notre Dame Press, 1989.

Walhout, Clarence. "Christianity, History, and Literary Criticism: Walter Ong's Global Vision." *Journal of the American Academy of Religion* LXII (1994): 435–460.

Waugh, Joanne, B. "Heraclitus: The Postmodern Presocratic?" *Monist* 74 (1991): 605–623.

Walzer, Michael. *Spheres of Justice.* New York: Basic Books, 1983.

Whitehead, Alfred North. *Science and the Modern World.* New York: Macmillan, 1925.

Wiebe, D. "The Prelogical Mentality Revisited." *Religion* 17 (1987): 29–61.

Wilson, Bryan R., ed. *Rationality.* New York: Harper & Row, 1970.

Winch, Peter. *The Idea of a Social Science and Its Relation to Philosophy.* London: Routledge & Kegan Paul, 1958.

Wittgenstein, Ludwig. *On Certainty.* Edited by G.E.M. Anscombe and G. H. von Wright. Translated by Denis Paul and G. E. M. Anscombe. New York: Harper & Row, 1969.

———. *Philosophical Investigations,* 3rd ed. Translated by G. E. M. Anscombe. New York: Macmillan, 1958.

Wolin, Sheldon. "Paradigms and Political Theories." In *Politics and Experience: Essays Presented to Michael Oakeshott*, pp. 125–152. Edited by P. King and B. C. Parekh. Cambridge: Cambridge University Press, 1968.

———. "Political Theory as a Vocation." *American Political Science Review* 63 (1969): 1062–1082.

———. *Politics and Vision: Continuity and Innovation in Western Political Thought.* Boston: Little, Brown and Company, 1960.

INDEX